CHRISTIAN ETHICS
AND MORAL
PHILOSOPHY

An Introduction to Issues and Approaches

Craig A. Boyd and Don Thorsen

Baker Academic

a division of Baker Publishing Group
Grand Rapids, Michigan

To

W. Richard Stephens Sr.

and

Laurence W. Wood

© 2018 by Craig A. Boyd and Don Thorsen

Published by Baker Academic
a division of Baker Publishing Group
PO Box 6287, Grand Rapids, MI 49516-6287
www.bakeracademic.com

Printed in the United States of America

Library of Congress Cataloging-in-Publication Data
Names: Boyd, Craig A., author. | Thorsen, Donald A. D., author.
Title: Christian ethics and moral philosophy : an introduction to issues and approaches / Craig A.
    Boyd and Don Thorsen.
Description: Grand Rapids, MI : Baker Academic, a division of Baker Publishing Group, [2018] |
    Includes bibliographical references and index.
Identifiers: LCCN 2018023225 | ISBN 9780801048234 (pbk. : alk. paper)
Subjects: LCSH: Christian ethics—Textbooks.
Classification: LCC BJ1251 .B69 2018 | DDC 241—dc23
LC record available at https://lccn.loc.gov/2018023225

Scripture quotations are from the New Revised Standard Version of the Bible, copyright © 1989, by the Division of Christian Education of the National Council of the Churches of Christ in the United States of America. Used by permission. All rights reserved.

18 19 20 21 22 23 24   7 6 5 4 3 2 1

Contents

List of Figures   v

1. Varieties of Ethics and Moral Thought   1
   Case Study: Violence against Women and Children

2. Ethics in the Hebrew Scriptures   21
   Case Study: Care for the Environment

3. Ethics in the Christian Scriptures   39
   Case Study: The Nearest and the Neediest

4. Divine Command Theory   55
   Case Study: Intervention, Exemptions, and Conscience

5. Natural Law Ethics   71
   Case Study: Human Sexuality

6. Individualistic Ethics   85
   Case Study: Abortion

7. Kantian Ethics   103
   Case Study: Capital Punishment

8. Utilitarianism   121
   Case Study: War

9. Continental Ethics   137
   Case Study: Euthanasia

iii

10. Virtue Ethics   155
    Case Study: Lying

    Epilogue: *Love and Christian Ethics*   173

    Glossary   181

    Further Reading   188

    Scripture Index   197

    Subject Index   199

Figures

1.1   The Intersection of Moral Philosophy and Moral Theology   4

1.2   The Domains of Moral Philosophy   8

1.3   Approaches to Moral Theology   11

1.4   Using the Quadrilateral for Applied Ethics   15

5.1   The Hierarchy of Law in Thomas Aquinas   79

7.1   Autonomy and Heteronomy in Kantian Ethics   113

8.1   The Trolley Problem   129

10.1   Courage as a Mean between Extremes   159

10.2   Sufficiency as a Mean between Extremes   160

10.3   The Priority of Prudence among the Cardinal Virtues   160

ONE

Varieties of Ethics and Moral Thought

Men go abroad to admire the heights of mountains, the mighty waves of the sea, the broad tides of rivers, the compass of the ocean, and the circuits of the stars, yet pass over the mystery of themselves without a thought.

—Augustine, *Confessions*

Words to Watch

agapistic ethics	ethics	moral theology
analytic ethics	general revelation	narrative ethics
applied ethics	*imago Dei*	natural law ethics
biblical ethics	metaethics	normative ethics
consequentialism	morality	quadrilateral
cultural relativism	moral philosophy	relativism
deontological ethics	moral relativism	special revelation
divine command ethics	morals	virtue ethics

Introduction

"Ethics" is a term that usually refers to the academic study of morals and moral systems. We rarely appeal to the general idea of ethics but most often appeal to some specific account that we have in mind, as indicated by the use

1

of a modifier. We might, for example, speak of professional ethics or personal ethics. These modifiers help us to be more precise with our discussions. We can also talk about the various approaches that people throughout the world adopt with regard to ethics, given their own religious, cultural, and philosophical commitments. As a result, there are Buddhist ethics, Jewish ethics, Hindu ethics, Muslim ethics, Maorian ethics, and Christian ethics.

There are also specifically philosophical approaches to ethics, including Kantianism, utilitarianism, contractarian ethical approaches, ethical relativism, continental ethical approaches, feminist ethics, natural law ethics, natural rights ethics, and virtue ethics. These lists are not exhaustive, but they show that we need to have some qualifications on the term "ethics." This book is about the relationship between two kinds of ethics: the theories of ethics found in philosophy and approaches found in Christian ethics. It is a conversation between philosophical ethical theories and the Christian tradition that many of these philosophical theories either emerged from or argued against.

What Is the Difference between Morality and Ethics?

We can begin by making an important distinction between morality and ethics. **Morality** concerns the principles and teachings about right and wrong that organize a group of people. These include, for example, prohibitions against lying, murder, and theft, as well as exhortations to honor one's parents and give aid to those who are suffering. All human communities practice morality in one way or another. Yet not all people take the time to think about the nature of these principles: why they apply, how they apply, and what motivates us to abide by them. Such reflection is the work of ethics, which requires asking important questions about the morality we practice. A contemporary definition of **ethics**, therefore, is the thoughtful reflection and evaluation of various systems of morality around which people organize their lives. We can see this distinction at work in an experience from the life of Augustine (354–430), who is one of the most important philosophical and theological figures in the Christian tradition.

In his spiritual autobiography, *Confessions*, Augustine recounts the story of how he stole some pears from a neighbor's orchard.[1] He says that one evening some of his friends encouraged him to go out and raid the neighbor's orchard for pears. The pears were not particularly delicious, but Augustine wanted to go along because there was no fun in stealing them alone. He wanted

---

1. Augustine, *Confessions* 2.27–35; see *The Confessions: With an Introduction and Contemporary Criticism*, trans. David Meconi, SJ (San Francisco: Ignatius Press, 2012).

"companions in crime." Augustine reflects that, had it not been for his morally suspect friends, he never would have stolen the pears, but there was a certain social dynamic that influenced his behavior. Years later Augustine still found occasion to reflect on this seemingly unimportant event to ask why he did what he did. What did he find pleasurable in the experience? To what extent was he personally responsible for his actions? To what extent can we place the blame for our sinful actions on other people?

In this brief narrative from the life of Augustine, we can see the difference between morals and ethics. **Morals** are the collective values we live by—the values we ascribe to certain activities and goods. Companionship is a value, but so too are self-restraint and respect for property that belongs to others. Augustine's morals as a young man had more to do with his desire for acceptance and pleasure than with a concern for integrity and respect. Some people value money above all else, while others see a life of self-sacrifice as most valuable. Some people pursue pleasure at all costs, while still others believe that honesty in all circumstances is to be valued. The point here is that all people have morals since we all value some behaviors over others. Yet we not only judge some moral behaviors as better than others; we also judge some moral systems as better than others. We can ask whether we were justified in some action, whether our intentions were the appropriate ones in a given situation, and whether we followed the guidance of our conscience. These and other questions begin the process of systematic reflection on morals—or what we call "ethics."

Among those professionals who engage in the practice of ethics, we'll focus on two kinds: philosophers and theologians. In general, philosophers consider life's ultimate questions without regard to holding specific theological assumptions. Historically, philosophy is the "love of wisdom" as developed by such figures as Socrates, Plato, and Aristotle. Philosophers often consider questions concerning the ultimate basis of reality, such as whether humans have free will, how knowledge is possible, and how the basic principles of logic work. They also consider questions concerning the ultimate meaning of human existence, such as the nature of the soul and what constitutes the "good life." On all the aforementioned questions, their work oftentimes overlaps with that of theologians. When philosophers look at questions raised by ethics, this is known as **moral philosophy**—that is, the reflection on and the evaluation of moral principles and norms from the perspective of philosophy.

Theologians, however, take beliefs about God to form the core of their ideas about life. They are not as concerned with proving God's existence as they are with understanding God's relationship to humanity and how reconciliation, salvation, and sanctification are possible. In light of these concerns, theologians are often interested in how God's relationship with humanity shapes and informs our behaviors toward one another and toward God. When theologians consider ethical questions, this is usually known as **moral theology**—that is, the reflection on the moral principles and narratives as found in the Scriptures and church tradition from the perspective of faith.

There is not always a clear distinction between philosophers and theologians (and between moral philosophy and moral theology), since some philosophers have religious commitments, while others do not. For example, Plato and Aristotle—two of the greatest Greek philosophers—both wrote extensively on ethical issues, including themes many Christians hold to be central to the life of faith such as justice, friendship, courage, and self-control. Other philosophers such as Friedrich Nietzsche and Jean-Paul Sartre were openly hostile to Christian beliefs. Still others like Augustine and Thomas Aquinas blur the lines considerably, since they not only engaged both philosophy and theology but also held to the idea that philosophy without the correcting influence of theology was fundamentally incomplete. As a result, we see that there is often a great deal of overlap between what counts as moral philosophy and what counts as moral theology (see figure 1.1).

Figure 1.1.
The Intersection of Moral Philosophy and Moral Theology

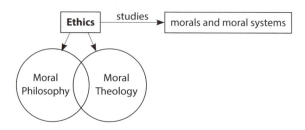

One of the tasks we have in this text is to treat both philosophical and theological approaches to ethics from a Christian perspective. Too often, texts in theological ethics ignore the importance of such thinkers as Plato, Aristotle, Immanuel Kant, and Friedrich Nietzsche, while texts in philosophical ethics ignore the work of theologians such as Augustine, Aquinas, John Calvin, John Wesley, and Søren Kierkegaard (many of whom are also considered "philosophers"). In reality, theological issues have influenced many so-called secular thinkers, and philosophers have influenced much of Christian thought on ethical issues. As a result, we intend to bring these two disciplines into conversation with each other. We begin by laying out some of the different approaches to these areas of ethics.

Right, Wrong, and the Good

Traditionally, moral theories have been divided between those that ascribe priority to the notion of what is right (and the corresponding idea of one's duty) and those that see the good (in terms of utility or interests) as the most important factor. Those ethical theories that advocate for the priority of the right are forms of **deontological ethics**,[2] while ethical theories that see the good as primary are forms of **consequentialism**.[3]

Deontologists emphasize the idea that an action is right or wrong regardless of the consequences. Moreover, one has a binding moral obligation to perform one's duty once it becomes known. For example, a deontologist would say that one is morally bound to keep one's promises regardless of any good that might come from breaking them, since one has a duty to fulfill as a result of the obligation freely entered into when making the promise.

Consequentialists see morality primarily in terms of the results of any given rule or action. They tend to avoid talk of duty and prefer to think in terms such as "the greatest good," "net utility," or "maximizing interests." A consequentialist would only see keeping a promise as valuable if it promoted good outcomes. Promise keeping, if adopted as a general rule, might promote overall good in some contexts. It all depends on what the consequences are. Lying might actually save someone's life or preserve a person's dignity in some situations.

The distinction between deontology and consequentialism often fails to account for theories such as virtue ethics, feminist ethics, and various forms of existentialism that resist being primarily concerned with either duty or consequences. These other theories emphasize such ideas as the development of specific virtues, authentic and responsible choices, or the practice of compassion.

Moral issues often take place at the intersection of all of these concerns. In both the Hebrew and Christian Scriptures, which together Christians view as their Bible, we see approaches that sometimes emphasize duty. In some instances, moral actions are associated with punishment and reward. At other times, development of personal character is encouraged. Children are told, "Honor your father and your mother . . . so that your days may be long and

2. Deontological theories include Kantianism, natural rights, and divine command theory.
3. Consequentialist theories include utilitarianism and egoism.

that it may go well with you in the land that the LORD your God is giving you" (Deut. 5:16). But at other times, God issues commands without qualification, lending to the idea that some actions are simply right in themselves—such as "You shall not murder" (Exod. 20:13). At still other times, people are told "to do justice, and to love kindness, and to walk humbly with [their] God" (Mic. 6:8).

We can see this conflict played out in contemporary situations when people try to judge among competing alternatives. Consider the case of war. Some Christians appeal to the idea that it may be important to kill in a "just war" so that there may be peace or to protect innocent lives from unjust aggressors. The appeal here is to a consequentialist intuition that God wants peace and that killing, while unfortunate, must be done to achieve peace. In contrast, there are some Christians who appeal to a deontological approach that sees the command against killing to be binding in all circumstances, regardless of the consequences. Others see the command to protect innocent life at all costs as another kind of moral obligation that does not permit exceptions. Still others look to the life of Jesus, when he tells Peter, "Put your sword back into its place; for all who take the sword will perish by the sword" (Matt. 26:52). The idea here is that a life of peacemaking and compassion cannot be understood entirely in terms of either doing one's duty or maximizing overall utility. In order to understand why Christians might take differing views on the question of killing, we must first consider how to understand the ways in which Christian ethics have been developed and applied.

Christian Ethics

Generally speaking, what makes Christian ethics "Christian" is the centrality of the person and teachings of Jesus Christ. The first place to look for guidance on questions of morals and how to develop an ethic, therefore, is in the Christian Scriptures. One of the most important passages in the Gospels concerns Jesus's teaching about the first or greatest commandment:

> One of the scribes came near and heard them disputing with one another, and seeing that he [Jesus] answered them well, he asked him, "Which commandment is the first of all?" Jesus answered, "The first is, 'Hear, O Israel: the Lord our God, the Lord is one; you shall love the Lord your God with all your heart, and with all your soul, and with all your mind, and with all your strength.' The second is this, 'You shall love your neighbor as yourself.' There is no other commandment greater than these." (Mark 12:28–31)

Of course, here we need to ask about what it means to love, how to love, and who are the various "neighbors" we are commanded to love.

Christians have not always been in agreement about the scope of love and what it requires. Questions about how love determines what is right or wrong and about what a good life is have puzzled all kinds of people, not just Christians. Yet these questions about love in particular—and how love informs our relationships with others—have animated important discussions among various Christian groups about how we should organize our lives around these important ideas.

Christians have tried to understand how this principle of love—as well as those principles that can be derived from it—has application to our lives in diverse ways. Is it ever permissible to lie? Are wars ever just? What should one think about human sexuality? Does one have obligations to care for the environment? Christians have often considered these and other questions in light of the teachings of Jesus and the various traditions of interpretation of his teachings. In turn, these traditions have been variously appropriated, altered, and challenged by many so-called secular theories as well. So we must consider the interaction between Christian ethics and those that offer alternatives to and modifications of the various traditions of Christian moral theology.

Methods in Ethics

Methodological approaches to ethics, at least in philosophy, generally ex- amine assumptions, look for validity and cogency in arguments, consider counterexamples, and attempt to build theories that will appeal to people regardless of their religious convictions. Some philosophers, such as Im- manuel Kant and John Stuart Mill, appeal to qualities such as universality and rationality, while others, such as Friedrich Nietzsche and Michel Fou- cault, attempt to undercut every theory as somehow illicitly motivated by a hidden desire for power.

What these various methodologies have in common is that they focus their attention on a consideration of values and principles without an explicit appeal to divine revelation. Some philosophers reject all forms of religious belief, while others see religious beliefs as confirming truths that can be known philosophically. Still other philosophers try to argue to religious truth from philosophical truths. When we consider the views of Kant or Nietzsche, for instance, we need to remember that they are not assuming that God speaks directly to human beings, that they harbor deep suspicions about the binding nature of religious obligations, and that they often think strictly religious approaches are misguided.

Areas of Ethics

Philosophers traditionally distinguish among three kinds of ethics: normative ethics, metaethics, and applied ethics. **Normative ethics** is an attempt to develop a theory about those central moral principles that should guide our lives. This is what people typically think of when they think of ethical theories. It considers questions concerning the content, motivation, and justification for morality: What should I do? Why should I do what I do? What is the nature of the good or the right?

Metaethics concerns questions regarding the meaning of moral language and the nature of moral properties. Does moral language describe things as they really are? Is there, for example, some real quality called "goodness" that we can point to in a moral act? Or is "goodness" merely a fiction we want to believe? Is moral language about prescribing moral behavior or about encouraging others to "go and do likewise"? Does moral language merely express the emotions of the speaker—such as praise and approval or disgust and condemnation? The focus in metaethics is typically on how we use and analyze moral terms.

Applied ethics is that discipline that engages specific moral issues from a particular moral perspective. Issues regarding capital punishment, care of the environment, treatment of animals, fair trade practices, genetic engineering,

Figure 1.2.
The Domains of Moral Philosophy

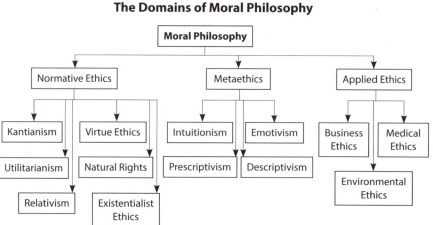

and patients' right to medical information are all part of the field of applied ethics. In short, any professional field has issues that can be regarded as applied ethics, and any legal area or domain that considers what people should or should not be permitted to do is part of applied ethics. In figure 1.2, various main categories are listed with common subcategories found within each of those major areas of ethics. In this book, we look primarily at the categories of normative ethics and how they are applied to various moral issues.

Philosophical Approaches

There is no one way to adjudicate among different approaches to philosophical ethics, since there are numerous approaches to the discipline of philosophy itself. The various approaches to philosophy include historical, analytic, continental, process, and Thomistic philosophy, among others. Each approach has various advocates, strengths, weaknesses, and insight into philosophical questions. For the purposes of this book, we focus primarily on the most relevant theories and how they intersect with Christian ethics.

Historical approaches to ethics focus primarily on two things: tracing the historical development of theories or concepts and asking how contemporary thinkers can benefit from the insights of past philosophers. Philosophers such as Plato, Aristotle, Augustine, Aquinas, Kant, and Kierkegaard can be valuable resources for addressing the various goods we should pursue, the kinds of virtues we should acquire, the importance of fulfilling our duties, and the centrality of relationship in the moral life.[4]

Analytic ethics derives primarily from Kant in the eighteenth century, and it represents a dominant trend in contemporary philosophy. Important analytic ethicists of the past one hundred years include G. E. Moore, A. J. Ayer, R. M. Hare, and John Rawls. Analytic moral philosophers focus on the meaning of moral language and the validity of the logic employed in ethical argumentation. As a result, much of analytic ethics is in the domain of metaethics.

Continental, especially existentialist, philosophy traces its origins to the work of Kierkegaard and Nietzsche up through twentieth-century philosophers such as Sartre, Martin Buber, Foucault, Emmanuel Levinas, and Jacques Derrida. Continental approaches to ethics focus on a variety of ideas including authentic choices, the existential encounter with "the other," and deconstructing the attempts of those in power to control the masses.

4. A helpful historical approach here is Arthur Holmes, *Fact, Value, and God* (Grand Rapids: Eerdmans, 1997).

Virtue ethics—and its theological versions, including narrative ethics—has tended to focus less on questions of what kinds of actions are praiseworthy and blameworthy and more on what it means to be a certain kind of person or to live a certain kind of life. According to virtue ethics, moral actions can only be understood within the context of the narrative of one's life and the character or virtues developed over one's lifetime. The cultivation of virtues or qualities of character such as justice, self-control, charity, and humility plays a central role in ethical discourse for virtue ethics.[5]

These various—and at times, competing—approaches to ethics are often treated in isolation from one another. It is our intention to be more integrative in this book, dialoguing among these approaches as well as between philosophy and theology, reason and faith.

Theological Approaches

There are a variety of ways in which to proceed in moral theology. Some begin with the biblical narrative and advocate biblical ethics, while others begin with theological commitments such as human depravity, divine transcendence, or the encounter with God. Some develop approaches systematically from a doctrine of God to an understanding of creation or to a theological anthropology, while still others emphasize the role of Christian churches in mediating the moral principles of the Bible to contemporary society.

Many Protestant Christians, especially those in the evangelical tradition, look first to the Bible for moral guidance. Texts such as the Decalogue, or Ten Commandments (Exod. 20:1–17; Deut. 5:6–21), and the Sermon on the Mount (Matt. 5–7) have a special place since they set out basic rules or principles that believers need to follow if they are to consider themselves true disciples. Protestants generally look to the Bible first and foremost and then to important theological figures who have interpreted the Bible in important ways. Such thinkers as Augustine, Luther, Calvin, and Wesley play important roles, but they are never on the same level of authority as Scripture.

In contrast, the Roman Catholic tradition holds that the Bible needs the authority of the church to address questions that Jesus and his disciples never faced. Catholics turn first to how their church has traditionally understood

---

5. See, e.g., Kevin Timpe and Craig A. Boyd, eds., *Virtues and Their Vices* (New York: Oxford University Press, 2014); Alasdair MacIntyre, *After Virtue: A Study in Moral Theory*, 3rd ed. (Notre Dame, IN: University of Notre Dame Press, 2007).

various passages and look especially to such figures as Augustine and Aquinas and how they interpreted and applied the tradition in their own historical and cultural contexts. For Catholics, one needs the necessary guidance of the church as found in such documents as the *Catechism of the Catholic Church*, papal encyclicals, and various ecumenical councils. From this perspective, Scripture cannot be read in isolation from the authoritative role of the Christian community.

Both Protestants and Catholics understand that the moral message of the Christian Scriptures has to be grasped, interpreted, and applied. How Christians do this requires thinking about the meaning of the text, the context of the text, and whether or not that text has a direct bearing on our contemporary discussions. Within the context of moral theology, there are five main alternatives: biblical ethics, divine command ethics, agapistic ethics, narrative ethics, and natural law ethics.

Figure 1.3.
Approaches to Moral Theology

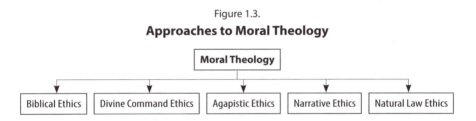

Biblical ethics | Divine Command Ethics | Agapistic Ethics | Narrative Ethics | Natural Law Ethics

Biblical ethics is an approach to Christian ethics that emphasizes the biblical text above all other authorities by attempting to apply the biblical text to contemporary situations. For example, one might ask whether sexual promiscuity is permissible and then look at the prohibitions from the Decalogue and the epistles of Paul to determine that there is a consistent message that it should be avoided. However, biblical ethics can run into difficulties with other ethical questions such as whether slavery is permissible. On the one hand, slavery was permitted in both ancient Israel and early Christian churches. On the other hand, Galatians 3:28 teaches, "There is no longer Jew or Greek, there is no longer slave or free, there is no longer male and female; for all of you are one in Christ Jesus." This verse suggests that in churches there should be no moral distinctions based on ethnicity, gender, or status. Here one has to take into account the meaning and interpretation of the texts and how they can or should be applied in contemporary contexts. (Cf. Paul's Letter to Philemon encouraging Philemon to receive Onesimus—a runaway slave—as a brother in Christ.)

Divine command ethics is an approach to Christian ethics that holds that whatever God commands is right, and whatever God forbids is wrong.[6] On this view, obedience to the commands of God (as found in the Bible) is the primary criterion of what makes for good and evil acts. But how do we know that it is God who commands these actions, and which commands to obey? When we ask which commands we should obey, we encounter some problems. For example, should we obey the dietary laws about not eating shellfish in the Hebrew Bible? How do we (or should we) apply these commands in the twenty-first century?

A third theological alternative is agapistic ethics.[7] **Agapistic ethics** is an approach to Christian ethics that takes the command to love as the central theme. This approach is based on Jesus's commands to his followers: "'You shall love the Lord your God with all your heart, and with all your soul, and with all your mind.' This is the greatest and first commandment. And a second is like it: 'You shall love your neighbor as yourself.' On these two commandments hang all the law and the prophets" (Matt. 22:37–40). Thinkers as diverse as Augustine, Aquinas, and Kierkegaard have all emphasized the primacy of this command. The issue here is not just the importance of the command but also its primacy. Another issue is how a person can acquire the ability to love not only one's friends and relatives but also one's enemies (Luke 6:27–28). Other questions concern whether there are some people who should be loved more than others and whether the intention to love is the only thing that matters.

Narrative ethics is an approach to Christian ethics that sees that virtues must be developed within the ongoing narrative of Christian churches and the practices they inculcate in their disciples. It shares a good deal with its philosophical counterpart, virtue ethics, but places virtue ethics within a larger narrative context. Theologian Stanley Hauerwas argues that for Christian ethics narrative is primary and that rules and principles are secondary. Discipleship, for Hauerwas, is more about being a certain kind of person than it is discovering the right rule that we should apply in any given context.[8] If one considers the rules of the Ten Commandments, for example, one finds that they begin with this verse: "I am the LORD your God, who brought you out of the land of Egypt, out of the house of slavery" (Exod. 20:2). According to narrative ethicists, the commandments make no sense apart from the ongoing story of God's faithfulness.

6. A comprehensive approach to divine command ethics is Janine Marie Idziak, *Divine Command Morality: Historical and Contemporary Readings* (New York: Mellen, 1978).

7. See Gene Outka, *Agape: An Ethical Analysis* (New Haven: Yale University Press, 1978).

8. Stanley Hauerwas, *The Peaceable Kingdom: A Primer in Christian Ethics* (Notre Dame, IN: University of Notre Dame Press, 1983).

A final alternative is **natural law ethics**, which is an option in both moral theology and moral philosophy. The tradition of natural law ethics holds that some moral principles are in all humans because of the ways in which God created humans. Reflection on human nature and human communities provides the content for much of human morality, and these principles are so "natural" that all people, regardless of culture or religion, can discover them. In moral philosophy, it serves as the basis for a kind of universal morality, wherein all people can agree on some basic moral norms. C. S. Lewis appeals to this kind of thinking when he argues that all societies share some universal moral principles, such as prohibitions on murder and lying.[9] In moral theology, natural law is often employed by Catholic theologians concerning issues of social justice, sanctity of life, and human sexuality. Here natural law is seen as a continuation and application of moral principles found in the Bible and applied to current issues in morality. Questions concerning the nature of marriage and divorce, although addressed in the Bible, have different contexts and implications some two thousand years later.

General and Special Revelation

When considering the moral message of the Christian Scriptures, we discover that there are at least two ways in which God communicates to humanity: general revelation and special revelation. **General revelation** has to do with what people can know through their natural abilities and by observation of the world in which they live. Such knowledge is available to everyone and is thought by some to reveal at least basic religious knowledge about God. Thomas Aquinas says the ability to know God through nature is due to the "light of natural reason" that God has implanted in every human being.[10] Psalm 19:1 says that "the heavens are telling the glory of God; and the firmament proclaims his handiwork," which suggests that the glory of God and God's existence can be known by observation of the created order of the world.

God's existence is thought to be communicated to all people, mysteriously by their observance of the world that God created. Such knowledge not only tells people about God, but the Bible says it also confirms their sinfulness and God's judgment on them. In Romans 1:18–19, the apostle Paul says: "Ever since the creation of the world his eternal power and divine nature, invisible though they are, have been understood and seen through the things he has

9. See, e.g., C. S. Lewis, *Mere Christianity* (New York: Macmillan, 1947); C. S. Lewis, *The Abolition of Man* (New York: Macmillan, 1952).
10. Thomas Aquinas, *Summa Theologica* 1.1.2, trans. Fathers of the English Dominican Province (New York: Benziger, 1947).

made. So, they are without excuse; for though they knew God, they did not honor him as God or give thanks to him, but they became futile in their thinking, and their senseless minds were darkened" (Rom. 1:20–21). An important concept here is that of sin, the separation or alienation from God and from one's neighbor. As a result, people fail to honor God and to live the kinds of lives to which they are called. What is needed is the restorative work of grace that can only be understood through the idea of special revelation.

In the Christian tradition, **special revelation** has to do with God's disclosure of particular knowledge required for salvation, especially as revealed through the gospel of Jesus Christ.[11] By grace, God makes it possible for people to be healed from sin and from those habits and behaviors that prevent them from living lives that reflect the *imago Dei*, or the image of God. The concept of the *imago Dei* has also been given to humans through special revelation (e.g., Gen. 1:26–27). God reveals in the early chapters of Genesis that humans have been created in God's own image, which gives them a unique value and responsibility in all creation. Hence murder is considered especially sinful since it is a kind of direct attack on the image of God and consequently an attack on the Creator.

Special revelation occurs in many ways but primarily through the Scriptures and most fully in the person of Jesus Christ. Oral traditions were written down and sometimes compiled by editors until a body of sacred writings emerged as the Hebrew Scriptures. During the first century, Jesus and first-generation Christians revered the sacred writings they received and exhorted others to live by them. The Beatitudes (Matt. 5:1–12), for example, were a particularly important set of ethical teachings for the early church. Yet how these teachings were transmitted and interpreted remained an open question.

Scripture, Tradition, Reason, and Experience

A helpful paradigm for understanding issues of religious authority for Christian ethics can be summarized by the so-called **quadrilateral**, which is an approach to Christian reasoning that includes reference to the authorities of Scripture, tradition, reason, and experience.[12] This paradigm does not resolve potential tensions among the four authorities, but it does provide useful categories and contexts for the study of Christian ethics and moral philosophy.

11. The Greek term for "gospel" is *euangelion*—"evangel" or "good news."
12. This concept is attributed to John Wesley's fourfold understanding of religious authority and theological method, which his followers describe as the "Wesleyan quadrilateral." See Don Thorsen, *The Wesleyan Quadrilateral* (1990; repr., Lexington: Emeth, 2005).

A great deal of knowledge is generally available to all people, regardless of their religious commitments. Such knowledge comes through reason and experience. Although historically some Christians have been suspicious of the extent of knowledge attainable through reason (e.g., critical thinking, philosophy, metaphysics) and experience (e.g., personal experience, social experiences, and the sciences), most Christians presuppose their general reliability. The success of the sciences since the time of the Renaissance is testimony to this. Whether we want to admit it or not, we all assume some degree of reliance on our reasoning and experiential capabilities (e.g., our ability to perceive words on the page of a book and to understand the words with our minds). Reason corresponds fairly well both to those truths we can gain through the discipline of philosophy and to what Christians call general revelation.

Even so-called special revelation requires the use of human abilities of reason and experience. In the Hebrew Scriptures, God revealed special knowledge to people through, for example, visions and dreams. The reception of such knowledge relies on our experiences and thoughtful reflection as much as it relies on divine agency in communicating special revelation. The reception of special revelation through the Bible also requires people's capabilities to read, interpret, and apply the subject matter theologically and ethically. Since the time when the Bible was canonized, some Christians have wanted to treat it as something untainted by human contact. Yet every interpreter of the Bible needs to understand the historical, literary, and cultural context of biblical revelation in order to interpret and apply it. Otherwise the result of one's reading of Scripture is merely an uninformed opinion on whatever the topic happens to be.

At the same time, Christians also affirm that church traditions have special relevance to understanding and applying biblically oriented beliefs, values, and practices. As we have seen, while Protestants generally relegate tradition to a subordinate role to the authority of Scripture, Roman Catholics view tradition—in terms of the authority of their church—as a necessary correlative of the Bible. Regardless of the specific religious tradition one inhabits

Figure 1.4.
Using the Quadrilateral for Applied Ethics

and the relative significance given to the role of tradition, the Bible together with tradition, reason, and experience provide useful categories for the study of moral theology. There is disagreement among Christians with regard to a right understanding and application of tradition, reason, and experience, just as there is disagreement with regard to a right understanding and application of the Bible. But at some point all religious authorities need to be considered and discerned in order to deal with the complex, real-life issues people face, especially when considering the various Christian approaches to ethics. For one way to understand how to use the quadrilateral for applied ethics, see figure 1.4.

Case Study: Violence against Women and Children

Around the world, many cultures maintain practices that can be viewed as promoting violence, especially against women and children. Among those socially approved practices are child marriages, human trafficking, and female genital mutilation. The International Center for Research on Women estimates that a third of all women worldwide are married before the age of eighteen. In many countries, they are married off before the age of fifteen and have little to no participation in the marriage contract. In some places a child bride can be married at age twelve or younger.

One version of **relativism**, the ethical theory that there are no universal moral truths, is **cultural relativism**, which holds to the idea that people in one culture cannot judge the actions of people living in another culture. On this view, no culture, religion, or temporal perspective is uniquely privileged. As a result, people living in Canada should not judge the behaviors of people living in Mozambique, and people living in Mozambique should refrain from judging people in Canada. It is only from *within* a culture that one can make moral judgments. To judge from the outside that the practice of child brides is wrong would be to misapply the judgments from another culture to this practice. Even a person who already lived within that culture could not criticize the practice, since this is what the culture already approves. In other words, whatever a culture does is right for that culture because it is what the culture does.

Another version of relativism is **moral relativism**, which is the idea that there are no universal moral principles that all people, regardless of their culture, recognize as obligatory. In this version, a person might say to another, "Well, that might be morally true for you, but it's not for me." A moral relativist thinks that all morality is relative to the individual and therefore subjective.

Questions of morality are not like questions of fact, since there is no truth that can be known about moral principles. For this view, universal moral principles simply do not exist. As a result, all moral convictions are merely matters of taste or preference. One person may like chocolate while another likes vanilla, but there is no truth to the question of whether chocolate or vanilla is better. In reducing all moral questions in a like manner, anything is permissible since there is no authority to which we can appeal. In this way, moral relativism is weaker than cultural relativism since the cultural relativist can at least appeal to social norms to provide a kind of authority higher than the individual's opinion.

One can see that relativism is a deeply flawed theory since it sanctions some truly horrific behaviors. For example, if a culture (or an individual) determined that public torture was morally permissible, then no one could say otherwise. Those from within the culture would not have the critical faculties necessary to criticize the practice, since they would naturally assent to it as part of the culture. Those outside the culture would not be able to criticize it, as it is not their culture. Further, one would not be able to make any kind of moral progress from within the culture. The work of abolitionists such as Frederick Douglass in America or William Wilberforce in England would have been impossible since, as members of a culture that practiced slavery, they could only assent to the practice without criticizing it. But clearly they were able to criticize the practice even from within the practicing culture.

If we agree that relativism is inadequate as an ethical theory, then we are still left with the question of how to employ the approaches of moral philosophy and moral theology to practices such as forcing children into marriages with adults. We might appeal to the idea of natural rights—that all people possess the right to self-determination and that this idea is inconsistent with the practice of selling a human being. Or we could ask the question of consequences. Utilitarians, for example, might ask who benefits and who is harmed from such a practice. The data show that many girls sold into marriages suffer abuse and can even be murdered. As a result, for both natural rights theorists and utilitarians, such a practice would be wrong.

Moral theology could offer a number of different approaches as well, all of which would likely agree that the practice is wrong. Consider the quadrilateral for guidance. The Bible, when understood in its historical and cultural context, might not initially be too helpful here, as the practice of marriage has changed considerably over the past two to three millennia. Yet we could look at more general biblical principles—such as Jesus's exhortation to "do to others as you would have them do to you" (Luke 6:31)—or look at Jesus's frequent exhortations to compassion. Such biblical passages would all need interpretation and application. We could even say that compassion is a basic principle throughout the Bible and that to fail to practice it would be wrong, regardless of the cultural context.

Reason might help us not only to interpret moral passages of the Bible but also to suggest how to think consistently about child marriages and how they parallel the issue of slavery. If we do not sanction slavery, then how could we possibly sanction child marriages? We could also employ logic here to the broader topic of relativism in order to undermine it as a theory. Consider the following valid argument:

> If relativism is true, then it is impossible to put an end to immoral practices.
> But it is possible to put an end to immoral practices (such as slavery).
> Therefore, relativism cannot be true.

Reason, therefore, asks questions of consistency, implication, and logical relations.

Tradition becomes a tricky source. The Christian tradition includes various strands of Protestantism as well as Catholic and Orthodox Churches. These faith traditions emphasize various aspects of the Christian message. Yet some cultures see their own traditions as fixed and unchanging. One could argue that tradition is the keeper of truth in the sense that a tradition might have a clear prohibition on, for example, killing innocent persons. However, sometimes traditions can serve to maintain deeply embedded prejudice, which is wrong regardless of how long it has been in existence.

Finally, one can consult experience. Hearing the stories of young women who have survived the experience of being sold off in a marriage contract can provide moral data for thoughtful people to consider. Scientific research on physical and physiological harm should also be weighed and evaluated.

In short, using the quadrilateral makes clear that the practice of child marriages is wrong, regardless of one's particular theological perspective. As we work through other theories and approaches throughout this book, we will see in greater depth how these approaches converge and diverge and how they could be used to answer similar questions.

How to Use This Book

This text is intended as an introduction. As such it does not cover every conceivable topic, nor does it intend to. Rather, the book attempts to lay out some basic options in both moral philosophy and Christian ethics.

Each chapter addresses at least one major foundational topic or normative theory. There is also the opportunity to consider a current applied issue
in order to facilitate the reader's understanding of how the theory works.

Each chapter can be read on its own without reading the prior chapters. At
the beginning of each chapter there are important terms that the reader should
know ("words to watch"), which are also provided in bold throughout the
text. The glossary at the end of the book will aid readers in quickly locating
key terms and their definitions. At the end of each chapter there are discussion
questions that are designed to aid readers—especially in classroom settings—to
consider how the theory in question might address specific moral issues.

Discussion Questions

1. What is the difference between ethics and morals? How is this distinction
   helpful? How would you define each of these terms in your own words?

2. What is the difference between right and wrong? How do determinations of right and wrong differ from determinations of the good? How
   is this distinction helpful?

3. What are the three basic areas of moral philosophy? How are they helpful in sorting out different moral problems?

4. What distinguishes Christian ethics from other approaches to ethics?
   What points of intersection do they share?

5. To what religious authorities do Christians specifically appeal in ethical decision-making? To what extent are these authorities helpful or
   potentially problematic?

6. Are the categories of Scripture, tradition, reason, and experience relevant
   in ethical decision-making? How might one apply these authorities to
   various issues like euthanasia, lying, and world hunger?

7. In what ways can both moral philosophy and moral theology respond
   to the challenge of cultural relativism?

TWO

Ethics in the Hebrew Scriptures

He has told you, O mortal, what is good;
and what does the Lord require of you
but to do justice, and to love kindness,
and to walk humbly with your God?
—Micah 6:8

Words to Watch

anthropocentrism	First Table	Second Table
apodictic law	Holiness Code	stewardship
casuistic law	*Ketuvim*	*Tanakh*
covenant	*Nevi'im*	*Torah*
Decalogue	ownership	
ecojustice	principle of proportionality	

Introduction

In the late 1950s the use of the pesticide DDT was prevalent throughout much of the United States as a means of controlling mosquitos and eliminating insects that could harm various crops. During this time Rachel Carson, a well-known scientist, began to suspect that use of DDT was a serious ecological threat to both humans and other animals. Yet her initial warnings did not find a sympathetic ear with the large chemical companies that produced DDT, and a number of them threatened lawsuits. By late 1962 Carson had amassed sufficient evidence for her landmark book, *Silent Spring*.[1] Carson was able to show that overuse of DDT contributed to the decrease in bird populations and poisoned an entire annual crop of cranberries so as to make them unsafe for human consumption. In addition to the direct harm pesticides could wreak on agriculture and animal and human life, insects could develop a tolerance to pesticides so that eventually the poisons would become ineffective.

By the late twentieth century people all around the world had come to see that humans have an interdependent relationship with the environment. The principle is akin to Newton's third law of motion that every action has an equal and opposite reaction. For every change in the environment, humans react, and for every action taken collectively by humans, the environment reacts. In response to the threat of hurricanes and earthquakes, people develop technology to protect their homes and environs. Likewise, when humans introduce new elements into the environment, the environment responds—as in the case of the pesticides that Carson documented.

A desire to care for the environment may spring from a variety of sources: self-interest, the interests of one's descendants, compassion for other animals, or a desire to maintain biodiversity. A concern for the land and the well-being of all life can even be seen in some of the earliest books of the Bible and their emphasis on agrarian culture and issues of righteousness. Indeed, the idyllic paradise described in Genesis 2 is a garden where all things are well-ordered. Even though we are removed millennia from the authors of the earliest biblical writings, many thoughtful people share their concern for the earth and all that is in it. Stewardship is one of the more important principles throughout the Bible. However, the idea of stewardship also must be understood within the wider context of God's covenantal relationship with humanity as well as with the righteousness that God requires from God's people.

In this chapter, we first look at the key elements of the Hebrew Scriptures and the principles that guided the children of Israel. Central to their way of life were the various covenants God established with them, but so too was the idea of stewardship and care not only for others but also for the land they inhabited. After our general treatment of those principles that shaped the ancient Hebrews, we return to this very contemporary issue of care for the environment and how the idea of stewardship (among other perspectives) might guide our thinking about important environmental problems facing us today.

1. Rachel Carson, *Silent Spring* (New York: Houghton-Mifflin, 1962).

The Torah

"Old Testament" is the traditional Christian name for the *Tanakh*, or Hebrew Scriptures, which consist of three major sections: *Torah* (Hebrew, "instruction" or "teaching"), *Nevi'im* (Hebrew, "prophets"), and *Ketuvim* (Hebrew, "writings").[2] The Hebrew Scriptures provide the foundational teachings for Christian understandings of morality found later in the New Testament, or Christian Scriptures, and are therefore central to both Jewish and Christian conceptions of ethics. They shape our views about God's holiness, righteousness, justice, wisdom, and steadfast love, and they develop the important themes of human sinfulness, redemption, the possibility of sanctification, and the importance of covenantal relationships between God and humanity. The first section of the Hebrew Scriptures, the **Torah**, provides the foundational understanding of these ideas from which the other two sections build. Here we look at two major themes in the Torah: covenant and holiness.

Covenantal Relationships

A **covenant** is a relationship between two parties based on love wherein they bind themselves to one another. A covenant is therefore not a business contract or transaction but a commitment of the entire self to the other person, much like a wedding vow. The covenants between God and Israel (and others) are the primary focus of the Hebrew Scriptures. Like contracts, there are stipulations for the covenant, which include laws, prohibitions, wisdom, and other moral imperatives by which God's people may show their love for God and their neighbors—including those on the margins of society. Yet a progressive revelation occurs in the Hebrew Scriptures that goes far beyond the minimum required by a contract to reveal more and more about God, God's holiness, and God's intention that people be holy. Throughout the Hebrew Bible we come to see, as Paul Ramsey says, God's "unwavering faithfulness" and "stubborn steadfastness" to the Jewish people.[3]

Covenantal relationships took place throughout all of the ancient Near East. Sometimes covenants (Hebrew, *berith*) occurred between God and people, between a ruler and a people, and between groups of people. In the Hebrew Scriptures, just as God initiated covenantal relationships with people, God's faithfulness also guaranteed their enforcement. Two of the most important covenants were the Abrahamic and Mosaic covenants.

2. The word *Tanakh* is therefore an acronym that includes the first Hebrew letter of each of the three sections in the Scriptures mentioned above.
3. Paul Ramsey, *Basic Christian Ethics* (Louisville: John Knox, 1993), 5.

Abraham, the founding patriarch of the Hebrew people, was thought to have had the most significant covenantal relationship with God. In Genesis 12–17, several aspects of this covenantal relationship occur between God and Abraham. In some instances, unconditional promises of land and descendants are made by God, and in other instances, conditional promises are made that are dependent on obedience to God, symbolized by male circumcision. God's covenantal relationship with Abraham was significant, and parts of it have continued to influence Jewish and Christian adherents. But the later covenantal relationship established between God and Moses effectually superseded this previous covenant.

The Mosaic Covenant is also known as the Sinaitic Covenant since it was given by God to Moses on Mount Sinai after the liberation, or exodus, of the Hebrew people from Egypt. It includes the **Decalogue**—also known as the Ten Commandments—as well as numerous other laws. The Decalogue has taken center stage in discussions of biblical ethics. It reads as follows:[4]

> Then God spoke all these words:
> I am the LORD your God, who brought you out of the land of Egypt,
>   out of the house of slavery; you shall have no other gods before me.
> You shall not make for yourself an idol. . . .
> You shall not make wrongful use of the name of the LORD your
>   God. . . .
> Remember the Sabbath day, and keep it holy. . . .
> Honor your father and your mother. . . .
> You shall not murder.
> You shall not commit adultery.
> You shall not steal.
> You shall not bear false witness against your neighbor.
> You shall not covet. . . .
>
> Exod. 20:1–17

It is significant that the Decalogue begins with a reminder of who God is and what God has done for the people. It is in this context that the list of commands is situated. The Ten Commandments do not contain the entirety of divine instruction in the Hebrew Scriptures, but they do serve as the touchstone for a kind of basic righteousness and a reminder of why the children of Israel should abide by them. They were the basis of God's covenantal relationship with the Hebrew people—part of a larger narrative wherein God continually acts on behalf of the people. The exodus event is

4. A second list occurs in Deuteronomy 5:1–22.

what gives the commands in the Decalogue their meaning and context. Walter Brueggemann says, "Reference to the Exodus suggests that the theological intention of the Ten Commandments is to institutionalize the Exodus: to establish perspectives, procedures, policies, and institutions that will generate Exodus-like social relationships. The reason the commandments are so urgent and insistent is that they are Yahweh's (and therefore Israel's) strategy for fending off a return to pre-Exodus conditions of exploitation and brutality within the community."[5] This covenant is to establish a new kind of relationship between God and Israel—a relationship that forbids the people from exploiting one another the way they were exploited when they were in Egypt. As John Rogerson says, "God did not liberate a people so that they could enslave or oppress each other."[6]

These commandments are what is called apodictic law. **Apodictic law** refers to commands that do not permit any exceptions and must be kept by all people who are part of the covenant. The commands break down according to what we could call our obligations to God and our obligations to our neighbors. The **First Table** consists of those commandments that pertain directly to God—the Creator and Liberator. They include prohibitions on other gods, idolatry, and making wrongful use of God's name, as well as the command to keep the Sabbath. The **Second Table** consists of those commandments that pertain to obligations to our neighbor. They include the exhortation to honor one's parents (since they are our first neighbors and the cause of our existence) and the prohibitions on murder, theft, adultery, bearing false witness, and coveting.

First Table: Commands Oriented to God	Second Table: Commands Oriented to Neighbor
1. No other gods	5. Honor your father and mother
2. No idols	6. Do not murder
3. Do not make wrongful use of God's name	7. Do not commit adultery
	8. Do not steal
4. Remember the Sabbath	9. Do not bear false witness
	10. Do not covet

These commandments not only provide the central moral teaching for the covenant between God and the Jewish people but also serve as a foundation for later Christian teachings (cf. Jesus's teaching in the Sermon on the Mount) as well as for much of secular moral philosophy.

5. Walter Brueggemann, *Theology of the Old Testament* (Minneapolis: Fortress, 1997), 184.

6. John Rogerson, "The Old Testament and Christian Ethics," in *The Cambridge Companion to Christian Ethics*, ed. Robin Gill (New York: Cambridge University Press, 2001), 37.

Obedience to God, including obedience to God's laws and prophets, represented a confession of Hebrew scriptural ethics. But being the people of God concerned more than mere obedience; it required a way of life, a way of being that holistically reflected the Hebrews' gratitude to God, who created, redeemed, and providentially cared for them. It required righteousness and holiness.

The Holiness Code

The commands following the Ten Commandments are referred to as the **Holiness Code** by Christians because of the prominence of the Hebrew Scriptures' discussion of God as holy and of God's expectation for how people should live holy lives. The idea of holiness, which includes righteousness and justice, is essential to understanding both the Decalogue and the covenant God establishes with the Israelites. Paul Ramsey has shown that God's justice gives shape to all human manifestations of justice in that it becomes the "plumb line for measuring the rightness of human relationships. . . . The core of the Old Testament ethic, its central organizing principle, is to be found underneath an abundance of external codes of law in God's active righteousness, which through the covenant became the 'nature of the kingdom.'"[7] When we understand that the notion of justice undergirds the specific laws throughout the Hebrew Scriptures, we can begin to see why some actions—which seem to us as odd, unnecessary, or irrelevant—could have significance to a people intent on being grateful for the unmerited grace bestowed on them by their God.

The Holiness Code—much of which is found in the book of Leviticus—includes commandments and prohibitions that pertain to the whole of life, religious and ethical, personal and social. The commandments include both prescriptions and prohibitions. The prohibitions mostly pertain to idolatry, murder, and sexual relations, though they also include other areas such as personal injury, theft, and economic relations. For example, some laws have to do with redeeming property or redeeming people who served as indentured slaves.

Dietary commandments are noteworthy because they were a point of controversy among early Christians, as described in the book of Acts. Dietary, or *kosher* (Hebrew, "fit" for consumption), commandments had to do with what could be eaten, how food was to be prepared, and how it was to be eaten. Kosher laws include avoiding eating animals with cloven hooves or seafood without scales and fins, including pigs and shellfish. There also

7. Ramsey, *Basic Christian Ethics*, 5.

exist numerous commandments about sexual conduct, which touch on many aspects of sexuality and usually pertain to the sexual conduct of men. For example, there were laws pertaining to sexual relations between men and close relatives (mothers and sisters, stepmothers and stepsisters, sisters-in-law, aunts, granddaughters), women and their daughters, ritually unclean women, neighbors' wives, other men, and animals. Although some of these sexual and dietary prescriptions may seem odd or unusual, they were a means by which the Israelites could distinguish themselves from people who practiced other religions. But since the laws were often not followed by the people, they needed to be reminded of the covenant God had established with them. This was the work of the prophets.

The Prophets

The *Nevi'im*—Hebrew for "prophets"—is the second section of the Hebrew Bible, which builds on the Mosaic covenant and nuances it in dramatic ways. The prophets did not present a new ethical perspective so much as they responded to different historical contexts, which highlighted aspects of the law in socially applicable ways but always in reference to the requirements of God's justice. In particular, the prophets emphasized the social, political, and economic implications of the law more poignantly than had been previously understood and applied.

For the prophets, holiness emphasized the righteousness and justice of God and the need for God's people to reflect that righteousness in their concern for and action on the part of justice and in their resistance of evil. An example of these emphases can be found in a lament by God about the city of Jerusalem (or Zion):

> Your princes are rebels
>   and companions of thieves.
> Everyone loves a bribe
>   and runs after gifts.
> They do not defend the orphan,
>   and the widow's cause does not come before them.
>
> Isa. 1:23

The lament does not have to do with the pursuit of justice in a legal context but with regard to how the poor and weak needlessly suffer. Increasingly, God's relationship with the Hebrews was seen not as an exclusive tribal relationship but as one that extended to all peoples and tribes in the world. As such, greater understanding and action was needed in caring for the full range of people's needs, socially as well as individually.

The prophet Amos pointedly observed that God did not desire a people who followed religious practices but who failed to care about the unjust treatment of others. Rather, God was especially concerned for the plight of the poor. Amos even said that God despised the Hebrews' festivals and assemblies, if they simultaneously refused to attend to weightier matters of social justice and the resistance of evil:

> I hate, I despise your festivals,
>> and I take no delight in your solemn assemblies.
> Even though you offer me your burnt offerings and grain offerings,
>> I will not accept them;
> and the offerings of well-being of your fatted animals
>> I will not look upon.
> Take away from me the noise of your songs;
>> I will not listen to the melody of your harps.
> But let justice roll down like waters,
>> and righteousness like an ever-flowing stream.
>
> Amos 5:21–24

The prophetic message here is that God's laws cannot be reduced to privatized ethics, even if performed conspicuously with solemnity and piety. The prophet Micah echoes this concern for the social dimensions of justice when he proclaims,

> He has told you, O mortal, what is good;
>> and what does the Lord require of you
> but to do justice, and to love kindness,
>> and to walk humbly with your God?
>
> Mic. 6:8

What is at work here is that the social aspects of righteousness had lamentably been ignored too often by the Israelites, and that ignorance—intentional or unintentional—transgressed the holistic ethics God intended to communicate.

In short, for the prophets the idea of holiness inevitably includes social relationships. As a result, there is no holiness but social holiness (as is often said in Methodist social ethics) since holiness applies to people's relations with their neighbors—including Hebrews and non-Hebrews. Consequently, if people are to become holy, as God commands them, then this will occur in both individual and collective contexts, with the benefits that communal life has for the common good (as later Christian authors would say) of all humanity, as well as for individual believers. The prophets thus emphasized social concern, social justice, and social advocacy to a greater extent than the earlier writings in the Hebrew Scriptures.[8]

The covenant (as seen in the Law) and the call to return to the covenant (as seen in the prophets) were two of the three central aspects of the teachings of the Hebrew Scriptures. But there was one more element, the practical words of wisdom or sayings and stories of venerated individuals, that people could adopt and integrate into their own lives. This was the work of the writings.

The Writings

The *Ketuvim*—Hebrew for "writings"—represent the third section of the *Tanakh*, the Hebrew Scriptures. This section consists of a variety of writings, both historical and poetic. The writings include the well-known poetic books of Job, Psalms, and Proverbs. Sometimes they are referred to as Wisdom literature, along with the books of Ecclesiastes and the Song of Songs, which focus on sayings from wise people, antiphonal songs between lovers, and practical advice for living a good life and avoiding wickedness. The two main themes in the writings are the pursuit of wisdom (which is always understood as a form of right living) and the recurring theme of justice.

In promoting wisdom, the writings broadly affirm moral emphases found elsewhere in the Hebrew Scriptures, but more emphasis is placed on a general understanding and appreciation for wisdom—sometimes personified as a woman (e.g., Prov. 8:15–21)—than on particular religious rituals or ethical teachings. Wisdom is the cultivation of a healthy relationship with God and with others. The book of Proverbs says,

> The fear of the LORD is the beginning of wisdom,
>   and the knowledge of the Holy One is insight.
> For by me your days will be multiplied,
>   and years will be added to your life.
>
> 9:10–11

---

8. Some biblical interpreters have considered this a radical change from previous teachings— e.g., by explaining it as a kind of Axial Age. Those who argue for the influence of an Axial Age posit that human understanding changed throughout the entire ancient world, maintaining that human civilization concurrently achieved an intellectual and socially conscious coming-of-age, so to speak. See, e.g., Karl Jaspers, *The Way to Wisdom: An Introduction to Philosophy*, 2nd ed. (New Haven: Yale University Press, 2003), 98.

Such wisdom contributes to the good in one's life as well as to determining right and wrong.

Wisdom also implies practicing justice. Many of the proverbs and psalms emphasize the importance of justice, as does the book of Job, whose well-known story of suffering is one also included in the writings. In this poetic narrative, Job is accused by his friends of failing to practice righteousness. They reason that God only punishes the wicked, so Job must have done something wrong. They also contend that the poor practice wickedness, and this reflects God's judgment. Gustavo Gutiérrez rejects this (and the arguments of Job's friends) by noting, "The obligation to care for the poor means that the poor are not persons being punished by God (as the doctrine of temporal retribution implicitly asserts) but rather God's friends. To give to the needy is therefore to give to God."[9]

Problematic Moral Passages in the Hebrew Bible

The Hebrew Scriptures are not unambiguously ethical or moral, as we generally understand the terms. Phyllis Trible considers a number of the actions perpetrated against women as inexcusable.[10] Women endured marital exploitation by a rigidly patriarchal society, rape without justice, violence that was unacceptable when done to men, and death, including the human sacrifice of daughters. Although Trible focuses on injustices done toward women, other examples such as slavery and genocide also exist.

Perhaps one of the chief moral problems contemporary readers see in the Hebrew Scriptures has to do with the widespread practice and patronage of slavery. There is no evidence of abolitionism practiced in either the Hebrew or Christian Scriptures, although there were restrictions placed on slaveholding. Biblical teachings about a year of Jubilee (Lev. 25; Deut. 15) did not seem to extend to slavery. Even though one can point to passages that advocate a more humane treatment of slaves in the Bible relative to other ancient Near Eastern civilizations, the practice of slavery remained the status quo among the Hebrew people. There did exist an abolitionist-oriented practice of setting free indentured slaves and other slaves who had been forcibly taken captive. Yet slave practices were widely accepted, and historically Christians long considered slavery to be grounded on explicit

9. Gustavo Gutiérrez, *On Job: God-Talk and the Suffering of the Innocent* (Maryknoll, NY: Orbis, 2005), 40.
10. Phyllis Trible, *Texts of Terror: Literary-Feminist Readings of Biblical Narratives* (Philadelphia: Fortress, 1984).

teachings in the Bible.[11] Indeed, slavery and the slave trade continued worldwide for centuries among Christians who believed that God and the Bible vouchsafed its practice. Not until the nineteenth century in Britain, with the social activism of William Wilberforce, was slavery and the slave trade considered a serious moral problem.

What changed? Had biblical interpreters gotten it wrong for thousands of years? Had the Bible gotten it wrong? Had God gotten it wrong? There are different perspectives on why Christians eventually moved toward abolitionism as the ethically preferred viewpoint in contrast to ongoing slave ownership, slave trade, and violence done to slaves. Some argued that Christians had interpreted the Bible incorrectly; the principles of salvation, fraternity in Jesus Christ, and human rights superseded the liabilities of slavery. Others argued that the Bible contains progressive revelation that at one time permitted slavery but no longer sanctioned it, due to liberative principles found especially in the Christian Scriptures. Although the Christian Scriptures seemed to affirm slavery as the status quo, a trajectory of egalitarianism among people superseded apparent class hierarchicalism among peoples: Jew and gentile, free and slave, and so on (see Gal. 3:28).

Another ethical problem in the Hebrew Scriptures has to do with genocidal practices, especially executed by the ancient Israelites after the exodus they experienced under the leadership of Moses. Many of these teachings—theological and ethical—trace back to the liberation of the Hebrew people from their enslavement by the Egyptians. Yet within a generation, the Israelites conquered the Canaanite people of ancient Palestine, enslaved non-Hebrews (e.g., Deut. 20:10–11), and killed entire populations of people—all seemingly under the command of God. Consider God's recorded words in Deuteronomy 7:1–2: "When the Lord your God brings you into the land that you are about to enter and occupy, and he clears away many nations before you—the Hittites, the Girgashites, the Amorites, the Canaanites, the Perizzites, the Hivites, and the Jebusites, seven nations mightier and more numerous than you—and when the Lord your God gives them over to you and you defeat them, then you must utterly destroy them. Make no covenant with them and show them no mercy." Although the Bible records that God wanted the Israelites to remain pure theologically and ethically and perhaps racially, the complete extermination of entire people groups seems incongruous at best with other teachings about holiness,

11. Bartolomé de las Casas, a Catholic thinker in the Renaissance era, argued that slavery was immoral, but his ideas did not gain any traction with the political leaders of his day.

righteousness, justice, wisdom, and steadfast love found elsewhere in the Hebrew Scriptures.[12]

Christians and the Ethics of the Hebrew Scriptures

Having seen above what the Hebrew Scriptures say about ethics, we turn now to how Christians have utilized them in their moral deliberations. Let us consider a few options. The first is complete acceptance of the ethics of the Hebrew Scriptures, emphasizing Jesus's claim to "fulfill" rather than "abolish" the law and the prophets (Matt. 5:17). Such acceptance assumes that the moral views in the Hebrew Bible are unassailable, arguing that moral ambiguities found are apparent and not actual. Extensive apologetic work is then offered in order to affirm all that the Hebrew Scriptures teach ethically.

A challenge to this approach is that, while in theory it sounds appealing to affirm all ethical teachings in the Hebrew Scriptures as universally valid and applicable, few Christians (or Jews, for that matter) consistently practice them. Consider homosexual behavior, for example. There are not many verses that address—directly or indirectly—homosexual behavior. Leviticus 18:22 says to male recipients of God's special revelation: "You shall not lie with a male as with a woman; it is an abomination." This command is repeated in Leviticus 20:13, now adding a punishment: "If a man lies with a male as with a woman, both of them have committed an abomination; they shall be put to death; their blood is upon them." The verses seem clear-cut, and yet few Christians advocate the death penalty for homosexual behavior—or for capital punishment in the case of other sins listed in the Holiness Code, such as adultery, various incestuous relationships, sexual behavior with animals, and disobedience toward parents. Moral inconsistency and hypocrisy seem to pose a serious problem unless all of the commandments are kept.

In discussing homosexuality and homosexual behavior, a question arises concerning whether the moral teachings of the Hebrew Scriptures have sufficient categories for adequately assessing the complexity of issues related to homosexuality. For example, Scripture does not make a distinction between homosexual orientation and behavior, which leads us to wonder whether people are morally accountable for attractions that may be unconscious impulses.

12. For example, see Laura Nasrallah and Elisabeth Schüssler Fiorenza, eds., *Prejudice and Christian Beginnings: Investigating Race, Gender, and Ethnicity in Early Christianity* (Grand Rapids: Eerdmans, 2009); and Thom Stark, *The Human Faces of God: What Scripture Reveals When It Gets God Wrong* (Eugene, OR: Wipf & Stock, 2011).

Regardless of whether such impulses are conscious or unconscious, biologically set or culturally nurtured, we can ask whether people are morally accountable for an orientation even if they do not act on it. What of those who practice celibacy in singleness and fidelity in homosexual marriage? Such questions make it difficult to determine from the Hebrew Scriptures a single, universal ethical view of homosexuality and other issues (rightly or wrongly) associated with it, such as gender identity, transgenderism, intersexed people, and cross-dressing.[13]

A second approach is to demythologize the Hebrew Scriptures, arguing that the existential dimension of divine revelation supersedes specific teachings contained within it. Encounters with God are more important than particular biblical teachings, which are subject to finite and sinful human interpretations.[14]

A third approach is to claim that there exist different dispensations (or eras) in the Bible and that God relates with people differently during different dispensations. Consequently, the teachings of the Hebrew Scriptures and even parts of the Christian Scriptures (e.g., Jesus's teachings prior to Pentecost) are not morally required in our contemporary context; instead, they are for either a past dispensation or a future one—a purported future millennial kingdom on earth.[15]

A fourth approach is to offer nuanced interpretations of these various moral teachings, bringing contemporary approaches to understanding them. This approach may use historical, critical, feminist, liberationist, postcolonial, and other interpretive methods to assess the meaning and application of the text.[16]

If one adds multicultural, multilingual, and multinational approaches to biblical interpretations of early Hebraic moral codes, then the viewpoints multiply rapidly. Yet all of these contextual approaches to the Bible help us to understand the breadth and the depth of biblical teachings, especially those concerning various moral practices. Since the Bible offers a variety of perspectives on, for example, how to treat the outsider, it follows that conversation with multiple theological and ethical views held throughout the world would be beneficial. Hospitable engagement with adherents of other religions might provide helpful insights since the other often offers insight and wisdom that one's own community does not possess. One need only consider the stories

---

13. For further discussion of this topic, see our case study in chapter 5.

14. For example, see Rudolf Bultmann, *Kerygma and Myth: A Theological Debate* (New York: Harper and Row, 1961).

15. For example, see Lewis Sperry Chafer, *Systematic Theology*, vol. 4 (Dallas: Dallas Seminary Press, 1948).

16. For example, see Miguel A. de la Torre, *Reading the Bible from the Margins* (Maryknoll, NY: Orbis Books, 2002.

of Ruth or the Roman centurion to appreciate this fact (see Ruth 4:1–22; Matt. 8:5–13).

In talking about biblical ethics, there exists an element of selectivity. For example, what moral emphases are most important in the Bible? Does the quantity of biblical references to particular ethical issues tell us what is most important? Should qualitative decisions about what issues are most important ethically in the Bible be made? In making these determinations, the question of proportionality arises.

The Principle of Proportionality

The **principle of proportionality** states that the more a topic is mentioned, the more important it is to an author. According to this principle, the more an idea or theme is repeated, the more central it is; the less frequently something is mentioned, the less important it is. For example, more than two thousand verses in the Bible point out God's concern for the poor and for justice, directly or indirectly, and the majority of those verses appear in the Hebrew Scriptures. Yet many Christians do not habitually care for or offer compassion to those who are poor or who are unjustly treated, and they argue that other ethical topics mentioned far less often in the Bible are more important. But this logic seems to betray what the Bible teaches.

Care for those who are poor represents one of the most prominent ethical themes of the Bible, especially in the Hebrew Scriptures. Jim Wallis finds that the two most prominent ethical themes in the Hebrew Scriptures are idolatry and poverty.[17] Although the sheer quantity of references does not confirm the quality or importance of ethical themes, their presence should at least remind us that such themes ought not to be neglected in Christians' beliefs, values, and practices. Ironically, Christians seem to say relatively little today about either idolatry or poverty, though probably for different reasons.

First, idolatry is too often thought about in the past tense—as an archaic practice by people in antiquity—and not relevant today, except perhaps in distant foreign countries. Historically idolatry had to do with the worship of gods other than the Hebrew God, Yahweh, and the worship of their images. The first two of the Ten Commandments explicitly prohibit such worship (Exod. 20:4–5). However, the worship of false gods extends beyond the worship of mythic gods and statuary; it pertains to any worship of or ultimate concern for someone or something that alienates people from the one true

---

17. Jim Wallis, *God's Politics: Why the Right Gets It Wrong and the Left Doesn't Get It* (San Francisco: HarperSanFrancisco, 2005), 212.

God. As such, greed, family, politics, patriotism, and even one's own righteousness can become an idol.

Second, poverty is mentioned throughout the Hebrew Scriptures, but often the causes of poverty are ignored by contemporary readers. Circumstances beyond one's control (e.g., malnutrition, illiteracy, accidents, illness) and structural challenges in society (e.g., economic and social forces, political and legal injustices) often are the causes of poverty. Even a cursory study of biblical references to care for the poor reveals that Christians are to have compassion for the poor and to advocate on behalf of those who are impoverished. The prophets, for example, harshly judge those who neglect the poor. According to the prophet Ezekiel, the sin of Sodom was that "she and her daughters had pride, excess of food, and prosperous ease, but did not aid the poor and needy" (Ezek. 16:49).

If numbers alone make a difference when studying the Bible, then Christians ought to focus more on the ethical problems related to idolatry and poverty. Not every moral problem from thousands of years ago still applies today, yet poverty remains and, when considered rightly, idolatry still seems to be a problem as well.

Case Study: Care for the Environment

Environmental degradation is a fact of the early twenty-first century, and human agency is an important factor in this process. Fossil-fuel-related pollution from the burning of oil, gasoline, natural gas, coal, wood, and other fossil fuels has contributed to immense amounts of carbon dioxide (CO_2), which imperils sustainability of the world's ecosystems and the quality of human life. Although the development of plastics has made convenience a way of life in industrialized Western societies, the pollution in the oceans has increased to the point that vast portions of the Pacific Ocean are covered with plastic refuse carried out to sea by the tides. The reduction of the rainforest in Brazil has contributed to the degradation of the ozone layer and the elimination of numerous animal species. Species extinction is now the highest ever in recorded human history. In addition, water supplies have dwindled over the past few years, putting cities at risk of running out of water and depriving entire crops of the water necessary for their growth. At the same time, the threat of rising sea water—due to climate changes—imperils coastlines around the world, which increases risk to human life and health in addition to the tremendous costs required to repair the damages done to homes, businesses, cities, and countries.

A further complication is the damage not merely to the environment itself but to other humans. Pollution affects the air we breathe, the water we drink, and the foods we eat. Some ethicists have called for principles of **ecojustice**, which is the practice of making certain that poor and marginalized groups do not unfairly bear the burden of ecological harms. Pollution, nuclear power plants, and toxic waste sites are often located near the poor and marginalized instead of near wealthy and politically powerful communities. The concern for principles of ecojustice can be seen as closely related to biblical principles of justice with regard to concern for the poor and the marginalized.

Humans not only alter the environment but are also part of it. As a result, there is a mutuality to the relationship. People have navigated that relationship in a variety of ways. The medieval Christian approach appealed to the idea of the uniqueness of humans in all creation and borrowed a good deal from Aristotle. The modernist approaches further divorced humans from the rest of creation. More recent approaches try to maintain that nature—even without God—has some basic value, even if only on utilitarian grounds. But a return to the biblical idea of stewardship might be the most viable approach of them all.

One of the problems with medieval Christianity was the tendency to see the created order as simply there for human interests and desires. Hearkening back to Aristotle, medieval Christians saw all nature as imbued with purpose (or *telos*; cf. teleology). Humans were created for the purpose of worshiping God. Animals, plants, and the seasons were all there to serve the interests of humans. Rain made the grass grow. Grass fed the cattle. Cattle provided milk and meat for human consumption. This was an anthropocentric view of the world. **Anthropocentrism** is the view that humans are at the center of everything and that even God "stood outside" the cosmos. Over a generation ago, Lynn White argued that the medieval approach was a kind of divinely endorsed utilitarianism that saw humans as having the only real value in all creation.[18] Practically speaking, this meant that humans acted as lords of creation (doing with it whatever they wanted). This attitude persisted until the modern era when—with the many discoveries of science—humans were dethroned.

Galileo and Descartes—among others—began to offer mathematical and empirical explanations for various natural phenomena. They could predict the patterns of the stars, planets, and other heavenly bodies much more accurately. Scientific explanations began to replace religious ones. With this came the further distancing of humans from creation. Nature was to be observed,

18. Lynn White, "The Historical Roots of Our Ecological Crisis," *Science* 155 (1967): 1203–7.

analyzed, and studied as an object. Animals, plants, minerals, and other natural objects had no value in themselves since they did not possess souls, freedom, or other human qualities. Again, humans could do whatever they wished with the natural order since now it did not even possess the status of creation but was merely nature.[19]

More recently some have appealed to the overall interests of beings inhabiting the planet.[20] Instead of seeing humans as singularly different from all other beings, these thinkers see humans as having the same moral value as all other sentient beings. The strength of this view is that it sees humans as part of the wider natural world. The weakness is that it fails to offer any substantive reason for why all sentient beings have value. It seems possible that those creatures—humans—that can intercede on behalf of all other sentient beings have more value because they have more responsibility.

A theological approach to the environment that emphasizes stewardship might offer a more reasonable alternative since it both (1) sees humans as part of the created order and (2) understands that humans occupy a special place in that order. Here we can distinguish stewardship from ownership. **Stewardship** is the habitual care of a gift entrusted to a person or persons. As care, stewardship has the interests, well-being, or integrity of that gift in mind. **Ownership**, however, is the possession of an object wherein the only interests belong to the owner. Consider parents' relationship with their children. The parents act as stewards of the child until the child reaches adulthood. The parents do not own the children, and as a result parents cannot do whatever they want to their children but must look to the well-being of the children.

In a similar way, humans should look to the well-being of other sentient animals and the basic integrity of the environment not simply because they are a part of the environment or because other animals might experience pain but also because the created order is a gift from the Creator. This seems to be the attitude expressed in the earliest narrative in the Bible. According to the early chapters of Genesis, Adam and Eve, the first humans, are called to be stewards of the garden. Their task is to tend it, care for it, and preserve its integrity.

Given the requirements of justice and the obligations of stewardship, a number of questions arise with regard to care for the environment: (1) What, if any, are the obligations of Christians to the environment? (2) What are the

19. Jeremy Bentham was an exception here, declaring: "The question is not, 'Can they reason?' nor 'Can they talk?' but 'Can they suffer?'" *An Introduction to the Principles of Morals and Legislation*, ed. J. H. Burns and H. L. A. Hart (Oxford: Oxford University Press, 1996), 283.

20. See, e.g., Bentham's intellectual descendant Peter Singer, *Animal Liberation* (London: Cape, 1990).

obligations of Christians to those in other parts of the world who also suffer the effects of environmental degradation? (3) What are the obligations of Christians to subsequent generations of people? (4) How does a conception of stewardship help to answer these questions? To these questions, others could be added. They are intended to inspire readers to think further about what it means to fulfill God's command to people to have "dominion" over the world (Gen. 1:26, 28).

Discussion Questions

1. How authoritative should laws of the Hebrew Scriptures be for Christians today? How does one distinguish between eternal and temporal ethical teachings in the Hebrew Scriptures?

2. How do the ethical teachings of the Ten Commandments compare with the Holiness Code? How consistent (or inconsistent) are people in obeying both the Ten Commandments and the Holiness Code? What of the prophets and writings of the Hebrew Scriptures?

3. To what degree are ethics aided by social accountability to others? To what degree are ethics social—that is, having to do with moral obligations to others collectively as well as to others individually?

4. To what degree is there continuity between the ethics of the Hebrew Scriptures and Christian Scriptures? To what degree is there discontinuity? Can you envision a balance?

5. What are your ethical views of idolatry and poverty? What are contemporary idols that alienate you (or others) from God? How strongly do the Hebrew Scriptures emphasize advocacy and compassion for the poor?

6. What kinds of obligations do people have to other sentient beings, and why? What are the obligations people have to the environment? What is the basis for those obligations?

THREE

Ethics in the Christian Scriptures

And now faith, hope, and love abide, these three; and the greatest of these is love.

—1 Corinthians 13:13

Words to Watch

agapē	counsels of perfection	love
analogy of Scripture	golden rule	love chapter
chesed	greatest commandment	*philia*
context	holiness	Sermon on the Mount

Introduction

A recent report from a comprehensive United Nations study showed that over 795 million people worldwide suffer from malnutrition or food insecurity.[1] Another study shows that every year over three million children die from starvation alone.[2] Yet in the United States, one in every three people

1. Food and Agriculture Organization of the United Nations, *The State of Food Insecurity in the World: Meeting the 2015 International Hunger Targets; Taking Stock of Uneven Progress* (Rome, 2015), http://www.fao.org/3/a-i4646e.pdf.
2. World Hunger Education Service, Hunger Notes, World Child Hunger Facts, 2011, https://www.worldhunger.org/world-child-hunger-facts/.

is overweight.[3] While 1.4 billion people live below the international poverty line, the richest 1 percent of the world's population controls 50 percent of its wealth. These data raise a host of questions, including how much wealth is enough, whether people should be permitted to accumulate as much wealth as they want, whether the wealthy have any obligations to the poor, and what role governments should play in encouraging access to opportunity, distribution of wealth, taxation, and minimum standards of health and well-being. Amid all of this is the fact that food and water are basic to any kind of human survival; without these basic needs being met, people die slowly and painfully.

There are a number of causes for food scarcity. Armed conflict in many places in the world prevents both agricultural production and food supply delivery. Political stability is thus a necessary condition for the development of agriculture and the economic growth of a society. In addition to the political conditions, poverty causes much malnutrition since without economic resources people cannot purchase what they need for survival. Environmental disasters are a third factor that accounts for many cases of starvation and malnutrition.

Concerns about food scarcity are not unique to the twenty-first century. Much of Jesus's preaching in the Christian Scriptures concerns food, which is often understood both literally and metaphorically. Jesus teaches that we need food for the body as well as food for the soul. In the famous **Sermon on the Mount**—Jesus's longest sermon (Matt. 5–7)—he explains how people are to live lives that are blessed (e.g., the Beatitudes), how they are to behave, how they are to love, and how they are to pray. With regard to salvation, Jesus says, "For I tell you, unless your righteousness exceeds that of the scribes and Pharisees, you will never enter the kingdom of heaven" (Matt. 5:20). Considering that the scribes and Pharisees were among the religious leaders thought to be the most holy and righteous of the Jews, Jesus's words were startling and disconcerting. They ran counter to much of the religious **context** with which first-century Jews were familiar. Generally speaking, context has to do with the situation—the particular place in time and circumstances—in which Scripture was written. Thus, in interpretation, it is important to investigate such matters as the genre, historical context, and literary context of a biblical passage.

While the ethical teachings in the Sermon on the Mount include Jesus's imperatives concerning anger, adultery, divorce, oaths, retaliation, love for

3. U.S. Department of Health and Human Services, National Institute of Diabetes and Digestive and Kidney Diseases, National Health and Nutrition Examination Survey (NHANES), 2013–2014, https://www.niddk.nih.gov/health-information/health-statistics/overweight-obesity.

enemies, almsgiving, fasting, the accumulation of wealth, worry, and judging others, the sermon culminates in what is known as the **golden rule**: "In everything do to others as you would have them do to you" (Matt. 7:12). These words of mutuality were not unique in antiquity; versions of it can also be found in other religions. Jesus did not see this imperative as new—or at least not radically new—since he immediately notes that this principle encapsulates "the law and the prophets" (Matt. 7:12). The golden rule epitomizes much of Jesus's morality, which is also found as the second part of his **greatest commandment**: "You shall love your neighbor as yourself"—a command also found in the Hebrew Scriptures (Lev. 19:18).

This chapter begins with a survey of the moral teachings of Jesus and the apostle Paul. We then consider the centrality of love and how love is an expression of holiness. Finally, we return to a recurring theme in the Christian Scriptures: How do we care for the neediest among us? That is, in a world of poverty, what are the obligations of those who are economically advantaged to those who are economically disadvantaged?

Jesus and the Sermon on the Mount

The central teachings in Christian ethics are found in those passages of the Christian Scriptures (traditionally referred to as the "New Testament") that reiterate the main teachings of the Hebrew Scriptures and in those new teachings that Jesus offers, especially in the Sermon on the Mount and at other key places in the Gospels. Much of the ethical decision-making among Christians hangs on particular interpretations one has of key texts in both the Hebrew and Christian Scriptures, and so in addition to the teachings themselves, interpretations of those teachings need to be considered.

The Sermon on the Mount addresses a number of moral issues, but these moral issues need to be interpreted since there is historical, literary, and cultural distance between Jesus's original audience and contemporary readers. The literary structure, sociocultural context, and enduring ethical significance are all important features that affected the meaning of the message for the original audience. The question is to what extent the ethics of his day are adequate for today. Have social, political, economic, national, and military contexts changed so much that Jesus's teachings have only limited application today?

There are several ways to interpret Jesus's Sermon on the Mount.[4] First, there is a literal or absolute way of interpretation. Consider Jesus's comparison

4. Craig Keener argues that "more than thirty-six discrete views exist, depending on how one counts them." *The Gospel of Matthew: A Socio-Rhetorical Commentary* (Grand Rapids:

of murder and anger: "You have heard that it was said to those of ancient times, 'You shall not murder'; and 'whoever murders shall be liable to judgment.' But I say to you that if you are angry with a brother or sister, you will be liable to judgment" (Matt. 5:21–22). Consider also Jesus's teaching about retaliation: "You have heard that it was said, 'An eye for an eye and a tooth for a tooth.' But I say to you, Do not resist an evildoer. But if anyone strikes you on the right cheek, turn the other also" (Matt. 5:38–39). Historically, those Christians who have followed these teachings literally are pacifists. However, the majority of Christians have not been pacifists, despite regular appearances of pacifists throughout church history (for example, Anabaptists). Other statements by Jesus have not typically been interpreted literally—for example, his imperative, "Be perfect, therefore, as your heavenly Father is perfect" (Matt. 5:48). Multiple qualifications of the latter imperative have been made. In general, Christians have had to nuance their understanding of Jesus's teachings in the Sermon on the Mount in order to make sense of it, rather than following the sermon in a literal or absolute way.

A number of nuanced interpretations of the Sermon on the Mount have arisen. Some have qualified Jesus's statements, claiming that parts of what he said are unreasonable or unwise. The qualifications, perhaps, are due to other passages in the Bible that mitigate (or eliminate) what Jesus said (a strategy known as the **analogy of Scripture**—that is, the interpretation of unclear biblical passages with clearer biblical passages on the same topic) or due to cultural differences between the first and subsequent centuries. For example, they might consider it unreasonable or unwise to turn the other cheek, to "give to everyone who begs from you and . . . not refuse anyone who wants to borrow from you" (Matt. 5:42), or to "love your enemies and pray for those who persecute you" (Matt. 5:44), and so on.

Another nuanced interpretation of the Sermon on the Mount recognizes how Jesus sometimes used the literary device of hyperbole, or exaggeration, in his preaching for the sake of oratorical flourish rather than ethical obligation. For example, when Jesus talks about the need to avoid adultery, he says the following about resisting lustful temptation:

> You have heard that it was said, "You shall not commit adultery." But I say to you that everyone who looks at a woman with lust has already committed adultery with her in her heart. If your right eye causes you to sin, tear it out and throw it away; it is better for you to lose one of your members than for your whole body to be thrown into hell. And if your right hand causes you to

---

Eerdmans, 2009), 160–62. For our discussion, we will only summarize main approaches to the interpretation of the Sermon on the Mount.

sin, cut it off and throw it away; it is better for you to lose one of your members than for your whole body to go into hell. (Matt. 5:27–30)

Because the Bible does not contain examples of Jesus's followers gouging out their eyes and cutting off their hands, these teachings are usually interpreted as figurative or symbolic in nature, emphasizing the need for caution but not of literal self-mutilation. This raises the question of whether the moral caution itself is as figurative as the examples of tearing out eyes and cutting off hands. Certainly, Jesus used figurative and symbolic language elsewhere in the sermon, such as when he talked about his followers being the "salt of the earth" and the "light of the world" (Matt. 5:13–14). Thus, some argue that Jesus's teachings may need to be nuanced in light of the rhetorical exaggerations in his sermon.

Another way to interpret the Sermon on the Mount is to consider the core of Jesus's teachings rather than specific applications of the principles. On this reading, explicit references to moral dos and don'ts are not crucial; instead readers are to discern ethical principles that underlie Jesus's teachings, leaving individuals to decide for themselves how to apply those principles in real-life situations. Consider Jesus's exhortation to almsgiving (Matt. 6:1–4). Today many Christians feel the need to restrict almsgiving, if they think that those seeking alms need to be taught a lesson of tough love for the sake of self-reliance rather than receiving gratuitous charity. From this perspective, collective almsgiving ought not to occur—either by churches or governments—since Jesus's ethics should be considered individualistic and not social, spiritual and not physical.

Similar to the aforementioned interpretation of the Sermon on the Mount is the belief that Christians' attitudes are more important than their actions. For example, Jesus often talks about the need for right attitudes with regard to anger, adultery, divorce, oaths, retaliation, and enemies. Because of the finitude of human existence and circumstances, and because of the corporate impact of sin on the world, some regard it as unrealistic (as well as unbiblical) to expect perfect performance of righteousness and justice from Christians. On this view, since people are saved by grace through faith rather than by works (Eph. 2:8–9), God does not expect perfection with the new covenant. God only expects people to be forgiven by the atonement of Jesus Christ. As such, Christians should endeavor to have right attitudes motivating their actions and accomplishments without concern that they have done enough to merit their salvation.

Still other Christians introduce boundaries on how the Sermon on the Mount ought to be understood and applied. Medieval Catholics talked about

counsels of perfection, which were instructions that Christians should obey if they want to go beyond the reception of salvation and fulfill Jesus's exhortation to become "perfect" (Matt. 5:48). These counsels of perfection were to be distinguished from the precepts of the gospel, which all should obey but which do not necessarily lead to perfection. Although it may be impossible for the majority of Christians to pursue Christlikeness in the challenges of their day-to-day lives, some may take on a more virtuous, ascetic lifestyle for the sake of achieving sainthood. Monastics were especially interested in pursuing these counsels of perfection, and many of them adhered literally to Jesus's teachings as found in the Sermon on the Mount and elsewhere without making such earnest living a requirement for average Christians. These counsels of perfection are rooted not only in the Sermon on the Mount but also in Jesus's exhortation to a rich young man. After saying that he had kept all the commandments (Matt. 19:17, 20), the rich young man was given an additional command by Jesus: "If you wish to be perfect, go, sell your possessions, and give the money to the poor, and you will have treasure in heaven; then come, follow me" (Matt. 19:21). Although the rich young man did not heed Jesus's additional command, it is argued that others ought to do so in pursuing spiritual and moral perfection.

One final approach to the interpretation of the Sermon on the Mount is the dispensationalist approach. Those holding this view have a specific eschatological understanding of Jesus's teachings and of much of what is found in the four Gospels. According to dispensationalism, there exist multiple eras (or dispensations) in world history in which God interacted with humanity through various covenants. Although there may be some similarities between the covenants, each is quite unique with distinct ways by which people are saved. Jesus lived prior to the start of the church dispensation, it is argued, which started at Pentecost. As such, his teachings are not intended for Christians and churches today but are instead for a future final dispensation known as the Millennial Kingdom, which Jesus will establish on earth in the end times (see Rev. 20:1–6). According to most dispensationalists, Jesus will physically return after a secret rapture and a seven-year period of tribulation and divine wrath on the earth. Thus, these dispensationalists argue that the ethics of Jesus—as found in the Sermon on the Mount and elsewhere—will apply fully in the final dispensation but apply only preliminarily and nonbindingly for Christians today.

From this brief survey of how Christians have interpreted the Sermon on the Mount, we can see that there is no unanimity with regard to how to understand Jesus's teachings in general and his ethics in particular. This does not mean that we are without any guidance with regard to learning about Jesus's beliefs, values, and practices. Certainly the Bible contains the primary starting point when determining Christian ethics. But Christians should be humble when making their claims about what Jesus and the Christian Scriptures state precisely about any particular ethical issue.

For some, the determination of Christian ethics is thought to be a deductive science, studying the whole of what the Christian Scriptures say about ethical issues. Such approaches often include claims to certainty and absolute truth with regard to their ethical conclusions, which can be appealing to those wanting clear-cut answers to questions they have. But for most, biblical studies are more of an inductive practice, which looks at the biblical evidence and to what may be found from church traditions, critical thinking, and relevant experience. Such determinations may not appear to be as confident or absolutistic as deductive approaches. But they are more rooted in a plausible reading of the Bible, given the diversity of ethical views that Christians have historically embraced.

Paul and Christian Ethics

Although Christians usually look to Jesus in deciding their ethics, the apostle Paul also powerfully influenced the early development of the church's ethics. Paul affirmed what he considered to be the divine or eternal laws of God, but he rejected what he considered to be ritual law, which he identified provisionally with Judaic traditions and not as enduring laws for Christians. It is thus difficult to determine a systematic understanding of Paul's ethical beliefs, values, and practices.[5] The difficulty is increased by the fact that biblical scholars question the authorship of some of the biblical letters. Consequently, multiple ways of understanding Paul's theology have arisen, including his view of Christian ethics. For the sake of brevity, we will discuss two of them, known as old and new perspectives on Paul.

After the Protestant Reformation, Lutheran and Reformed (Calvinist) interpretations of Paul emphasized the discontinuity between Judaism and Christianity and minimized the need of good works, which pertains to obedience to the laws of God. Luther and Calvin argued that good works do not factor into salvation in Paul's letters. For example, Ephesians 2:8–9 says: "For by grace you have been saved through faith, and this is not your own doing; it is the gift of God—not the result of works, so that no one may boast." Although good

---

5. For a table of the Pauline virtues and their citations, see David P. Gushee and Glen H. Stassen, *Kingdom Ethics: Following Jesus in Contemporary Context*, 2nd ed. (Grand Rapids: Eerdmans, 2017), 50.

works may be considered virtuous, they do not impact salvation that comes by "grace alone" (Latin, *sola gratia*) and "faith alone" (Latin, *sola fide*)—two key slogans of the Protestant Reformation. Focus is placed on the irresistibility of God's election of people for salvation, for there are no conditions for people's atonement; it is God alone who determines their salvation. Luther and Calvin disagreed with regard to the uses of the law. Luther emphasized the spiritual and civil uses of the law, while Calvin advocated a third use, which considered the laws of God to be morally instructive and beneficial to decent, orderly living. Christians were to obey the law not in order to merit salvation but as an obedient act of praise and thanks to God for salvation, which had practical benefits for life.

The so-called new perspective on Paul emphasizes a greater continuity between Paul's view of grace and faith, including God's role in providing for people's salvation, and the conditionality of their choosing to assent, repent, and act faithfully. Consider Ephesians 2:10, which follows the aforementioned passage by Paul: "For we are what he has made us, created in Christ Jesus for good works, which God prepared beforehand to be our way of life." Good works may not merit salvation, but they are inextricably bound up with it. Thus, good works ought not to be excluded from the discussion of people's authentic faith and salvation, despite anticipated paradoxes involved with their inclusion in discussing the Christian life.

It is somewhat of a misnomer to talk about old and new perspectives on Paul since the so-called old perspective is identified mostly with the Protestant Reformation. In some respects, the new perspective on Paul reclaims theological and ethical views that predate the sixteenth century. Roman Catholic and Orthodox Christians have long emphasized how God voluntarily chose to limit sovereign control over humanity in order that people might have sufficient power—afforded to them by divine grace—to choose freely to accept or reject God's will for their lives. With regard to decisions about both their ethical obedience and their eternal salvation, God provided grace preveniently so that, despite the limitations of finite existence and of sin, people may decide for themselves freely, without the constraint of external factors, necessity, or fate. Like the conditionality of God's covenant relationships established with people (and groups of people) in the Hebrew Scriptures, people are conditionally subject to the new covenant, with which God wants people to cooperate with divine grace in order to receive eternal life and then live Christlike lives by the power of the Holy Spirit.

Paul did not consider the Christian life to be one of spiritual and ethical passivity. He did not think of Christianity in terms of adherence to ritualistic circumcision, dietary laws, and the keeping of Jewish festivals. But he did consider the Christian life to be decisive and active, and he was hopeful with regard to living Christlike lives, ethically as well as spiritually. In Galatians 5:6, he says, "For in Christ Jesus neither circumcision nor uncircumcision counts for anything; the only thing that counts is faith working through love." Paul goes on to say that Christians are "called to freedom" but that they ought not "to use [their] freedom as an opportunity for self-indulgence" (Gal. 5:13). Finally, echoing the words of Jesus, Paul says, "For the whole law is summed up in a single commandment, 'You shall love your neighbor as yourself'" (Gal. 5:14). Paul did not offer principles without specific guidance with regard to responsible moral living. He still provided a list of vices that Christians should avoid, which he described as "works of the flesh" (Gal. 5:19–21), and a list of virtues ("fruit of the Spirit") they should pursue as they are guided by the Holy Spirit (Gal. 5:22–26). So Paul affirms Jesus's law of love as a love that can be ethically identified and willfully obeyed with the aid of God's grace.

Moral Responsibility

Although Christians have had divergent opinions on the degree to which obedience to God's laws relates to the gospel message of salvation, they agree that people are responsible for their moral choices. There are several ways in which people are responsible: spiritually in relationship with God, individually in relationship with others, and socially as members of a group. The Christian Scriptures address all of these relationships, providing guidance and warnings for the decisions we make.

In the Gospels, Jesus often speaks about the moral responsibilities his followers undertake when they choose to become disciples. An important passage that addresses these concerns is found in Matthew 25 in a story known as the great judgment or the sheep and the goats. In this passage, the people of all nations are gathered before the "Son of Man" as he separates the "sheep" (the righteous) on his right from the "goats" (the unrighteous) on his left:

> Then the king will say to those at his right hand, "Come, you that are blessed by my Father, inherit the kingdom prepared for you from the foundation of the world; for I was hungry and you gave me food, I was thirsty and you gave me something to drink, I was a stranger and you welcomed me, I was naked and you gave me clothing, I was sick and you took care of me, I was in prison and you visited me." Then the righteous will answer him, "Lord, when was it that we saw you hungry and gave you food, or thirsty and gave you something to drink? And when was it that we saw you a stranger and welcomed you, or naked and gave you clothing? And when was it that we saw you sick or in prison

and visited you?" And the king will answer them, "Truly I tell you, just as you did it to one of the least of these who are members of my family, you did it to me." (Matt. 25:34–40)

Those who practice compassion on the most vulnerable are the true disciples. They are not merely hearers of the word; they are also doers of the word (James 1:22). The ones who receive their reward are not those who profess their love for God, nor those who possess the right doctrine, but those who practice compassion to those who are on the margins of society. Those would-be disciples who fail to do this are condemned to eternal punishment.

It is in this famous passage that we see the three kinds of responsibility at work. We are responsible to God by keeping God's command to practice compassion. We are responsible as individuals when we visit the sick and care for the most vulnerable. And we are responsible socially when we recognize that this is our task not merely as isolated individuals but as people living in community. Although the Bible speaks to God's loving and forgiving character, it also speaks to God's justice. God requires responsibility on the part of those who would be disciples, but God also provides hope, which is grounded in the message of Jesus Christ.

Ethics of Love

Jesus, Paul, and the other authors of the Christian Scriptures focus time and again on the importance of love—of loving God and of loving one's neighbor as oneself. The greatest ethical command that Jesus gave had to do with love, and this principle is echoed throughout the Christian Scriptures. The Bible progressively reveals that the greatest motivation of God toward humanity was based on love. Perhaps the best-known verse in the Bible is John 3:16, which tells of God's love for the world: "For God so loved the world that he gave his only Son, so that everyone who believes in him may not perish but may have eternal life." God's love for us is echoed in Paul's letter to the Romans: "But God proves his love for us in that while we still were sinners Christ died for us" (5:8). This theme of God's love throughout the Christian Scriptures sharpens the emphasis found in the Hebrew Scriptures about God's *chesed*—God's "steadfast love" for humanity (e.g., Exod. 15:13; 34:6; Num. 14:18; Deut. 5:10).

Although love is central to understanding Jesus, Scripture, and the whole of Christianity, there is no consensual definition of the term. In the Greek language, several words are used to describe love, which will be discussed below. However, in the English language the word "love" is used to describe many dimensions of affection and commitment. The highest love is thought to be attributable only to God, and yet people are called to love as well. As one of the so-called theological virtues, love is thought to be a gracious *gift* from God, as well as a *task* that people are to undertake—aided by the Holy Spirit—in loving God with their whole heart, soul, mind, and strength, and their neighbors as themselves (Mark 12:28–31). As such, **love** has to do with our proper relationship with God, others, and ourselves, characterized—at least—by holiness, righteousness, and justice. Historically, love was thought to be the highest virtue, which mediated between the deficiency of selfishness and the excess of enablement.

One of the greatest biblical descriptions of love was written by Paul in his letter to the Corinthian church. In 1 Corinthians 13, the so-called love chapter, Paul talks about the "more excellent way," surpassing all other gifts, charisms, and virtues, including faith and hope (1 Cor. 12:31; cf. 13:13). First Corinthians 13 provides both the theological and ethical foundation for other counsels that Paul gives. It is noteworthy that Paul used the Greek word *agapē* (translated as love) throughout the chapter, as we shall see below.

Christians have discussed the different types of Greek words for love used in the Christian Scriptures—three in particular. The first is *agapē*, which suggests a higher, more holy, unconditional type of love, divinely aided by grace. *Agapē* is used to describe the love of God and Jesus for humanity and also the kind of love that humans should have for God. In addition, a second word for love is *philia*, which connotes more of a brotherly or sisterly love, as in the love between friends. Sometimes the word *philia* is translated as friendship. Such love is important for relations among people, including family, friends, and neighbors. But in the Christian Scriptures the more unconditional type of love, *agapē*, is the preferred type of love to which Christians should aspire in fulfilling the law of love. A third word translated as love is *philostorgosa*, which is a combination of *philos* (beloved, friendly) and *storgē* (natural affection, filial love). For example, Romans 12:10 translates the word as "mutual affection." This variation of love also suggests friendly regard, especially toward one's kindred.[6]

6. A fourth Greek word sometimes translated as love is *eros*, which has to do with erotic love and is not mentioned explicitly in the Christian Scriptures—perhaps because it is also the name of a Greek god. These terms do not always operate in precisely defined ways; etymological and grammatical considerations of the Greek language alter their meaning. Consider some examples from the Gospel of John. First, when John talks about how the "Father loves the Son," sometimes the word *agapē* is used (e.g., John 3:35), and sometimes the word *philia* is used (e.g., John 5:20), signifying the interchangeability of the words in describing God's love in the book of John. Second, people were described as having *agapē*-type love, but their love was not for God or others but for their self-interests (e.g., John 3:19; 12:43).

Love and Holiness

Love and holiness are affiliated throughout the Christian Scriptures. **Holiness** is an attribute that has to do not just with righteousness and justice but with the very character of God as revealed in the Hebrew Scriptures and with the holistic ways in which God relates with people: spiritually and physically, individually and collectively. Thus, the love Christians are to have for God, for themselves, and for their neighbors ought also to reflect a holistic character. For example, when Jesus says that we are to love our neighbor as ourselves, this love is not directed only to single individuals with whom we come into contact. Love extends to our neighbor collectively, including aliens, strangers, and foreigners. Although we must have wise boundaries with regard to how we are to love our neighbors, our love is to be more inclusive rather than exclusive of others who are somehow different or who are not of our tribe or family.

Since the modern era—initiated by the scientific revolution, the rise of the nation-state, and the Protestant Reformation—Christians and churches, especially in Western civilization, have been individualistically oriented. The so-called rugged individual who makes it on his or her own is an ideal that reflects our sociocultural context more than it reflects biblical ideals. The Bible balances individual standing before God and others, just as it cares about how both individuals and groups relate to others, individually and collectively. With regard to ethics, there is no biblical distinction between personal and social ethics; instead, ethics are thought to impact people holistically. Even ethical decisions thought to be private and publicly inconsequential have an impact on others, directly or indirectly. Likewise, ethical decisions thought to be public and privately inconsequential have an impact on people individually, directly or indirectly.

Because of the impact of people's sociocultural context on their understanding of the Bible and of ethics, Christians have become increasingly concerned about understanding their own context—their situatedness—as well as the context of the Bible and of historic views of Christian ethics. As a result, Christians have reread the Bible in light of contemporary concerns about such matters as the liberation of people from that which binds them physically and spiritually. Such bondage may occur due to the marginalization, oppression, or persecution of people based on their class, race, gender, ability, or some other reason for discrimination. Indeed, there may be reason to be concerned about unethical treatment of the ecological environment in which people live since the Bible says that people are entrusted with having "dominion" over the world, being caretakers rather than exploiters in their care of creation (Gen. 1:28). Too often such issues have been dismissed as trivial and not perceived as genuinely ethical issues for which Christians ought to be concerned. But there are no bounds to the holistic nature of biblical ethics because they embrace all people, at all times, and in all places, extending even to the created world in which we live. Christians may disagree on the precise ways in which they are to be engaged in such social, political, economic, and environmental issues, but it is difficult to argue that the Bible is indifferent to them.

Jesus serves as an exemplar for Christian ethics and not just as someone concerned with a privatized, truncated view of right living. Jesus presented a completely holy way of living, which translated into a holistic understanding of Christian ethics. His love for others included compassion ministries that cared for the symptoms of suffering—for example, poverty and bigotry due to racial, ethnic, or religious differences. His love also included advocacy ministries that cared for the causes of suffering—for example, due to the hypocrisy of leaders who oppressed people spiritually, economic abuses of money changers who oppressed poor worshipers, and colonial leaders who oppressed people politically and militarily.

Case Study: The Nearest and the Neediest

The result of what Jesus teaches in the Christian Scriptures is that everyone is my neighbor. People are called to love not only their friends and relatives but also strangers and enemies. This seems to be a radical departure from basic human impulses since it seems to view all people in a radically egalitarian manner, and it thus raises a number of questions: Can I no longer privilege my children over those of a stranger or an enemy? Should I take the time to entertain my enemies as I do my friends? How do I deal with the demands of those most in need? In contemporary ethical discussion, these questions can be framed in terms of the nearest and the neediest. Do I have greater obligations to one or the other? If so, what are the consequences? Philosopher Joshua Greene presents an adaptation from one of Peter Unger's many thought experiments to illustrate the problem:

> You are driving along a country road when you hear a plea for help coming from some roadside bushes. You pull over and encounter a man whose legs are covered with blood. The man explains that he has had an accident while hiking and asks you to take him to a nearby hospital. Your initial reaction is to help this man, who will probably lose his leg if he does not get to the hospital soon. However, if you give this man a lift, his blood will ruin the leather upholstery

of your car. Is it appropriate to leave this man by the side of the road in order to preserve your leather upholstery?[7]

Here most people believe that it is morally wrong to fail to help the wounded person. Simply to drive off without attending to that person's needs evokes a sense of moral outrage on the part of those interviewed since a person's well-being compared with the inconvenience of having one's upholstery ruined seems to trivialize the victim's health and welfare. However, Greene asks us to consider another case:

> You are at home one day when the mail arrives. You receive a letter from a reputable organization. The letter asks you to make a donation of two hundred dollars to their organization. The letter explains that a two-hundred-dollar donation will allow this organization to provide needed medical attention to some poor people in another part of the world. Is it appropriate for you not to make a donation to this organization in order to save money?[8]

Most people find that it is morally permissible to withhold the donation to the relief organization. Since we have no immediate prima facie obligation or emotional pull to those who are halfway across the globe, many people feel that it is morally acceptable to refuse the request. But the question then arises: Have we not trivialized the lives of those at risk in just the same way as we would have trivialized the well-being of the injured hiker? Why do we make these different judgments? The reason is that in the case of the wounded hiker, we have a clear instance of a personal moral violation. In the case of the relief organization, however, it represents an impersonal moral violation. The only difference between the two cases is the proximity of the person in need to the potential aid-giver.

Garth Hallett, a Christian ethicist, raises a similar problem.[9] A couple could spend $50,000 a year sending their child to an elite private liberal arts college or let the child go to a community college for free. The $50,000 savings could then be sent to a reputable world relief organization. If all people have equal value before God, then it follows that for the parents to spend that money on their child is to refuse the demands of the neediest. The Christian tradition is quite clear that the neediest have the greater demands on our resources. But the couple could object that, since they brought their children into the

7. Joshua Greene, "From Neural 'Is' to Moral 'Ought': What Are the Moral Implications of Neuroscientific Moral Psychology?," *Nature Reviews and Neuroscience* 4 (2003): 848.

8. Greene, "From Neural," 848.

9. Garth Hallett, *Priorities and Christian Ethics* (New York: Cambridge University Press, 1997).

world, they are responsible for them, while they had nothing to do with the circumstances of these other people and their misfortune. On this view, the neediest aren't neighbors in a recognizable sense.

The parable of the good Samaritan raises a question about the idea of proximity as it relates to the question of who is a neighbor. Is my neighbor merely the closest person to me physically, as in the case of the person who lives next door to me? Or is my neighbor the person who is closest to me in terms of social status and familiarity? Or does the concept of neighbor go beyond these two meanings? The good Samaritan in the parable tends to a needy person who is both physically near to him and also socially distant. Given the proximity of all people in a global environment in which we navigate by means of computers, social media, and instant news, are there truly any people who are not our neighbors?

Discussion Questions

1. How do you interpret Jesus's ethics in the Sermon on the Mount? Do you think Jesus's moral teachings should be followed literally, or do you think they need to be nuanced? If so, then how do you nuance Jesus's ethics?

2. With which interpretation of Paul's ethics do you agree: the so-called old view, which emphasizes salvation by grace through faith alone and rejects the relevance of good works (and ethical obedience) for salvation, or the new view, which emphasizes how genuine salvation by grace through faith is inextricably bound up with good works?

3. Although Christians have been forgiven for their sins, to what degree does God hold them accountable for ethical obedience (or disobedience) to biblical teachings?

4. What is the relationship between love and Christian ethics? How do distinctions between the Greek words for love—especially *agapē* and *philia*—help us gain a greater understanding of Christian living?

5. Why is it important to remember that the ethics of Jesus and the Christian Scriptures apply to ethical issues pertaining to people socially and individually? In addition to ministering compassionately on behalf of the poor, how might Christians advocate on their behalf?

FOUR

Divine Command Theory

> God's will is so much the highest rule of righteousness that whatever he wills, by the very fact that he wills it, must be considered righteous. When, therefore, one asks why God has so done, we must reply: because he has so willed, you are seeking something greater and higher than God's will, which cannot be found.
>
> —John Calvin, *Institutes of the Christian Religion*

Words to Watch

conscience	hubris	voluntarism
depravity	intellectualism	weak divine command
divine sovereignty	strong divine command	morality
Euthyphro Dilemma	morality	

Introduction

In one of the most famous—and problematic—episodes in the Hebrew Bible, God tells Abraham to take his only son, Isaac, to Mount Moriah and to offer him there as a sacrifice (Gen. 22). The reader is not told what Abraham is thinking or what he might have said to his wife, Sarah, or even much of what was said to Isaac. Abraham obeys and takes Isaac on a three-day journey to offer him on the mountain as a sacrifice to God. On arrival at the mountain, Isaac asks, "Where is the lamb for a burnt offering?" (Gen. 22:7). Abraham replies cryptically, "God himself will provide the lamb" (Gen. 22:8). Abraham then takes the boy, binds him, lays him on the altar they have built, and raises a knife to kill his son. At the last moment, God intervenes and rescinds the command. We are told that God did this only to "test" Abraham, and that by Abraham's act of obedience God learns that Abraham was indeed willing to offer that which was most precious to him (see Gen. 22:1). This particular story raises a host of difficult problems, not the least of which is the question of whether God can command us to do what is morally reprehensible in our eyes.

A related question raised by the Abraham-Isaac narrative concerns God's moral character. Throughout the Hebrew Bible, God's commands may seem to reflect a somewhat inconsistent or seemingly arbitrary moral character. Let us begin with a consideration of the Decalogue (or Ten Commandments):

> [1] You shall have no other gods before me. [2] You shall not make for yourself an idol. . . . [3] You shall not make wrongful use of the name of the LORD your God. . . . [4] Remember the Sabbath day, and keep it holy. . . . [5] Honor your father and your mother. . . . [6] You shall not murder. [7] You shall not commit adultery. [8] You shall not steal. [9] You shall not bear false witness against your neighbor. [10] You shall not covet. (Exod. 20:1–17)

Some of these commands make perfect sense to us today, regardless of our particular religious commitments. For example, not giving a false testimony in a court of law is especially important for legal justice. Telling the truth not only plays an important part in the justice system but also is part of what makes society function well. The prohibition on theft is recognized by almost every society in the world as important for securing personal property. Not committing murder is important to the development of the peaceful coexistence of every human society.

However, these are not the only commands God gives to various characters in the Hebrew Bible. We also find a number of other more puzzling commands:

- Do not eat of the tree of the knowledge of good and evil—to Adam and Eve (Gen. 2:17).
- Do not touch the skin of a pig (Deut. 14:8).
- Do not boil a young goat in its mother's milk (Exod. 23:19).
- Circumcise your male children (Gen. 17:12).
- Do not eat shellfish (Lev. 11:9–12).

This list seems neither contrary to the precepts of the Decalogue nor an affirmation of the precepts. Rather, these seem to be specific commands to a specific people that require a peculiar social context to understand completely. Many of these seem to reflect some specific concerns that a particular people had in an entirely different social and cultural context from the one we now inhabit.

Finally, there are those rare commands in Scripture—like the command to Abraham to sacrifice Isaac—that seem contrary to our most basic moral impulses and even contrary to the precepts of the Decalogue. In addition to the Abraham narrative, we also find the command to the Israelites to "plunder the Egyptians"—that is, to take whatever they want from them (Exod. 3:22)—on their journey to the promised land (Exod. 12), the edict to destroy all the inhabitants of Canaan (Deut. 7), and the command for Hosea to marry Gomer, the prostitute (Hosea 1). These seem bizarre and highly unusual at best. At worst, they seem irrational and immoral. So how do we make sense of the wide range of commands God seems to give? Are actions morally right because God commands them? Or does God command certain actions because those actions are right? Must God abide by some absolute moral laws? Or is God free to command whatever God feels like commanding? Could God command us to torture innocent children? Could God command us to kill another human being? Would God ever ask us to lie? In this chapter we look at divine command theory, its origins in the Scriptures, its theological commitments, and the criticisms that both Christians and non-Christians level against it. We also consider various cases of people who think God commands specific actions that would run contrary to what are generally accepted moral practices, such as those who claim God does not sanction the use of inoculations or fanatics who think God prefers some ethnic groups to others.

The Divine Command Tradition

Divine command morality—the idea that all of morality rests upon God's commands and nothing else—traces its origins to the Bible. Since Christians believe God speaks through special revelation, the Bible's prescriptions and prohibitions are taken seriously. This does not mean that the Bible has no need for interpretation or that some precepts that were social constructs still apply. Rather, it means that if God—whom Christians take to be personal—communicates to believers in and through the Scriptures, then we must assign these commands a special place of authority that may transcend the political or private spheres.

As we have seen, the Bible contains a great variety of commands ranging from specific instructions to particular individuals to the general prescriptions that conventional morality would require. However, there are also those unusual commands that seem to contravene the commandments against murder, theft, and adultery. These were seen as exceptions to the Decalogue and became a topic of concern for many medieval theologians.

Thomas Aquinas, John Duns Scotus, and William of Ockham all commented on these exceptions, and they provided different answers to how it was that God could seemingly contradict the commands of the Decalogue.[1] The three major instances in the Bible were (1) the command to Abraham to sacrifice Isaac, (2) the command to the Israelites to steal from the Egyptians at the start of the exodus, and (3) the command for Hosea to take the prostitute Gomer as his wife. These three thinkers gave different answers based on their understanding of God's nature.

For Thomas Aquinas and others who followed him like John Wesley and C. S. Lewis, God's wisdom, or intellect, was the defining feature of God's nature. God's creation is rational and orderly because God is Reason, the divine *Logos*. The intellect, therefore, is above the will, and so these thinkers are called intellectualists. **Intellectualism** is the idea that ethics can be understood by the human intellect because it is ultimately based in the divine Reason, who commands all things according to his nature. For Thomas, God could not dispense with any of the Ten Commandments since all of them ordered people to God as God is their ultimate end or goal—that is, since God desires communion with humanity, God's commands must direct them to himself. However, there were those who held that the divine will was the key feature in God's nature.

Thomas held that God could command the sacrifice of Isaac since all people are guilty of sin and sin is punishable by death. Thus, Abraham was merely executing a form of divine justice. Further, since the Israelites were held as captives for four hundred years, God was merely giving them their just reward for those centuries of slavery. For Thomas, God had a reason—based on principles of divine justice—that permitted exceptions to these commands.

In contrast, thinkers like Scotus and Ockham thought that divine power, which was based in the divine will, was the defining characteristic of God. These thinkers believed that God could command whatever God willed and was not constrained by the intellect. These thinkers were known as voluntarists (from the Latin, *voluntas*, "will"). **Voluntarism** is the view that the will is the central element in the commands of God. For these two thinkers, God was not absolutely bound to the Ten Commandments.

For Scotus, God must command creatures to love him and worship him. Accordingly, Scotus thought that God had to command the first few commandments. Consider, for example, the commandment to "have no other

1. For a survey of these thinkers and the primary texts, see Thomas E. Davitt, *The Nature of Law* (St. Louis: Herder, 1951).

gods." Since God created humans for union with God, God had to command all people to love God and not have other gods. The other commandments about murder, false witness, and stealing could be dispensed with since they were merely what God willed to be the case.

Ockham goes further than Scotus, emphasizing divine power in saying that the divine will can command whatever God wants—even hatred of God. This seems puzzling, but Ockham wanted to emphasize that there are no limits on what God could command. It is against this background that thinkers such as Martin Luther and John Calvin developed their ideas about divine power and divine commands.

As we can see from this brief survey, there might be a number of reasons why divine command theory commends itself to Christians. First, it seems as if we need a divine command to tell us what we ought to do. Second, it places Jesus's teachings at the center of our moral concerns. Third, it forces us to recognize our own limitations. Finally, it insists that there is nothing above God or independent of the divine will.

The Christocentric Nature of Divine Command Morality

In the Christian Scriptures, Jesus and others give commands that defy conventional wisdom: "love your enemies and pray for those who persecute you" (Matt. 5:44); "take up [your] cross and follow me" (Matt. 16:24); "do not repay evil for evil or abuse for abuse; but, on the contrary, repay with a blessing" (1 Pet. 3:9). Jesus and his teachings are pivotal to many Christian defenses of divine command theory since no investigation of nature, human virtue, or common sense would ever seem to yield these kinds of prescriptions. Jesus's command to love one's enemies offers a new way of thinking about others that transforms the conventional wisdom of the day.

In Matthew's Gospel, Jesus repeats the refrain, "You have heard that it was said . . . but I say to you . . ." (Matt. 5:21–22; cf. 5:27–28, 31–32, 33–34). Jesus's commands provide new content to the believer's moral system. Traditional morality fails to account for the radical revision in our moral thinking that Jesus demands. Divine commands show that the old maxim, "An eye for an eye only succeeds in making the whole world blind," is not what God desires. Rather, at times genuine Christian faith requires a radical conversion away from conventional morality. Only when this happens can there be genuine and peaceful coexistence.

Traditional morality contends that we should love our family more than our friends and our friends more than mere acquaintances. We have no obligations to the stranger, and we should hate our enemies. But Christ calls us to love all people without exception. The parable of the good Samaritan illustrates that the divine command to love crosses all ethnic and social boundaries, even to the point of loving one's enemies.

Some divine command theorists insist that their theory is the only one that rightly places Jesus Christ at the center of their moral vision. In this view, divine commands are seen as an expression not only of Christ's teaching but also of his centrality to Christian faith. Belief in Christ is the sine qua non of Christian faith. Only faith in Jesus can save, and therefore obedience to his commands—as an expression of our faithfulness—is what is required of the believer. To think of any other teaching or of any other way of pleasing God is to commit a kind of idolatry. One's ultimate loyalty is to Christ and not to an abstract principle such as the moral law, duty, or the greatest good for the greatest number. Only Christ—and the disciple's relationship to him—can serve as the basis for moral obligation. As a result, obedience becomes the chief virtue for adherents of divine command theory.

Divine Commands as a Remedy for Human Arrogance

For some defenders of divine command theory, human arrogance is a disease that requires divine grace to cure. Sinful arrogance, or hubris, permeates all human activity. **Hubris** is the idea that humans can determine their own rules and that they overreach themselves when they attempt to instruct God on what God can and cannot do. There are no virtuous pagans "since all have sinned and fall short of the glory of God" (Rom. 3:23). **Depravity** infects all human activity; humans are so sinful that they cannot know God's commands. Even if they could know what God requires, they could not succeed in keeping God's commandments, since sin would prevent them.

Not only does Christ command a truly radical enemy love; God also requires humility as the way to genuine virtue. Again, no traditional accounts of morality, whether derived from Plato or Aristotle, consider humility as a virtue. Only when we see ourselves in our proper relationship to God can we understand who we are and what is required of us. We cannot understand our place in the world apart from a proper belief in God.

Divine command theorists contend that attempts to base morality on any principle other than the grace of God in Jesus Christ are human arrogance. Only those who understand themselves as servants of Jesus can truly be moral. Any attempt to establish morality on a merely human principle is simply another example of humans trying to establish themselves before God on their own terms rather than on the grace of God.

Divine Commands and the Sovereignty of God

A basic belief of all orthodox Christians is found in the Nicene Creed: "We believe in one God, the Almighty, maker of heaven and earth, and of all things visible and invisible."[2] For defenders of divine command theory, this is not merely a throwaway doctrine but is an affirmation that nothing is entirely independent of God. The doctrine of **divine sovereignty** is the view that God has complete control over the entire creation. All things depend on God for their being, and there is nothing that God did not make or does not have absolute control over.

Consider the prologue of John's Gospel: "All things came into being through him, and without him not one thing came into being" (1:3). Here the idea of *creatio ex nihilo* ("creation from nothing") becomes important to defenders of divine command theory. Since God created everything in the cosmos, there is no domain over which God does not exercise sovereignty. All things depend for their being on God—or more philosophically we could say that all things in the cosmos except God are contingent beings. All things depend for their being on God, and God could have created them otherwise. This is easy to see with regard to humans. People could have been different than they are; they could have been shorter or taller, or had red or blonde hair instead of black hair. So too with the principles of morality: they are contingent and depend for their being on God. As such, God is not beholden to some external principle of morality, since there is no such thing. Since God is the absolute sovereign of the universe, God is free to command whatever God chooses. To suggest otherwise would be for a citizen of the realm to usurp the proper authority of the king.

The Divine Command Dilemma

Plato's earliest dialogue, *Euthyphro*, addresses the question of God's relationship to the principles of morality.[3] Socrates meets Euthyphro on their way to the Athenian courts, where Socrates is to be prosecuted for allegations of corrupting the youth and atheism. He asks Euthyphro why he is going to court, and Euthyphro explains that he is prosecuting his own father for the crime of killing a slave. Socrates asks him why he would prosecute his own

2. See Joseph Wilhelm, "The Nicene Creed," *The Catholic Encyclopedia*, vol. 11 (New York: Appleton, 1911), http://www.newadvent.org/cathen/11049a.htm. In Western liturgy, the words "We believe" may be replaced by "I believe."

3. Plato, *Euthyphro*, in *Plato: The Collected Dialogues*, ed. Edith Hamilton and Huntington Cairns, trans. Lance Cooper (Princeton: Princeton University Press, 1961), 169–85.

father. Euthyphro replies that it is what the gods demand. Socrates, therefore, poses the following dilemma, which has come to be known as the **Euthyphro Dilemma**:

1. If the gods' command makes an act right, then morality is arbitrary.
2. If the gods command an act because it is right, then the command is not essential to morality.
3. Either the gods' command makes an act right or the gods command an act because it is right.
4. Thus, either morality is arbitrary or the gods' command is not essential to morality.

Many religious believers have found this dilemma perplexing. Christians want to affirm God's omnipotence—that God can do anything—but they also want to affirm the idea that there is a kind of objectivity to morality. If we choose the first option, then we are committed to saying that God could command anything—even things that we find objectionable—and we would be obligated to obey the command. God could, for example, command the torture of innocent children, and we would be obligated to obey. Further, if we choose the first option, then it undercuts our confidence in the idea that there are enduring moral truths independent of time and culture.

If we choose the second option, then we are committed to saying that even God must obey the precepts of morality—that there is a standard apart from God that even God must obey. In this case, we have to wonder what the point is of God commanding an action if we already know it to be obligatory. God thus seems to be morally superfluous.

People of faith find themselves torn between wanting to affirm an objective foundation for morality and wanting to affirm God's sovereignty over all creation. Those who subscribe to divine command theory hold that the rightness of an action is determined primarily by the command of God.[4] What makes actions right or wrong is the command of God and nothing else. On this view, God's omnipotence is not subject to some external standard of morality—as if that were possible—but God can command whatever God chooses. As a result, the command of God alone is the basis of obligation.

---

4. Defenders of divine command theory include theologians such as Emil Brunner and Helmut Thielicke. See Emil Brunner, *The Divine Imperative: A Study in Christian Ethics*, trans. Olive Wyon (London: Lutterworth, 1937); Helmut Thielicke, *Theological Ethics,* vol. 1 (Philadelphia: Fortress, 1966).

Strong and Weak Divine Command Theories

Topic	Strong	Weak
Meaning of omnipotence	God can do anything without qualification	God can do all things that do not include logical contradictions
Divine commands	God can command anything whatsoever including commands for people to "hate God," or to "torture infants"	God can command anything that does not violate (or run contrary to) God's loving nature
Central divine attribute	Power	Love
Central human virtue	Obedience	Love prompted by obedience

Strong and Weak Divine Command Theories

Defenders of divine command ethics tend to fall into two groups: those who see God as having the power to command anything whatsoever and those who see God's power as constrained by God's goodness. The first version, which we might call **strong divine command morality**, is the contention that God can command anything whatsoever since God's power is not inhibited by any constraints. Thinkers such as William Ockham, Martin Luther, and John Calvin seem to subscribe to this version of divine command theory. Ockham contends that God could even command us to hate God. Similarly, Luther comments on the absolute divine freedom to do whatever God wants when he says, "God is He for whose will no cause or ground may be laid down as its rule and standard; for nothing is on a level with it or above it. . . . What God wills is not right because He ought or was bound so to will; on the contrary, what takes place must be right, because He so wills."[5] God's power, in the strong version, is absolute in the sense that there are no constraints whatsoever keeping God from commanding things that seem to us to be horrifically wrong. Yet there are others who think that God's loving nature would prevent God from doing that. Thus, God's love is not independent of who God is.

The second version, which we might call **weak divine command morality**, is the contention that God's commands are constrained by God's character. This theory has become the favorite of more recent Christian theologians and philosophers. This view is also called the modified divine command theory since it attempts to respond directly to the problem posed by the Euthyphro Dilemma.[6]

5. Martin Luther, *Martin Luther: Selections from His Writings*, ed. John Dillenberger (Garden City, NY: Doubleday, 1961), 195–96.
6. Robert Merrihew Adams and John Hare are two prominent defenders of the weak theory of divine commands. See Robert Merrihew Adams, "A Modified Divine Command Theory

According to the weaker view of divine command theory, although God has the power to command the torture of innocent children, we can rest assured that God will not command this. A central part of this belief system is that God is loving and good and would never do this since to torture innocent children would contradict God's very nature. It is only when we consider God's power in isolation from God's love or goodness that we can come up with these strange and revolting scenarios. Since God's power is intimately connected to God's love, we can rest assured that anytime we obey a command from God, it is for our own good. In this way defenders of the weak version hope to avoid the problem that if God's command determines the nature of morality, then morality is arbitrary. Since God's command does determine the nature of morality, and since God is loving, then the content of morality is not arbitrary.

Criticisms of Divine Command Theory

Historically, most of the criticisms of divine command theory are leveled against the strong version. Here we find people charging divine command theory with the claim that morality is arbitrary since it depends on the whim of God.[7] But just as troubling is the idea that the only people capable of determining good and evil are those religious people who hold to the right doctrines. Clearly non-Christians are very often moral people who know that murder, lying, and theft are wrong, and they do not need a divine command to tell them so. Consequently, either non-Christians who abide by moral principles are immoral, or they do have some notion of morality. If they do have some notion of morality, then they did not get it by a divine command. Thus, it is argued, divine commands cannot suffice as the basis of morality.

A second objection, also leveled primarily against the strong view, is that it elevates divine power over divine goodness. C. S. Lewis raises this objection:

> If God's moral judgment differs from ours so that our "black" may be His "white," we can mean nothing by calling Him good; for to say "God is good," while asserting that His goodness is wholly other than ours, is really only to say "God is we know not what." And an utterly unknown quality in God cannot give

---

of Ethical Wrongness," in *Religion and Morality*, ed. Gene Outka (Garden City, NY: Anchor, 1973); John Hare, *God's Call: Moral Realism, God's Commands, and Human Autonomy* (Grand Rapids: Eerdmans, 2000).

7. See, e.g., A. C. Ewing, "The Autonomy of Ethics," in *Divine Command Morality: Historical and Contemporary Readings*, ed. Janine Marie Idziak (Lewiston, NY: Edwin Mellen, 1979), 224–30.

us moral grounds for loving or obeying Him. If He is not (in our sense) "good," we shall obey, if at all, only through fear—and should be equally ready to obey an omnipotent Fiend. The doctrine of Total Depravity—when the consequence is drawn that, since we are totally depraved, our idea of good is worth simply nothing—may thus turn Christianity into a form of devil-worship.[8]

Although Lewis's criticism seems to be leveled against the strong version, defenders of the weak theory would argue that it does not address their rebuttal of the Euthyphro Dilemma. But this may not be the end of the matter.

If defenders of the weak version of divine command theory contend, "We know God is loving so we need not fear that God will not give a horrific command," then they have to answer the question, "How do you know God is loving?" They may respond that God does loving things such as keeping promises, caring for the oppressed, and so on, but such a response acknowledges that we already know that such activities are morally good. In that case, the divine command theorist must admit that there is a prior understanding of morality that God must abide by that is given to us through nature or intuition. In this case, we may wonder what advantage the divine command theorist has over those who defend natural law theory or virtue ethics.

A final criticism is that divine command theory seems to function more as a theory of obligation than as a theory of morality. God's command becomes the source of obligation even though the normative nature of the command may rest in the created order as the natural law theorist contends. Creatures are morally obligated to God as Creator, but the Creator acts on the basis of what is objectively good for creatures. The fact that many non-Christians may engage in the same moral behaviors that Christians do seems to be an indication that creatures naturally know some kinds of good behavior, even though they may not explicitly believe in God or see God as their Creator. The result is that the most important—and most central—virtue for the divine command theorist is obedience, which seems mistaken on at least two counts. First, obedience is a virtue usually reserved for the young and immature. It is insulting to be told by someone else, "Because I said so," when you are no longer a child. Second, the Scriptures quite plainly teach that the most important of the virtues is love, not obedience. Although obedience might lead to love, obedience can at best be only instrumental in achieving the aims of love.

8. C. S. Lewis, *The Problem of Pain* (New York: Macmillan, 1962), 37–38. It may seem that Lewis is unusually harsh in his criticism of the divine command theory and the doctrine of total depravity. However, Lewis's point that we must have some sense of "the good" that is congruent with God's commands seems to be accurate. Otherwise it is difficult to see how we could possibly know that God's commands were good.

Case Study: Intervention, Exemptions, and Conscience

As we have seen, the Bible is full of instances of God telling people what to do and what not to do. But often these biblical commands are to specific people at specific times, and as a result appeals to Scripture must always be understood in their proper context, interpreted reasonably, and applied judiciously. Some commands, as in the case of the Decalogue, have enduring significance and applicability.

Yet people continue to insist that God has told them to engage in various kinds of behavior—such as killing other people, robbing banks, and committing other kinds of immoral actions. In so doing, they claim that they have divine sanction for their activities. In these cases, as in the case of Abraham and Isaac, if the person obeys, then real harm may come to someone. Moreover, God could command someone to act in ways that do not violate any particular rule to which most people ascribe. God seems to have the power to command particular actions that do not raise any clear warning flags. For example, God could command a driver to stop and give money to a homeless person on the side of the road since this would not contradict any basic precepts of common morality—but likely fulfills them. However, things get more problematic as we consider other commands.

Let's look more closely at the problem posed by the story of Abraham and Isaac. Suppose you are on a hike in the mountains, and you see a man and a young boy heading to the summit. You greet them and ask the man, "What are you doing?" To your surprise, he says, "I heard the voice of God tell me to take my son and offer him as a sacrifice." What do you do? It seems there are at least three options:

1. Assist the man.
2. Do nothing.
3. Try to stop the man.

Assisting the man means setting aside traditional morality that forbids murder—even religiously sanctioned murder. It also means believing that God told this man to kill his child. Many people would reject this view on the basis that God does not command evil actions.

Doing nothing would mean removing yourself from the entire situation. After all, you are not the person hearing the voice of God and intent on killing your own child. From this perspective, you would be taking the view that noninvolvement, regardless of the seriousness of the situation, is the best alternative. Moreover, it means that you do not have to make a judgment about the man's mental well-being or whether he really did hear the voice of God. In this case, however, your inaction could be seen as condemning an innocent child to death, which seems morally unacceptable.

In trying to stop the man, you would be assuming either (1) that God did not tell this specific man to kill his son or (2) that as a rule God does not or cannot make these demands on people. In either case, you would believe yourself to have a moral obligation to prevent harm to the boy. While this scenario may seem far-fetched to most people, there is another situation in which people believe that God may command actions that result in harm to a child.

Consider a more contemporary and plausible scenario. Many people object to the use of vaccines. For some, like Christian Scientists, this refusal to be vaccinated is a religious duty based on a divine command. Others are simply skeptical of the medical value of vaccines. But in both cases there is a judgment of **conscience** at work. Conscience is the moral agent's subjective judgment concerning any specific course of action. In some circumstances it can affirm that a specific action is required or permitted. But in other circumstances it can determine that a specific action is wrong. In this case, the Christian Scientists determine that the vaccination would be wrong because it seems to contravene what they think is a divine command. There are also questions about potential risks and harm to their children. But at least two methodological points might be considered first: (1) Are there relevant teachings in the Christian Scriptures that might speak to this issue directly or by analogy? (2) Does science—as a form of using reason and experience—have any bearing on the issues? Once people consider these two questions, they can turn their attention to other more specific aspects.

One of the key issues at stake here is that of weighing an individual's conscience against that of the society's—or others'—interests more generally. In Catholic moral theology, for example, a person's conscience is morally binding. If one truly and sincerely believes an act to be wrong, then one has an obligation to avoid that action. Conversely, if one believes that failing to act would be wrong, then one has the obligation to act. As Ralph McInerny has claimed, even when people are mistaken, they should follow their conscience since it is always wrong—from the perspective of moral psychology—to disobey the judgment of conscience.[9] But a person's conscience, while morally binding, is not infallible. There are countless instances of people acting on their conscience that we see to be wrong.

Consider the case of fanatical racists who believe that God wants them to kill people of other races. There are at least two problems here. First, we

9. Ralph McInerny, *Ethica Thomistica: The Moral Philosophy of Thomas Aquinas* (Washington, DC: Catholic University of America Press, 1989).

can see that the individual's actions extend to others. In the case of parents who refuse health care for their children, the children suffer directly, not the parents. This is not like the case of Rastafarians, for example, who smoke marijuana for religious reasons. Even the Rastafarians can claim that their actions affect only themselves and not others. In the case of the parents who refuse medical treatment for their children, their behavior can—and often does—result in real harm to the children. So the question here is whether a judgment of an individual conscience should be permitted to harm others. If so, then it seems that it is morally permissible to act in ways that harm others because their convictions are so strongly felt. Moral feeling becomes the primary aspect of the decision. But this is clearly problematic since the feeling of a conviction cannot be a substitute for questions of truth. I may, for example, feel very strongly that the square root of 81 is 7, but my conviction is obviously wrong.

Second, some individuals often refuse to entertain the notion that they could be wrong. Radical adherence to the belief that "God has unequivocally said so" precludes other moral values such as humility, charity, and justice. Is it not possible—at least in some respect—that the person could be wrong? And if so, isn't it better to promote life and health than to harm it?

In a way similar to how individuals often claim infallibility based on God's commands, political institutions also fail the infallibility test. Again, numerous instances of systemic racism and sexism have allegedly been based on God's commands. These include activities ranging from refusing to give women and specific minority groups basic rights—like the right to vote—to altering admissions requirements for colleges and universities. It may be that a person's religious conscience can act as a balance to political oppression, racism, and sexism. But even here it can become a battle of competing consciences—that is, my conscience may tell me to do one thing while yours tells you to do the opposite. And, if we take this one step further, then people on one side of an issue can claim that God told them to refuse to engage in a certain kind of activity, while those on the other side can respond that God told them to actively engage in that activity. How can we determine which side is right other than by comparing who has the biggest God?

Discussion Questions

1. How would you respond to someone who was about to kill his or her own child and says to you, "God told me to do this"? How would you

respond to people who refuse to inoculate their children because "God said so"?

2. Are there limits to what you believe God can command? If so, what are they?

3. Do you think it is a limitation on God's power if God cannot command some kinds of activities? If so, why? If not, why not?

4. To what extent can Christians appeal to a divine command moral theory when they live in a society that separates personal religious morality from a public pluralistic morality?

5. To what extent should a people's religious convictions influence their views on politics and social issues? Should religious convictions be the basis for civil disobedience? If so, in what circumstances?

FIVE

Natural Law Ethics

These, then, are the two points I wanted to make. First, that human beings, all over the earth, have this curious idea that they ought to behave in a certain way, and cannot really get rid of it. Secondly, that they do not in fact behave in that way. They know the Law of Nature; they break it. These two facts are the foundation of all clear thinking about ourselves.

—C. S. Lewis, *Mere Christianity*

Words to Watch

divine law	methodological atheism	primary precepts
eternal law	moral precepts	secondary precepts
human law	natural law	*telos*
imperfect happiness	perfect happiness	

Introduction

In Sophocles's tragic play *Antigone*, we find the first hints in Western culture of what later comes to be known as **natural law** ethics, which is the idea that there are in human nature abiding moral principles that all people can and do understand.[1] Antigone is the bereaved sister to Polyneices, who died fighting against King Creon. The king has decreed—as a punishment—that Polyneices

1. Sophocles, *Antigone*, trans. Paul Woodruff (Indianapolis: Hackett, 2001).

cannot be buried. Instead, his body will be left to the vultures and wild beasts to devour. Antigone is rightly disturbed that this could happen to her brother's lifeless body and chooses civil disobedience in order to satisfy the moral requirements of a higher law. In defiance of the edict, Antigone secretly buries her brother but is caught and brought in for questioning by the king. She protests that the king has no power over what all people know to be right and good and that even if he decrees something against this **eternal law**—a law established by the gods for all time—it stands over and above all human proclamations. Certainly Creon may punish those who violate his so-called law, but all people seem to know that this is not a legitimate law.

Twenty-five centuries later Martin Luther King Jr. sat in a Birmingham jail and wrote a famous letter in which he appeals to Augustine, Thomas Aquinas, and others in the Christian tradition who all proclaimed that the laws of the state must conform to natural law in order to have legitimacy. King turned to the natural law tradition as a means to combat institutionalized racism, and alluding to Augustine, he proclaimed, "An unjust law is no law at all," in the sense that an unjust law has no binding moral force on those who must suffer under it.[2]

King and Sophocles believed that all people possess an intuitive awareness of some common precepts of morality, regardless of an individual's adherence to any specific religious tradition. A religious tradition that claimed to know that murder was right and that torture was permissible should be rejected outright as false. In King's case, a religious tradition that sanctioned slavery, lynching, Jim Crow laws, and other forms of institutional racism was a false religion.

One of the more notable and popular writers on natural law ethics in the twentieth century was C. S. Lewis, who repeatedly defends natural law ethics in his various works.[3] For Lewis, there were some moral truths that all people in all cultures recognize as morally binding. The natural laws are instilled in human nature so that no one can avoid them. It is, therefore, possible to read the natural law from an understanding of human nature.

In this chapter we consider the historical development of natural law theory in both the secular and Christian traditions and to what extent it is still a viable moral theory. We conclude the chapter by noting how a natural law theory might engage topics of human sexuality, especially same-sex relationships.

2. Martin Luther King Jr., "Letter from Birmingham Jail," April 16, 1963, http://kingen cyclopedia.stanford.edu/encyclopedia/documentsentry/annotated_letter_from_birmingham /index.html.
3. See C. S. Lewis, *Mere Christianity* (New York: Macmillan, 1943); C. S. Lewis, *The Abolition of Man* (New York: Macmillan, 1947).

Basic Natural Law Theory

We can summarize the basic elements of natural law ethics in the following statements:

1. All humans share a common nature.
2. Moral principles are grounded in that shared nature.
3. The basic moral principles cannot change (unless human nature changes).
4. These principles direct humans to their proper ends or goods.
5. All people know what the basic moral principles are.[4]

By saying that humans share a common nature, we mean that there is some basic essence or nature that each member shares with every other member of that species. We can see that all mammals share common traits such as being warm-blooded, giving birth to live young, having hair, and having mammary glands. In a similar way, natural law theory supposes that there is a common nature to human beings, and this nature is transcultural. Regardless of the culture or geographic location, certain kinds of activities will always necessarily be required for living in society—and the assumption here is that humans are social animals. Although the manifestations of these principles may vary from culture to culture, the principles will remain the same. For example, all cultures believe that children should show respect to their parents. In some cultures, this may mean silence in the presence of one's parents, and in others it may mean caring for them when they become incapacitated. Finally, a common human nature applies to both members of the sexes equally. Although there are biological differences between men and women, there are no differences in terms of their moral value. This common nature also serves as the basis for our moral obligations.

The second element concerns what we might call philosophical anthropology —that is, one must first know what a human is before one can know what a good human is. Certain kinds of unethical activities will thwart or frustrate our nature just as certain kinds of foods will frustrate our bodily health. Eating cyanide will kill us physically, but murdering a fellow human may kill us morally. The natural law guides us to those goods that are appropriate to us as reflective, social beings who also possess bodily desires and appetites. Since we have both rational and bodily desires, the natural law instructs us to pursue the truth, speak truthfully, practice peace, be courageous, refrain from sexual promiscuity, and so on.

4. Cf. Craig A. Boyd, *A Shared Morality: A Narrative Defense of Natural Law Ethics* (Grand Rapids: Brazos, 2007).

The third element of natural law is that **moral precepts** do not change unless human nature changes. Certainly, if human nature changes, then there is the possibility that the most basic precepts of natural law morality may change as well. Nevertheless, it seems that it would always be the case that we are required to practice justice and seek truth since these principles would act as necessary constraints on human behaviors, given our social nature.

The fourth element of natural law morality concerns its teleological dimension—that is, the ways in which our activities presuppose some particular end or goal (from *telos*, the Greek word for end). The idea that shapes this principle derives from Aristotle, who claimed that there is a specific "human function." By that he meant that humans possess a unique goal or purpose in life based on their nature. For Aristotle, this meant that all humans desire happiness and that this goal could only be attained by the thoughtful and judicious use of reason and the acquisition of the virtues.

Thomas Aquinas and other Christian writers in the natural law tradition have understood happiness as both imperfect and perfect. **Imperfect happiness** is that kind of happiness anyone—Christian or not—could possess in this life, while **perfect happiness** is the beatific vision of God. The various precepts of the natural law not only order our lives to peaceful coexistence with one another but also start us on the road to communion with God. But we must add that pointing in the direction of God is meant only as part of the moral life. It does not encompass the entirety of our moral lives.

The natural law does not delineate every detail of the moral life; rather, it lays down those commonly understood truths that provide the bare minimum for human coexistence. This means that natural law morality is not a complete moral system but requires the development and practice of the virtues as perfecting the agent. Thomas Aquinas says, "All acts of virtue are prescribed by natural law: since each one's reason naturally dictates to him to act virtuously."[5] All the acts of the virtues fall under the sphere of the natural law since they are prescribed by reason.[6] However, the natural law does not dictate precisely how one is to act according to reason. For Thomas, the

5. Thomas Aquinas, *Summa Theologica* 1-2.94.3, trans. Fathers of the English Dominican Province (New York: Benziger, 1947). Thomas says that the virtues are good habits that perfect the various powers of the soul. Thus, there are intellectual virtues that perfect the rational powers of the soul. Included in these virtues are understanding, wisdom, science, prudence, and art (1-2.57). The moral virtues perfect the appetitive powers of the soul and must be shaped by human reason and its grasp of the peculiarly human goods (1-2.60). In the case of both types of virtue, reason and not instinct understands what the good is and guides the agent to its proper end.

6. Thomas Aquinas, *Summa Theologica* 1-2.94.3. For further discussion on the relationship between virtue and natural law, see Vernon Bourke, "Is Thomas Aquinas a Natural Law Ethician?," *The Monist* 58 (1974): 52–66.

natural law simply indicates what specific kinds of actions are per se good and those that are evil, but he does not specify in his theory of the natural law just how one goes about determining what kind of behavior is required. Natural law morality does not simply provide prima facie obligations; it also requires the development of virtue, which enables a person to act consistently for the right reasons and in the right circumstances.

The final point concerning the nature of natural law is that its basic precepts are available to all humans whose reason is functioning in a normal fashion. The divine spark in all humans enables all people to apprehend the basic precepts of natural law morality. Thinkers from the apostle John to Lewis have affirmed the ability of humans to know what the natural law requires. For the apostle Paul, it consisted in natural revelation; for Augustine it was divine illumination; for Thomas Aquinas it was the natural light of reason. There is a normative capacity in all human cultures to understand these moral principles. Moreover, these principles have their goal-oriented nature based in a relatively stable human nature that is accessible to anyone who will consult it. Thus, even non-Christians have developed natural law theories since this moral information is available to all people. And so there seems to be general agreement among peoples of different cultures and religions concerning basic moral norms.

Secular Sources for Natural Law Ethics

As early as the time of Sophocles, there was an intuitive claim that the principles of morality do not change but hold universally—for king and subjects alike. The most important thinkers in the secular domain who contributed to the development of natural law morality were Plato and Aristotle. Both of these thinkers appeal to the ideal that (1) humans share a common nature, (2) this nature does not change, and (3) all people know what that nature is.

Plato and Natural Law

In Plato's most famous work, the *Republic*, we find Socrates defending an understanding of justice that is resistant to the charges of moral relativism—namely, the idea that morals have no objective basis.[7] Socrates's interlocutor in the early part of the dialogue is Thrasymachus. Thrasymachus contends that justice is the interest of the strong. There is no overarching principle for right and wrong on this view. There is only what the powerful declare to be law,

7. Plato, *Republic*, in *Plato: The Collected Dialogues*, ed. Edith Hamilton and Huntington Cairns, trans. Lance Cooper (Princeton: Princeton University Press, 1961), 575–844.

which changes from ruler to ruler. Socrates rejects this claim as philosophically naive. For Socrates, the rightly ordered soul is one wherein reason rules the emotional and appetitive elements, and as a result a person can come to know those moral principles that are enduring and embedded in our nature.

Later in the dialogue Socrates develops a philosophy of education, a political theory, and an account of justice that ultimately depends on a theory of human nature that applies to all humans. All people are composed of reason, emotion, and sensual appetite. Further, each component part has a specific function it is to fulfill. Reason controls the soul; emotion pursues honor; and appetite desires the sensual goods of food, drink, and sex.

In order for there to be justice in the soul, reason must maintain its control, and the emotional and appetitive components must obey. If this does not happen, then the soul becomes disordered. From this, Socrates defends certain conventional norms of ethics such as the goodness of rendering to others what is their due and the avoidance of murder and theft. But Plato's description is primarily in terms of the virtue of justice and not of law.

Aristotle on Right Reason

Plato's student Aristotle also had a view of human nature that determined what his ethical views were. All humans are "rational animals." Our "shared nature" consists of both our animal appetites and emotions and our rational abilities.[8] For Aristotle, like Plato, it was important for reason to guide our actions and not merely let our appetites or emotions determine our behavior by themselves.

For Aristotle, humans have appetites for food, drink, and sex, but they also have emotions such as fear and anger. If we let our lives be directed by any of these without the guidance of reason, then we fail to be truly human. Reason, therefore, tells us where, when, and how we should act. As a result, we see that certain kinds of actions such as adultery or cowardice are evil since they arise from unchecked emotion or desire. Moreover, all people know that these kinds of activities are wrong.

Natural Law and Christian Ethics

Christian defenders of natural law ethics find themselves in an interesting position. They want to affirm the truth of the Christian tradition as found

---

8. Aristotle, *Nicomachean Ethics*, books 1 and 2, trans. Terence Irwin (Indianapolis: Hackett, 1984).

in the unique revelation of Jesus Christ and the Scriptures while simultaneously wanting to affirm the idea that all people know the most basic truths of morality.

C. S. Lewis attempts to combine both elements in his defense of natural law when he claims that all people know the law of nature, but they also know that they have violated the law of nature. Lewis is thus able to defend the universal knowledge of natural law while simultaneously showing that grace is necessary. The Christian natural law theorist will want to demonstrate that the Bible does not speak against natural law. But more positively, many Christians have claimed that the Bible supports natural law ethics.

Natural Law and the Bible

The Bible does not give a theory of ethics; it speaks to various moral contexts such as marriage, the family, the village, the temple, synagogues, and churches. The first book of the Bible, Genesis, indicates that God creates "living creatures of every kind" (1:24), thereby establishing an understanding for natural law theorists that each creature has a specific nature. This includes the human creature whose nature is ordered to God in worship and praise.

In Exodus, we find the Decalogue, which elaborates on how we are to honor and worship God and how we are to treat our neighbor (Exod. 20:1–17). Although the Decalogue is part of the covenant God established with the children of Israel, most Christian thinkers have asserted that these precepts apply to all people, regardless of their race or religion. The precepts of the Decalogue apply to both Christian and Jewish ethics, and the teachings of the Qur'an echo these commands as well. At the very minimum, then, the great monotheistic faiths agree on these basic precepts of morality. In the Christian tradition, there is continuity between the precepts of the Decalogue and the teachings of the Christian Scriptures.

The prologue to the Gospel of John indicates that the pre-incarnate Christ is the one who illuminates all humanity with regard to questions of truth—including moral truth. If this is so, then all people have access to some basic truths about morality, and this truth is made possible through the creative activity of Christ. The Gospel of John seems to indicate that one need not explicitly confess faith in Christ in order to know the natural law.

In the first chapter of Paul's Epistle to the Romans, we find what has become the traditional starting point for Christian natural law ethics. Paul writes, "For what can be known about God is plain to them, because God has shown it to them. Ever since the creation of the world his eternal power and divine nature, invisible though they are, have been understood and seen through the things he has made. So they are without excuse; for though they knew God, they did not honor him as God or give thanks to him" (Rom. 1:19–21). The idea here is that all people know these basic truths because they can see them in nature. Paul explicitly states that even nonbelievers have access to basic moral knowledge and that God holds all people accountable for acting in accordance with this moral knowledge regardless of their religious traditions or beliefs.

Natural Law and the Christian Tradition

Augustine developed an idea of natural law from Cicero and thought that the law was "inscribed on the human soul."[9] For Augustine, natural law enabled all people to see basic moral truths, such as that murder is wrong, that lying is evil, and that we should practice justice. Thomas Aquinas further developed the Christian tradition of natural law by identifying in it the following features:

1. It is made possible through the divine *Logos* (reason) in creation.
2. It is discoverable through the "light of natural reason."
3. It applies universally to all people.
4. It does not change.
5. It is established by God for "the common good."[10]

For Aquinas, the natural law participates in the eternal law, and the eternal law is Jesus Christ himself. As John writes, "All things came into being through him" (John 1:3), which means that the natural law was part of the creation that the pre-incarnate Christ created. Therefore, all people—since they are created by God and possess reason—can know the natural law.

The light of natural reason is that ability all humans possess—inasmuch as they can think about the created order without special assistance from God. One need not be a Christian to know that murder is wrong. Muslims, Jews, Buddhists, agnostics, and atheists know this to be true. The fact that all these diverse groups of people can understand the basic precepts of natural law speaks to a third element: the universality of the natural law.

The natural law applies to all people in all cultures. This is because all cultures have rules promoting honesty, forbidding murder, requiring the care of the elderly and the young, and so on. No culture or society of any kind would be possible if these precepts were not applied. However, it does not mean

9. Augustine, *On the Free Choice of the Will* 1.6, trans. Thomas Williams (Indianapolis: Hackett, 1993).
10. Thomas Aquinas, *Summa Theologica* 1-2.94.

that these precepts will look the same in each and every society. Honoring the elderly in China might mean becoming silent in their presence, while in New York City it might mean offering them a seat on a crowded bus.

Figure 5.1.
The Hierarchy of Law in Thomas Aquinas

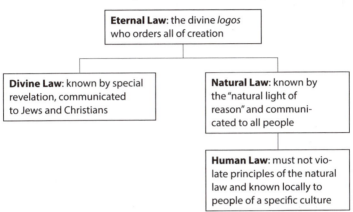

Since the basic precepts of the natural law apply to all people, it would seem that they do not change over time. Murder was wrong two thousand years ago, and it will still be wrong two thousand years from now. The reason for this is that the social nature of humanity cannot change. Defenders of natural law argue that all human society is based on at least two basic precepts: not harming one another and basic honesty with regard to keeping faith with one another.[11] No society is imaginable apart from these precepts. These precepts that do not change and are binding on all people regardless of culture are known as **primary precepts** of natural law. Thomas Aquinas includes other precepts as well, such as that all people should pursue virtue and the truth about God and that we must always practice justice. These precepts never permit exceptions.

There are also other precepts of natural law that are known as secondary precepts. **Secondary precepts** of natural law are precepts that are binding in the majority of cases but not in each and every instance. They function as general rules. Thomas asks us to consider the following example. It is a primary precept of natural law that we should always practice justice. Usually justice requires that we return borrowed items to their rightful owners. Yet what if I have a weapon that I have borrowed from my neighbor, and he wants it back

11. See Thomas Aquinas, *Summa Theologica* 1-2.94.2; Lewis, *The Abolition of Man.*

for the purpose of a revolution against the state? Assuming that the state is a just and peaceful state and that my neighbor has either a wicked intention or has some psychological instability, this is a time when I should not return the borrowed item, since it would be an instance of injustice as I would be aiding and abetting an evil action. Often these secondary precepts are made into **human law** for the general benefit of society, but we can see that they do permit exceptions in rare cases.

Criticisms of Natural Law Ethics

Criticisms of natural law ethics come from two very different sources: theists who claim that the theory is not religious enough and nontheists who claim that it is too religious. Others claim that the theory is archaic in the sense that it appeals to a view of human nature that is outmoded.

Some see natural law as a kind of methodological atheism.[12] **Methodological atheism** is the idea that our moral deliberations have no need of God; we can act—and reason—as if there is no God. The argument runs like this: A Christian should have ultimate allegiance to God. If there is a moral system that does not require God, then this moral system would have effectively turned into a kind of atheism by rendering God morally irrelevant. But a Christian cannot see God as irrelevant to morality. Thus, a Christian should reject natural law theory as a basis for ethics.

A defender of natural law ethics would say that God is the one who establishes natural law as **divine law** and that the worship of God is one of the precepts of natural law. As a result, natural law is not an atheistic moral theory but is one that appeals both directly and indirectly to a divine lawgiver.

Some nonreligious people see natural law theory as too firmly indebted to a theistic universe, wherein all things are appointed to their end by a divine lawgiver. If there is no God, then there can be no natural law.[13] This attack, however, switches the ground of the argument from ethics to the philosophy of religion.

A third criticism comes from biology. If humans have evolved over millions of years, then there is no permanent human nature.[14] Human nature changes over time, and so the kinds of behaviors natural law prescribes cannot remain

12. Edward Collins Vacek, SJ, "Divine-Command, Natural-Law, and Mutual-Love Ethics," *Theological Studies* 57 (1996): 633–53.

13. This is the view of Jean-Paul Sartre, *Existentialism and Humanism*, trans. Philip Mairet (London: Eyre Methuen, 1973), 27.

14. Ian Tattersall, *Becoming Human: Evolution and Human Uniqueness* (New York: Harcourt Brace, 1998), 198.

constant. If evolution is true, then it might seem that a kind of moral relativism would be the best that anyone could hope for. But even granted the truth of human evolution, it could be argued that humans have evolved in ways that point to some behaviors that promote cooperation and survival so that even on an evolutionary account of human nature's origins, there are a few core principles that remain.[15]

Case Study: Human Sexuality

As we have seen, natural law ethics takes human nature seriously in the sense that our biological and rational nature gives an indication of how we ought to behave. Since we are social animals, behaviors that encourage getting along peacefully are required. As a result, practicing justice is a precept of the natural law. So too is prohibiting murder since this also tears down the social fabric of society. But what about other kinds of activities that threaten interpersonal and community relationships—especially various kinds of sexual behaviors?

Biblical sources on human sexuality permit some practices that are not acceptable today, such as polygamy. Yet regarding activities like autoeroticism the Bible seems to be silent. Although the Israelites are told that a man is not to lie with another man, the term "homosexuality" (as well as the related term "heterosexuality") does not appear in the Bible but was coined in the nineteenth century. Although sexual relations are regulated throughout numerous passages in the Bible, the only rule governing sexual behavior that appears in the Decalogue is the prohibition on adultery.

In the Gospels, Jesus does not condemn the woman caught in adultery, but he does tell her not to sin again (John 8:11). The passages about sexual conduct in the Pauline Epistles are often found in lists of practices to be avoided and serve to differentiate Christian churches from the surrounding religious culture of the Greeks and Romans.

Historically, moral theologians and philosophers with Christian commitments have often employed natural law morality as an interpretation of the Bible, especially regarding sexual ethics.[16] When the Scriptures speak of animals being created "of every kind" (Gen. 1:24, 25), this phrase serves as a way to think about some actions as contrary to nature and others as in accordance with nature. What kinds of sexual behaviors are appropriate to humans? Here

---

15. Stephen Pope, *Evolution and Christian Ethics* (Cambridge: Cambridge University Press, 2007).

16. See, e.g., Servais Pinckaers, *The Sources of Christian Ethics* (Washington, DC: Catholic University of America Press, 1995).

the idea of a *telos*, a "natural end," for a behavior became the determining factor. Human sexuality is essentially for the purpose of procreation, and so sexual union and procreation are linked together intrinsically. Those activities that do not contribute to procreation are disordered acts. All sexual activity, on this view, must be for the purpose of procreation. Consequently, sexual acts that could not ever result in pregnancy were not allowed. Birth control, masturbation, homosexual activities, and all other kinds of nonprocreative sexual activity were condemned.

Since sexual union is ordered to procreation, other moral features follow. Sexual union should not take place outside the bonds of marriage. Sexual reproduction should be between two people committed to each other and to the raising of children. Without the bonds of marriage, men might not commit to raising their children. This also was an important consideration in the prohibition of adultery. If women were sexually promiscuous, then a man might not know whether the infant belonged to him or to some other man. This had not only biological and familial implications but also economic implications. If a child was born out of an adulterous encounter, and that child inherited the bulk of the cuckolded man's estate, then that act would amount to theft. But although adultery could be understood as both an economic evil and a sexually disordered act, homosexual behaviors lacked the economic feature.

Homosexual acts were seen as disordered in the sense that (1) they took place outside the bonds of marriage, (2) they could not in principle result in the birth of a child, and (3) they thwarted the design of human genitalia. Yet, as times change, we can question the reasons why these prohibitions on homosexuality continue to exist.[17] Some cultural factors will vary from place to place and time to time. Scientific research also enables us to know more about human sexuality than people did two thousand years ago (e.g., that some people may have excess hormonal activity or may be resistant to specific hormones or may have genetic markers that alter their appearance or behavior).[18] In addition to various developments in the sciences, political changes since the rise of the nation-states over four hundred years ago have also altered the ways in which people think about their freedoms and individual rights.

Many countries now permit same-sex marriages, where marriage is seen primarily in terms of a contract for partnering with another adult that is

17. For brief arguments on both sides of the homosexuality debate, see Dan O. Via and Robert Gagnon, *Homosexuality and the Bible: Two Views* (Minneapolis: Fortress, 2003).
18. For more on these issues, see Adrian Thatcher, ed., *The Oxford Handbook of Theology, Sexuality, and Gender* (New York: Oxford University Press, 2015).

recognized by the state. People pool their resources, share a life together, and engage in intimate behaviors with one another. The conditions for this are that the persons are of legal age and that they freely enter into the state-recognized contract. Consent is the primary requirement for marriage, and a child, an animal, or an inanimate object cannot give consent.

However, for most Christians, marriage is more than a contract; it is a covenant. Marriage consists in the radical commitment of one person to another. It is not merely a business relationship based on mutual self-interest. Yet if marriage is a covenant, then it could be argued that there must be conditions set on the participants, such as that it be between "one man and one woman." Early societies—including the patriarchs in the Bible—practiced polygamy. It seems that cultural factors have clearly influenced the ways in which modern-day Christians have appropriated the cultural practice of marriage in the Hebrew Bible. Is there something unique to marriage that requires it be only for one man and one woman? Does the raising of children, for example, provide the essential element? Or is heterosexuality itself the requirement for a covenantal understanding of marriage?

Second, although homosexual activity does not result in the birth of an infant, there are many other sexual activities that also do not result in the birth of an infant. Young women and men who are incapable of producing viable gametes would be prohibited from engaging in sexual activity. Postmenopausal women would be forbidden to engage in sex, as would men who had vasectomies. All forms of autoeroticism would also be prohibited. Yet homosexual relationships are often seen as especially problematic or singled out as being significantly more disordered—or as being more morally wrong—than these other sexual practices. This raises some important questions: Should sexual activity be restricted only to those who are able to have children, who are married to each other, and who engage only in sex that can in principle result in a pregnancy? What is the purpose of marriage? Are there reasons other than procreation for engaging in sexual activity? Does a long-standing traditional condemnation of homosexual behavior provide a compelling reason for its continued prohibition?

Third, male genitalia seem designed for female genitalia in a way that we could say that teeth are designed for chewing or legs are designed for walking. In other words, specific body parts are designed for specific purposes. But it seems that we can use various body parts for different functions. Science shows that our adaptations can function in multiple ways. So the question arises: Do male and female genitalia have one and only one function? If so, then it is wrong to use those parts in ways that nature—and nature's God—deem inappropriate.

Discussion Questions

1. Do you think there is a natural law? If so, then how do you know what it is? Do all people know it? How would you argue with someone who would claim that there is no natural law?

2. Are there certain kinds of behavior that are natural or unnatural? If so, then what is it in human nature that makes the acts natural or unnatural?

3. Is it possible for Christians and non-Christians to agree on the basic truths of morality? If so, then what is the basis for that agreement?

4. Do you think natural law theory makes Christian faith in divine revelation irrelevant?

5. What is the nature and purpose of human sexuality? Of marriage?

6. To what extent should governments enact laws governing sexual practices? What principles would you appeal to in your response?

SIX

Individualistic Ethics

We hold these truths to be self-evident, that all men are created
equal, that they are endowed by their Creator with certain unalienable Rights, that among these are Life, Liberty and the pursuit of
Happiness.

— The United States Declaration of Independence

Words to Watch

consistent ethic of life	individualism	selfishness
deism	law of nature	state of nature
egoism	natural rights	tacit consent
ethical egoism	objectivist ethics	
explicit consent	psychological egoism	

Introduction

In 1951 an African American woman named Henrietta Lacks died in a hospital
in Baltimore, Maryland.[1] She had cervical cancer that had metastasized. Her
death was the result of uremic poisoning brought on by her doctor's failed
treatments of the disease. While she was sick, doctors took her cells without
her permission or knowledge and grew them in cultures, since they found
that these cells could reproduce outside the human body. These cells are now
known as HeLa cells and have been used in some of the most famous medical

1. Rebecca Skloot, *The Immortal Life of Henrietta Lacks* (New York: Random, 2010).

85

experiments of the past half century. They have also spawned a multimillion-dollar industry just for their production, sale, and distribution.

Lacks died poor and in obscurity. Her cells were taken from her without her consent and without any remuneration for them. Many ethicists see this as a violation of her rights, since all people have a basic right to their own bodies and what happens to them.

The idea that we have individual human rights was famously articulated in the United States Declaration of Independence and Constitution. In 1776 the American Colonies declared their independence from their English rulers. Thomas Jefferson, along with his editor Benjamin Franklin, authored the now famous Declaration of Independence, delineating the reasons for their separation. Among those causes was the idea of "no taxation without representation." The basic problem for the colonists was one that concerned their rights to self-determination. The English had serious debts and fiscal obligations, and they felt little compunction about taxing the colonists who, in turn, felt their rights had been violated. Jefferson wrote, "We hold these truths to be self-evident, that all men are created equal, that they are endowed by their Creator with certain unalienable Rights, that among these are Life, Liberty and the pursuit of Happiness."[2] In the original version of the document, Jefferson had written "sacred" instead of "self-evident." But Franklin, ever the modernist, rejected the idea of "sacred" for that of "self-evident."

By this time many people in Europe blamed their interminable wars on religion, and although religion was one causal factor, there were many other issues at work, including ethnic tensions and economic gain. Religion, therefore, increasingly became a matter of private opinion and conviction, and Enlightenment philosophical ideas dominated public and political discourse. Jefferson and Franklin were basically appealing to the ideas of John Locke and Hugo Grotius, who had formulated the ideas of international political principles and **natural rights**. These natural rights were understood as entitlements to moral treatment grounded in the nature that all people share as human beings.

Although Jefferson and Locke both appealed to God as a kind of divine lawgiver, their notion of God was not specifically Christian. Rather, their commitments were those of **deism**—that is, the belief that God created humans and established a moral order to the universe but has little (or no) ongoing interaction with it. Those with specific religious commitments could join together with those who had a more minimalistic understanding of religion by rallying around the idea of a right that was bestowed on all people by a divine being.

---

2. "The Declaration of Independence," July 4, 1776, http://www.ushistory.org/declaration/document/.

The idea of rights has led people to think in terms of ownership over their own lives in interesting ways. Both sides of the abortion argument use the idea of rights to defend their views. Pro-life advocates believe that a fetus is a person (usually from the time of conception) and that, as a person, the fetus has a "right to life."[3] On the other side of the argument are pro-choice advocates who believe that a woman has a "right to privacy" or a "right to her own body" that supersedes any rights that the fetus may have.

Natural rights theory is part of a larger modern movement known as **individualism**, the view wherein persons—and not communities of people—are the most important features of social order. Natural rights is a deontological manifestation of individualism in the sense that a person is morally obligated to respect others' rights without regard to the consequences. Egoism is also an individualistic moral theory and is the idea that people pursue their own self-interest and that they are morally justified in doing so. But in contrast to the deontological orientation of rights theory, egoism is a consequentialist theory in the sense that the consequences of a person's actions are the only morally relevant issues.[4] In this chapter, we consider both natural rights theory and egoism and then examine how a rights-based theory would approach the issue of abortion.

Natural Rights Theory

The State of Nature and the Law of Nature

John Locke (1632–1704) is widely regarded as the founder of the modernist theory of natural rights.[5] In contrast to much of the patristic and medieval Christian tradition, he believed that specific religious traditions could not provide the kind of consensus that appeals to reason could. Locke attempted to give a moral defense of the political order by invoking ideas that were not specifically religious but were widely held, regardless of people's faith commitments. Since religious ideas were biased in favor of one specific God over another, explicit appeals to theology were not permitted. But Locke did think that values had to be grounded in some generic idea of God in order to provide an objective basis for his rights-based theory.

Instead of starting with a theological premise about creation, Locke began with a secular idea that has little or no theological suppositions—namely, that

3. Logically, the word "pro-life" is not the opposite of "pro-choice"; instead, the opposite of "pro-life" is "anti-life," and the opposite of "pro-choice" is "anti-choice."

4. For a discussion of deontological ethics, see chapter 7; for consequentialism, see chapter 8.

5. John Locke, *Two Treatises of Government*, ed. Peter Laslett (New York: New American Library, 1963).

of the **state of nature**. This state of nature was a precontractual condition of all people where they are completely free to pursue their own interests and abide by the law of nature. In Locke's state of nature, we find neither civil government nor political authorities to rule over people. In this first stage of the state of nature, people are free to grow crops, gather food, and hunt, provided that they do not take property from other people.

Locke writes that "the state of nature has a law of nature to govern it, which obliges every one: and reason, which is that law, teaches all mankind, who will but consult it, that being equal and independent, no one ought to harm another in his life, health, liberty or possessions."[6] This law indicates that all humans are to respect the lives, freedoms, and property of others. All rational people know the law of nature. This **law of nature** is the basic moral principle that governs all human interaction, regardless of religious commitments or cultural contexts. Since all humans are rational, Locke maintains that all people know it to be true. Everywhere one encounters any kind of human interaction, one finds that murder, assault, and theft are prohibited.

THE LAW OF NATURE

1. All people have rights to life, liberty, and property—these are *natural rights*.
2. All people have the ability to recognize these basic rights—this is because God has endowed all people with the rights and with the rationality to perceive those rights.
3. All people are morally bound to respect those rights—this is the *law of nature*.

In the second stage of the state of nature, we find some humans violating the laws of nature. A person might steal property from others or illicitly prevent other people from exercising their freedom. And as a result, we find a derivative right: the right to punish.[7] Thus, the state of nature and its moral principles cannot continue without alteration. Suppose a child steals mushrooms from a man's garden. What kind of punishment should the man give the child if he catches the child? Are there any punishments that would be too severe? Would it be permissible to amputate the child's hand? Or even to kill the child as a punishment? These questions might seem absurd to us, but

6. Locke, *Two Treatises of Government*, 311.
7. Locke, *Two Treatises of Government*, 314.

they illustrate this point: we are often biased in our own cases, and we fail to make objective and therefore fair judgments. Locke claims that we are so badly biased about situations where others trespass the law of nature against us that we need an objective arbiter to judge for us—and this is the second problem with the state of nature.

Since there is no known and unprejudiced judge who will effectively and objectively decide on the enforcement of the laws of nature, there needs to be an alternative. In the state of nature, there is a distinction between power and right. Those who may be in the right might not have the requisite power to enforce their rights; conversely, those who have power may not have the right to use it. A civil society will provide us with a union of power and right. As a result, we should lay down our right to judge in our own case and hand it over to an objective arbiter who also possesses the power to do what is right.

Social Contract and Consent

Locke held that there was a natural drive for every human to organize socially. He says, "God . . . put him under strong obligations of necessity, convenience, and inclination to drive him into society, as well as fixed him with understanding and language to continue and enjoy it."[8] The means by which humans formally enter into society is by the social contract.

People enter into the social contract with one another for greater security against one another as well as against external threats to society. But the agreement is with one another, not with the sovereign who rules them. In addition, they must give their consent to abide by majority rule. The majority can decide what laws will govern the country provided there is no illegitimate taking of property, freedom, or life.

For Locke, the key to the original contract—and its continuation—is consent. There are two types of consent. The first is **explicit consent** by which the original parties agree to the contract. An explicit consent is the verbal or written agreement a person makes to the social contract or constitution. **Tacit consent** is the second means by which all subsequent parties agree to the contract. A tacit consent is an agreement that is understood to apply to persons born into a society who, by continuing to live there, agree to abide by the principles of that society as articulated in the social contract. Those who are not party to the original contract and live in the society tacitly agree to abide by its laws. If they decide that they no longer wish to be part of the society, then they are free to leave and give their explicit consent to another nation. In

8. Locke, *Two Treatises of Government*, 361–62.

many countries today, people who are born into that country give their tacit consent to abide by the laws, while those who are immigrants give explicit consent, usually by swearing allegiance to the country and its constitution.

The government derives its legitimacy from the consent of the people, and therefore the laws that it promulgates are just since they have both (1) moral legitimacy, as based on their consent, and (2) the task of preserving the people's natural rights. Laws, therefore, are for the good of its citizens. Specific principles will follow from the preservation of the natural rights to life, liberty, and property.

Consent also plays an important role in other spheres of life. In order for a person to sell property or to engage in any kind of transaction, consent is required. No one can take advantage of another person by means of force or fraud since these two kinds of activities undermine consent. Consent, therefore, is not only the moral foundation on which all market transactions take place but also the foundation on which the government itself is permitted to rule.

Property

In the natural rights tradition, one of the most basic rights is the right to property. The generic sense of property (i.e., including one's life and liberty) is a natural moral claim to own something—that it belongs to a person. On this view, one naturally owns one's own life and freedom. Moreover, one may use one's life and liberty to acquire those things (property, in the more specific sense) necessary for self-preservation.[9] Since we all have the right to life, it follows that we all have the right to a certain amount of property necessary to preserve our lives. I thus have a right to food, water, shelter, and anything else that may help me preserve my life. Property, therefore, is a basic right.

We acquire property in the state of nature by mixing our labor with an object and thus acquiring it. For example, a farmer tills the land, plants the seeds, and harvests the crop. The wheat then belongs to the farmer. Or a person goes to a river or lake and removes water, thereby coming to own the water. Or someone goes to a public water fountain and drinks, thereby coming to own the water by drinking it.

A person will also have the right to the fruits of one's labor. When one has taken the water from the lake, one has a right to do with the water what one wants: wash clothes, irrigate a garden, or make ice. However, there are limits to property. One can use only so much before resources begin to go to waste.

The very nature of food and other forms of property led to the invention of money. Since many forms of property (e.g., food) are subject to spoilage,

9. Locke, *Two Treatises of Government*, 337.

and others have an extremely unwieldy nature (e.g., entire herds of animals), people developed the use of money because of its durability and convenience. Gold, silver, bronze, and other valuable metals served to substitute for the goods themselves. Since coins do not spoil, one may accumulate as much money as one can. For Locke, a just appropriation of goods from the state of nature was permitted as long as one did not prevent others from doing the same. But with the development of money, the appropriation of wealth became unlimited.

Rights and Religion

Since all people know the law of nature without recourse to divine revelation, it follows that the social contract and the moral principles it protects are founded on the basis of reason. For Locke, reason and religion do not conflict: the most reasonable of people will also invariably be the most religious. Yet Locke does not appeal to religion as the basis for his ethics and politics, since religion and the state serve two different and distinct purposes. The role of the state is to preserve the rights of all its citizens, not merely the ones who subscribe to a particular set of religious beliefs. The role of the church is to foster and develop the worship of God. The state—or the "civil government," in Locke's terms—secures our rights to life, liberty, and property. Beyond that, people are free to do as they please.

The freedom of religion, therefore, is a freedom that can only be secured when the civil state defends everyone's rights to freedom. Moreover, the basic aim of religion is entirely different from that of the civil government.[10] There are three reasons for this. First, civil governors do not have the spiritual care of the people as part of their proper responsibilities. For Locke, the civil magistrate is there only to protect the rights of the citizens. Second, civil authorities ought to use their power only in cases when coercion is needed. Religious beliefs, or personal convictions, are not the domain where governments should coerce people to believe or not to believe, since religion is a matter of "inward persuasion of the mind."[11] Third, if religion were to be enforced by the state, then religion would simply be a matter of one's nationality and not of one's conscience—and it would infringe on the basic natural right to liberty.

These natural rights and the freedoms they permit place individuals and their freedoms at the center of morality. Yet another approach to normative ethics—that of egoism—also places the individual at the center but considers matters in a more radically self-centered fashion.

10. John Locke, *A Letter concerning Toleration* (Buffalo, NY: Prometheus, 1990).
11. Locke, *Letter concerning Toleration*, 25.

Egoism

Psychological Egoism

Psychological egoism is an attempt at a description of how people invariably behave. It tells us about what factor or factors cause a person to act in particular ways. For the psychological egoist, all human activity is guided by self-interest. Every conscious endeavor we attempt is for the purpose of gratifying one or more of our desires. Exercise aims at longer life. Eating chocolate torte satisfies my desire for culinary delights. Buying a puppy pleases me since it pleases my children. These kinds of activities can readily be understood as egoistic. Even so-called heroic acts, such as soldiers throwing themselves on a grenade to save their companions or a good Samaritan helping a stranded motorist, are examples for the psychological egoist of selfish behavior. It is selfish because for the egoist every act is based on some kind of psychological satisfaction for the agent. Even though heroism and acts of kindness appear to be altruistic, they are nevertheless based on the agent's satisfaction. If the agents did not desire these things deep down, they would not do them.

Ethical Egoism

Ethical egoism is the view that even if we can desire another's good, we should act on our own behalf since everyone else does the same. Ethical egoism thus represents a more modest version of egoism. Unlike psychological egoism, which insists that all actions are based on egoistic considerations, ethical egoism allows for the rare exceptions of Mother Teresa, Dietrich Bonhoeffer, Mahatma Gandhi, and especially Jesus. The difference between psychological egoism and ethical egoism is that the former theory is an attempt at describing human behavior, while the latter is an attempt at prescribing human behavior.

Hobbes's Egoism

In the modern era, the philosopher Thomas Hobbes (1588–1679) was the first to advance a theory of psychological egoism.[12] For Hobbes, all people exist in a state of basic competition with one another. This condition he referred to as the "state of nature." It is a condition of a "war of all against all." Since there is this basic conflict among all people, Hobbes famously claims that the condition of each person is "nasty, solitary, brutish and short."[13] Like

12. Thomas Hobbes, *Leviathan*, ed. C. B. MacPherson (New York: Penguin, 1951).
13. Hobbes, *Leviathan*, 186.

Locke, Hobbes proposes a social contract, an agreement by which all people surrender their own liberties to an all-powerful government, "a Leviathan," that ensures their safety against the threats they pose to one another. In other words, people realize that in order to get what they really want, they must give up some of their freedoms. Immediate self-interest is sacrificed for long-term self-interest.

Hobbes held that all people were controlled by their desires. Everyone wanted to have material things that made their lives easier, and they also realized that they needed security from others who might take their things. Hobbes assumed that individuals would always maximize their own interests and that their interests were primarily shaped by the desires for property and security. As a result, Hobbes believed that humans would naturally seek to form a social contract in order to secure their property. Since Hobbes believed that the most serious problem was how to regulate the social interaction of a population of egoists, he devoted much of his writing to political matters rather than to strictly moral concerns.

Hobbes sees egoism simply as a fact of life. Since people are all psychological egoists, we should set up society so that it constrains people's self-interested actions by what is good for everyone. In his view, altruism is not a possibility, since it runs contrary to human nature. All people desire material possessions and relative safety. People enter into society not because they like one another but to protect themselves from one another. Self-interest drives us into the social contract.

Ayn Rand's Objectivism

Possibly the best-known egoist of the twentieth century is the novelist Ayn Rand (1905–82), who developed what she called **objectivist ethics**, which was the idea that a person's own life and individual happiness was the ultimate good.[14] Although Rand's work found great popularity in some circles, especially among economists, her ideas never took hold among professional philosophers or ethicists. Her primary interest lay in the attempt to recover the idea of **selfishness** as the central virtue in the moral life. Yet her definition of what constituted the moral and the immoral differed considerably from most common intuitions.

For Rand, there were three types of ethical theories that were fundamentally misguided: (1) the mystical, (2) the social, and (3) the subjective. Each one of these theories failed because they refused to place the individual person at the

14. Ayn Rand, *The Virtue of Selfishness* (New York: Signet, 1964).

center of all value judgments. The mystical approach to ethics "is explicitly based on the premise that the standard of value of man's ethics is set beyond the grave, by the laws or requirements of another, supernatural dimension."[15] Any biblically based ethics, divine command theory, theologically based virtue ethics, or theistic natural law theories fall under this heading. The mystic, she claims, has abandoned the rationality of this life for the so-called eternal rewards promised in religion. The individual's goods are sacrificed for the whims of the make-believe deity.

The social approach to ethics is a variation on the mystical approach in the sense that one's community replaces God as the standard of values. Individuals must sacrifice their individual good for the good of society. People meekly consent to let their own good be overridden by net utility or some other socially constructed fiction. Marxism, utilitarianism, and social contract theories are all forms of the social approach that we should reject, according to Rand, since they each require the denial of the individual's good.

For Rand, the subjectivist approach is possibly the worst since she claims that it is a "negation of ethics."[16] Since it denies any objective basis for ethics, there can be no standard. Rationality has been exiled from moral discourse, and there is now simply irrational indeterminacy where there should be rational egoism. A leap of faith, for example, is the complete antithesis of her own views since individuals sacrifice themselves in an act of complete irrationality. Abraham's willingness to sacrifice Isaac on the basis of faith, for example, was a completely irrational act.[17]

On Rand's account, a moral theory must have as its primary goal the good of the individual. She writes, "Objectivist ethics holds man's life as the *standard* of value—and *his own life* as the ethical *purpose* of every individual man."[18] Individual persons can and should pursue their own self-interest since this is the only possible value anyone could ever have.

For Rand, an individual's life should never be wasted on other humans. If we adopt the view that altruism is to be praised and emulated, then we rob people of that which is most important. We ask them to sacrifice their lives on behalf of others. We give away everything we will ever have. Our lives are our own, and it is immoral—from her perspective—to ever turn oneself into a "sacrificial animal" that places others' interests and goods above one's

15. Rand, *Virtue of Selfishness*, 38.
16. Rand, *Virtue of Selfishness*, 38.
17. One need not subscribe to Rand's account of normative ethics to claim that Abraham's action was irrational, since a utilitarian or a Kantian might come to the same conclusion on the basis of other considerations.
18. Rand, *Virtue of Selfishness*, 27, italics in original.

own.[19] In contrast, an ethical egoist would claim that this flies in the face of common sense since the ethical egoist thinks that our lives are our own to do with as we please—that we have a kind of absolute right to dispose of our lives as we see fit. Ethical egoists thus claim that they are the only ones who take seriously our common-sense intuitions that our lives are our own.

The altruist says that the standard of value is the common good and that each individual person's purpose is to contribute to the common good. But, for Rand, this has the effect of negating the idea of the individual's good since any attempt to promote the "common good" is merely a mask for the "moochers" of society to take advantage of the producers. As a result, we must radically revise the virtues and vices of traditional morality.

Rand proposes a completely objectivized list of virtues that includes rationality, integrity, honesty, justice, independence, productiveness, and pride. Each one of these virtues is defined with reference primarily to the good of the individual. Thus, justice is defined by Rand as "not accepting or giving anything that is unearned or undeserved."[20] Honesty is defined as not "faking reality"; integrity is defined somewhat strikingly as "not ever sacrificing one's own convictions for the wishes of others."[21]

Criticisms of Individualist Ethics

Individualist approaches have a number of criticisms leveled against them. Some of these criticisms are of the theory of human nature offered while others are of the specific aspects of the ethical systems. Psychological egoism has at least one major problem that calls its validity as a theory into question. If we consider the claim that each and every act is performed for selfish reasons, then it follows that there is no such thing as an altruistic act. This claim is problematic for at least two reasons. First, the claim seems to be radically contrary to our basic moral intuitions about altruism, compassion, and concern for others. Almost everyone has the experience of doing something for a selfish reason, but so too do we have the experience of doing something for an altruistic reason. But even if people were to deny their own individual experience of altruism, then we could consider the cases of well-known moral exemplars: Mother Teresa, Dietrich Bonhoeffer, Mahatma Gandhi, or countless others who have sacrificed their lives for others. If psychological egoism is true, then it follows that moral exemplars and saints are all acting on behalf

19. Rand, *Virtue of Selfishness*, 29.
20. Rand, *Virtue of Selfishness*, 28.
21. Rand, *Virtue of Selfishness*, 28.

of their own selfish interests either intentionally or unintentionally. If they are acting selfishly and know that they are acting selfishly, then they cannot be moral exemplars but are deceivers. If they are acting selfishly in an unintentional manner, then they are deceived. If so, then they are either stupid or insane. But both of these options seem contrary to common sense.

A second problem for the psychological egoist is the fact that the argument appeals only to those people who already believe that all people act out of purely selfish motives. In logic, this is known as begging the question—attempting to prove something you have already assumed to be true. It is only when we already believe that all acts of apparent altruism are selfish that we can conveniently provide an explanation—no matter how tortured—that altruistic actions are somehow fundamentally selfish.

The moral problems of Rand's objectivism center on the notion of justice. Rand's claim that justice is not accepting or giving anything that is unearned or undeserved is simply absurd since all people owe even their very existence to others and the care others have provided to us in the form of nurturing, education, and personal development. Every human has been given life. It is no accident that Rand's protagonists in her novels all pick themselves up by their bootstraps, so to speak, and earn everything they have.[22] The reality of the situation is that much of our lives cannot be accounted for through Rand's idiosyncratic definition of justice as not accepting anything that is unearned.

For their part, natural rights theories seem unable to adjudicate among competing rights. Which right is most important: life, property, or liberty? For some people the answers may be obvious, but philosophers have argued over this for more than two centuries. Many contemporary Christians, for example, assume that life is the most important issue. They think that without life the other rights are meaningless. In order to possess property or to express oneself freely, one must first be alive. Arguments about abortion usually proceed along these lines since the right to life is the one that allegedly guarantees the others. Although these arguments might make some intuitive sense, it can become more difficult if we see them all as having equal value—which seems to be Locke's own view, though some scholars have argued that Locke saw property as the most basic right. How do we judge, for example, between people's freedom to express themselves and others' freedom not to view something objectionable? Suppose a person wants to advertise a product on a billboard with a person in a sexually suggestive pose. Does that

22. For example, see Ayn Rand's novels *The Fountainhead* (New York: Bobbs-Merrill, 1943) and *Atlas Shrugged* (New York: Random House, 1957).

advertiser's right to expression supersede another person's right not to see it? It is difficult to make such a determination based on natural rights alone.

Individualism and Christian Ethics

The individualistic approach of Rand is inconsistent with any Christian account of ethics since Jesus preached an ethic of sacrificial love and compassion, and an account of justice that resists reduction to mere economic exchange. However, many Christians have come to employ natural rights arguments for and against specific issues such as abortion or war. Oftentimes the rights argument is understood as consistent with basic Christian ethics since in the traditional accounts of rights God-language is invoked as the source of the rights themselves. Christians often invoke a person's God-given right to engage in a particular activity. What makes the appeal so attractive to many North American Christians is that, as we discussed above, the Declaration of Independence asserts: "We hold these truths to be self-evident, that all men are created equal, that they are endowed by their Creator with certain unalienable Rights, that among these are Life, Liberty and the pursuit of Happiness."[23] Although God-language is invoked, it does not follow that natural rights is a specifically Christian theory, since Muslims, Jews, and even deists can affirm the theory. Natural rights therefore can provide the basis for a political ethic but not for a distinctively Christian personal ethic. Yet, while this approach to a political ethic might be prima facie appealing, there are at least three potential problems.

The first problem regards the assumption that we can coherently speak in terms of a political ethic and a personal ethic. Some would argue that this fails to understand the nature of a Christian ethic. If Christian ethics is to have any meaning at all, then it seems to follow that one's Christian commitment should be primary and not subordinated to what the state labels as right and wrong. Rather than seeing rights as primary and understanding Christian commitment within the rights-based political order, a person committed to a decidedly Christian ethic would see the narrative and exhortations of Christ as primary and rights as secondary. A second problem is that rights-based ethic seems to assume the priority of the individual over that of the community. For the advocate of natural rights, the individual can act against the common good of the society. However, the Christian sees the good of the kingdom of God as being more important than any individual's exercise of a specific right.

---

23. "The Declaration of Independence," July 4, 1776, http://www.ushistory.org/declaration /document/.

A third problem with a rights-based approach to ethics is that although it indicates specific wrongs a person should avoid, it does not prescribe positive obligations we have to others. In the parable of the good Samaritan in Luke's Gospel, the priest and the Levite have done nothing wrong—on the natural rights approach—since they did not violate the man's rights to life and liberty. Yet, Christ tells his followers that more is required. An active participation in the lives of others goes beyond that a natural rights approach would prescribe. At best, a natural rights ethics is incomplete from a Christian perspective. At worst, it enables people to think that they have done their Christian duty by not harming others.

Case Study: Abortion

In 1973 the US Supreme Court ruled in the case *Roe v. Wade* that a woman's constitutional right to privacy "is broad enough to encompass a woman's decision whether or not to terminate her pregnancy."[24] The right to an abortion is not an absolute right, since it does not encompass the death of the fetus. The court ruled that states could regulate abortions after the first three months of a pregnancy. The court also held that the fetus is not legally a person in "the whole sense."[25] And as a result, it does not have rights that could be violated.

Much of the discussion of abortion concerns the conflict of rights and the notion of personhood. Here we look at arguments on both sides of the issues, beginning with the pro-choice arguments and then moving to the pro-life arguments. Since abortion is both a political and a moral issue, it is helpful to delineate the issues at stake. First, to be pro-choice is to argue that one has a political right to an abortion on the basis of one's right to privacy—as construed in the *Roe v. Wade* decision—and that this right includes the right to terminate a pregnancy in the first three months. The pro-choice argument does not necessarily indicate whether the action is a morally good act but simply establishes that it is a person's right to obtain an abortion. There are people who are morally opposed to abortion but still consider it a woman's right to procure one. In a similar way, there are people who think that pornography should be legal in a free society even though they have moral objections to its use. On this view, the right a woman exercises is the right to control her own body—that is, her uterus—to the extent that the fetus can only occupy it if the woman gives her consent. Since the fetus is not a person in "the whole sense" of the term, the woman's action does not amount to murder.

24. Roe v. Wade, 410 U.S. 113 (1973).
25. Roe v. Wade, 410 U.S. 113 (1973).

The issue of personhood for the pro-choice defender is one wherein the fetus is not a person until birth. Here the argument depends on what is often a contentious conception of personhood. Mary Anne Warren famously argued that there are five necessary conditions for personhood: consciousness, reasoning, self-motivated activity, the capacity to communicate, and the presence of self-concepts.[26] If beings do not exhibit these capacities, then they cannot be persons in the relevant sense. This definition, however, would sanction the killing of newborn babies as well, and for this reason many people have found this kind of attempt at defining personhood unacceptable. A further complication here is that the one who makes the decision is the woman who is carrying the fetus, and this seems to be an arbitrary judgment based on purely subjective grounds. Does a person's choice—and that choice alone—confer or deny personhood? Shouldn't there be some kind of objective standard that determines who is, or is not, a person? It is on this issue of personhood that the pro-life defenders launch their counterargument.

For a pro-life supporter, it is merely a biological triviality that the moment of birth determines whether one is a person. John Noonan observes that historically "the criterion for humanity . . . was simple and all-embracing: if you are conceived by human parents, you are human."[27] Pro-life supporters point out that it is inconsistent to affirm that infants who are born prematurely—for example, at eight months—are considered persons, while fetuses still in utero at nine months are not. The idea behind the pro-life argument is that there is a gradual differentiation of the fetus from the moment of conception—where it has a complete set of DNA—until the time of its birth. To decide at any point in that process that the fetus becomes a person is an arbitrary judgment.

Since the fetus is a person in the relevant sense, the pro-life argument next appeals to the idea that all persons are endowed with the rights to life, liberty, and the pursuit of happiness. The most foundational of all the rights is the right to life since without it there can be no other rights. Moreover, a right to life is more fundamental to a person than any notion of a right to privacy. Abortion, therefore, not only is immoral but also should be illegal since it unjustly takes the life of a person. The difficulty in this position, as pro-choice advocates point out, is that there can be a conceptual distinction between being human and being a person. Consider individuals who have suffered a traumatic brain injury and have lost higher brain functions. The pro-choice advocate would acknowledge that those individuals are human

26. Mary Anne Warren, "On the Moral and Legal Status of Abortion," *The Monist* 57.4 (1973): 1–9.

27. John T. Noonan Jr., "An Almost Absolute Value in Human History," in *The Morality of Abortion*, ed. John T. Noonan Jr. (Cambridge, MA: Harvard University Press, 1970), 51.

since they possess human DNA, but they would argue that such individuals are no longer persons since they no longer possess the capacities necessary for personhood.

Judith Jarvis Thompson has argued that even if a fetus is a person in the relevant sense, its rights cannot outweigh the mother's right to her own body. To make her argument, she offers a thought experiment about a famous violinist.[28] She asks you to imagine that you (a man) wake up one day in a hospital bed next to a famous violinist who is unconscious. The violinist needs your kidneys to survive for nine months, and he has been connected to you by a rogue group of music lovers who drugged you and kidnapped you in the night. To disconnect him from you would kill him.

In such a scenario, do you have the right to disconnect him? Thompson says that you do since you have a right to your own body that the violinist does not share. She claims this is analogous to abortion, but her claim has two problems. First, it seems that her thought experiment is only analogous to abortion in the case of rape. Second, Thompson is arguing for a political right—based on the assumption that people have an absolute right to their own bodies—but even if a person does have a political right to an abortion, does that entail that it is the morally good or right thing to do?

From the other end of the spectrum, the late Cardinal Bernardin has argued that the issue of abortion is part of a larger domain of life-related issues.[29] He has proposed a **consistent ethic of life**, or a "seamless garment" approach, which is the view that being pro-life means being against war, euthanasia, and capital punishment and in favor of issues like universal health care and education. In other words, people cannot pick and choose what issues they want to defend on the basis of being pro-life. If all human life has dignity and is worthy of respect and affirmation, then for consistency's sake one has to also approach these other issues in the same way. For Cardinal Bernardin, to fail to apply this consistently is a moral failure.

Discussion Questions

1. Can a natural rights (or any individualistic) approach to ethics accommodate the basic intuitions we have concerning helping others? Is it

28. Judith Jarvis Thompson, "A Defense of Abortion," *Philosophy and Public Affairs* 1.1 (1971): 54–66.

29. Joseph L. Bernardin, *The Seamless Garment: Writings on the Consistent Ethic of Life*, ed. Thomas A. Nairn (New York: Orbis, 2008).

morally adequate simply not to harm other people? Or are there actions that it would be wrong to refrain from doing?

2. Do natural rights have a universal appeal? Or are they merely an invention of Western societies?

3. If people have natural rights to their own bodies, then do they have an absolute right to their own life?

4. Does a fetus have a natural right to life? If so, then what is the extent of that right? Does it preclude the mother's rights, including her own right to life in the case of a life-threatening pregnancy?

5. If a fetus has a right to life, then should an infant have a natural right to health care? If not, why not?

6. How might Christians think about the issue of abortion in a political system based on natural rights? Given that in many countries abortion is a political right, is there more than one way to consider the issue?

SEVEN

Kantian Ethics

Two things fill me with ever increasing awe: the starry heavens above and the moral law within.

—Immanuel Kant, *Critique of Pure Reason*

Words to Watch

actions contrary to duty	duty	rules of skill
actions for the sake of duty	heteronomous will	therapeutic theory
actions in accordance	hypothetical imperatives	of punishment
with duty	imperfect duty	universalizability
autonomous will	means-end formulation	
categorical imperative	of the categorical	
counsel of prudence	imperative	
deterrence theory	perfect duty	
of punishment	retributivism	

Introduction

When Adolf Hitler launched his plan to exterminate Jews during World War II, many people chose to harbor Jews secretly and to conspire to help them escape from the Nazi-occupied territories to safe lands such as the United Kingdom and the United States. Sympathizers would hide the refugees in basements, attics, and even specially constructed secret rooms. One of the best known of the Holocaust rescuers was Corrie ten Boom, a Dutch woman who helped many Jews to safety. In her autobiography she claims that when the Germans came to her family's house searching for the Jews, they never hesitated to tell the Germans the truth—yet the soldiers never believed them. She held to the conviction that it was always wrong to tell a lie—even to someone who was bent on murdering innocent people.

Dietrich Bonhoeffer, a well-known theologian and contemporary of Ten Boom, publicly resisted Hitler and paid for it with his life. He held that there are some people, by virtue of their unique relationships, who deserve to know the truth and some people who do not. We must be careful with how we divulge the truth and to whom. For Bonhoeffer, there were other moral principles that might make us think twice about telling the truth to someone who may intend to harm others or to exploit that knowledge for less than noble purposes.[1]

The examples of Ten Boom and Bonhoeffer raise a difficult moral question: Is it always a duty to tell the truth? Are we always obliged to tell others what we really think about their clothes, their new hairstyle, or their latest financial plan to get rich quick? Some philosophers have thought that we should always tell the truth and let the consequences sort themselves out. One such thinker was Immanuel Kant (1724–1804), the Enlightenment philosopher known for his development of the **categorical imperative**, his emphasis on the concept of **duty**, and his insistence that we should always tell the truth regardless of the circumstances or consequences.

We see here that Kantian ethics represents a deontological approach to normative theory in that it emphasizes duty, not the consequences of action, as having central moral importance. In this chapter we consider the key elements in Kantian ethics, including the good will, the categorical imperative, and the various kinds of duties. We will also consider how a Kantian—and others—would view the issues of capital punishment.

The Unqualified Good

Philosophers have perpetually argued about what the meaning of the term "good" is and how it can play a role in the moral life of everyday people. Kant's work was a continuation of this philosophical project, and his moral agenda was to develop a theory that best explained how people have always thought about morality. Kant saw his work as a philosophical defense of Jesus's golden rule: "Do to others as you would have them do to you" (Matt. 7:12).

At the beginning of his *Foundations of the Metaphysics of Morals* (a truly intimidating title for an introduction to ethics!), he asks his readers

1. Dietrich Bonhoeffer, *Ethics*, ed. Eberhard Bethge, trans. Neville Horton Smith (New York: Macmillan, 1963).

to imagine the "only unqualified good thing."[2] Is money an unqualified good? No, because we can use money for all kinds of devious purposes: to bribe a judge, to pay a hitman, to cheat on a test, or to buy a flashy new car that we really do not need in order to impress our friends. Is health an unqualified good? No, because it too can be used for evil purposes. We can use our health to focus only on ourselves, to harm others, or to elevate ourselves above those who are less fit than we are. What, then, constitutes the only unqualified good thing imaginable? Kant's answer to this question is "the good will." Those who possess a good will are those who wish to be good and to do the right thing regardless of what others may think of them. They are the people who truly deserve to be called good, since their motives are pure: they wish only that the good should be done without any appeal to an ulterior motive. But this raises the question: How do they come into possession of a good will? Or, in other words, how do we make certain that our intentions are not tainted by self-interest, vanity, or some other less-than-virtuous motive?

Hypothetical Imperatives

We inevitably find ourselves making decisions about what to do. What clothes should I wear today? What should I eat for lunch? Should I give money to the homeless person on the street? Should I turn up the thermostat to appease my child? Should I go to the U2 concert on Friday? Should I wash the car today? Should I lie to my boss? Some of these decisions are more important than others, and we might even say that some are moral and that others are amoral. Some questions rise to the level of moral importance, such as those that involve honesty, mercy, and compassion, while others seem to be aesthetic matters or merely questions of efficiency. How do we distinguish between questions that are moral and those that are not? How do these questions relate to the problem of determining whether someone has a good will?

For Kant, in order to determine what a good will is, we must first think about ways in which the will is determined. By this expression, he means that we must think about the reasons why we act. Here Kant considers two different kinds of motives for actions: those that take the form of an "If . . . then . . ." construction and those that apply universally without reference to any particular goal. The former are called "hypothetical imperatives," while the latter are called "categorical imperatives."

2. Immanuel Kant, *Foundations of the Metaphysics of Morals*, trans. Lewis White Beck (New York: Bobbs-Merrill, 1959), 9.

A **hypothetical imperative** is a kind of conditional guide to action. There are two types of hypothetical imperatives: rules of skill and counsels of prudence. **Rules of skill** refer to those kinds of activities where our end (i.e., our reason for action) is variable, and therefore our means to that end will also be variable. For example, I may want to find the best auto mechanic in town, the least expensive route from Los Angeles to Chicago, or a good Italian restaurant within ten miles of my home. How do I go about finding this information? I could ask my friends, search the internet, or consult an expert. The answers will vary accordingly, and I may get different answers by consulting different friends since their opinions, tastes, and judgments will differ. Those who are particularly adept at figuring these things out are not necessarily moral in their behavior; rather, they are shrewd.

A rule of skill always takes the form of an "If . . . then . . ." statement. What follows the "If" is called the "antecedent," and what follows the "then" is called the "consequent." The consequent is always determined by the antecedent. In other words, the interests and goals we hope to accomplish will always determine how we go about successfully accomplishing them. For Kant, this kind of imperative does not rise to the level of a properly moral judgment. Rather, it is a practical judgment that is amoral—that is, neither moral nor immoral. Consider the following rule of skill: if I want my office to be pleasing to me, then I will put a Van Gogh print above my desk. This is a purely aesthetic judgment based on my individual tastes, and we do not usually consider this judgment a moral one nor one that we would apply to all people by virtue of their common humanity.

The second kind of hypothetical syllogism, a counsel of prudence, is one where the end is not variable, but the means may be. A **counsel of prudence**, according to Kant, is a means by which we may attain happiness. All people desire to be happy, but not everyone agrees on the means of finding happiness. In this kind of hypothetical imperative, we always supply what follows the "If" with the desire to be happy, but what follows the "then" may vary from person to person. It takes the following form: "If you want to be happy, then . . ." The antecedent does not vary here, but the consequent will. Since all people want to be happy, the phrase following the antecedent remains constant. As Aristotle said, all people desire happiness; even those who intend evil things such as murder, theft, or adultery mistakenly believe that these actions will somehow make them happy. A counsel of prudence, therefore, is a means of attaining happiness.

But people define happiness in many different ways. Some think that happiness is found in wealth, others in health, and still others in friends, limiting desires, doing the will of God, satisfying every desire, or obtaining power. Kant

HYPOTHETICAL IMPERATIVES

1. **Rules of Skill:** always take the form of an "If . . . then . . ." construction where both the end and the means are variable.
2. **Counsel of Prudence:** always takes the form of "If you want to be happy, then . . ." where the end of happiness is universal but the means to achieving happiness is variable.

sees these disagreements as problematic. For Kant, the fact that we disagree on happiness raises two unpleasant consequences.

First, there is no universally accepted definition of happiness. Kant writes, "Unfortunately, the concept of happiness is such an indeterminate one that even though everyone wishes to attain happiness, yet he can never say definitely and consistently what it is he really wishes and wills."[3] We all have a vague, indefinite notion of happiness. We say we want to be happy, but we really do not know what that means. As proof Kant says that we can never define "happiness" to everyone's satisfaction. You may define happiness differently from me, and my happiness might conflict with your happiness. I may think that happiness consists in doing the will of God, and you may think that happiness consists in making as much money as possible. The fact that we disagree, combined with the plausibility that I might never get you to agree with me, indicates that "happiness" is not a term that everyone understands in the same way.

Second, achieving happiness is uncertain. For the sake of argument, we could assume that there was a universally agreed-upon definition for happiness. Even so, it does not follow that all good people actually achieve it. Consider, for example, the famous case of Oedipus from the Greek tragedy. Oedipus thought that marrying the newly widowed queen after saving the city of Thebes from the Sphinx would help secure the stability of the government. Unfortunately, as we come to find out, he was responsible for killing his own father and marrying his mother! This horrific series of events caused the terrible famine the city experienced, since the gods were punishing the city—and Oedipus. He desired—like all of us—to be happy, but unfortunately for him (and the entire city of Thebes), his actions caused grievous harm. Kant suggests that although all people desire happiness, they really should aim to be "worthy of happiness." Being worthy of happiness is a superior motive for doing one's duty, but it cannot supply the content of ethics. Many

---

3. Immanuel Kant, "Ethical Philosophy: 'Grounding for the Metaphysics of Morals,'" in *Ethical Philosophy*, 2nd ed., trans. James W. Ellington (Indianapolis: Hackett, 1995), 27.

times, those who deserve to be happy are not, and those who do not deserve to be happy are. Duty, however, is immune to the vicissitudes of life. The fleeting glimpses of happiness that some are fortunate enough to grasp can never function as the foundation for a moral system. Thus, Kant says, "The practical law, derived from the motive of happiness, I term pragmatic (rule of prudence), and the law, if there is such a law, which has no other motive than *worthiness of being happy*, I term moral (law of morality)."[4]

Categorical Imperatives

Since we cannot place happiness at the center of a normative theory, we must look elsewhere. Kant thinks that we must appeal to a priori principles of morality—principles that are necessary and universally binding. In order that there be no ambiguity in discovering our duty, Kant thinks we must appeal to reason. In his view, reason—not our emotions or our desire for happiness—is the only unambiguous moral authority. Any moral principle must apply to *all* people *all* of the time without any exceptions. If there were exceptions, then morality would be deeply problematic since we could never be certain if we were doing the right thing. His attempt to rid morality of any ambiguity is expressed in terms of his categorical imperative, which cannot vary according to place or time and cannot apply contingently. He offers four formulations of the categorical imperative.[5]

THE CATEGORICAL IMPERATIVE

Formula 1

Act only on that maxim through which you can at the same time will that it become a universal law.

Formula 2

Act as if the maxim of your action were to become through your will a universal law of nature.

Formula 3

Act in such a way that you always treat humanity, whether in your own person or in the person of any other, never simply as a means, but always at the same time as an end.

4. Immanuel Kant, *Critique of Pure Reason*, trans. Norman Kemp Smith (New York: St. Martin's, 1965), 636 (emphasis added).
5. Kant, "Grounding for the Metaphysics of Morals," 24–44.

Formula 4

All maxims as proceeding from our own making of law ought to harmonize with a possible kingdom of ends as a kingdom of nature.

The **universalizability** of an ethical principle is central to Kant's agenda and is the main criterion of the first formula of the categorical imperative. Any maxim (i.e., any subjective principle of action) must be capable of being universalized. Consider the maxim "I should help others in need." For Kant, this means that not only should *I* help others in need but also *all* people should help others in need. That is, I universalize the principle of helping those in need. But consider a different maxim: "I should take out a loan even though I have no intention of repaying it." I cannot universalize this maxim, since it would undercut the trust the entire banking system is based on. That is, I want everyone else to repay their loans while I take advantage of an exception for myself. But the principles of morality must apply universally to everyone without exception, otherwise they are not universal.

In formula 2, Kant alters the language slightly so that the maxim could become a universal law *of nature*. Here Kant appeals to the idea of the laws of nature as a basis for the categorical imperative. The Newtonian world, with which Kant was fascinated, postulated universal laws that governed all material objects without exception. Indeed, this is part of the very idea of law—namely, that objects invariably obey the laws that govern them. Gravity holds without exception. In Kant's epistemology, we find that it is impossible for us even to think without conceiving of some kind of lawlike governing structure for the world of the phenomena. So too in moral philosophy, we must have moral principles that apply with lawlike regularity.

Formula 3 introduces the idea of the human person as an end in himself— that is, the person is valued for himself and not for some other purpose or end. This is often known as the **means-end formulation of the categorical imperative**. Kant sees all human beings—insofar as they are rational—as beings that have an intrinsic dignity. As rational beings, all people deserve respect and to be treated as having equal value. Persons are valuable in themselves, not merely as objects of desire or means to our own ends. According to Kant, the idea that people are ends in themselves is a basic moral intuition; that is, it is a pure practical idea of reason that cannot be proved. We *must* think this way about human dignity and value even though there is no empirical proof for it.

In the fourth formula, we see that rational agents must think of themselves as "legislating for a kingdom of ends."[6] Here, Kant bridges the gap between individuals thinking for themselves and people in communities who must agree to basic principles of cooperation. For Kant, we need to see ourselves and our own actions as part of a social fabric that includes all rational beings. This helps us avoid acting out of selfish desires and motives by seeing that all people are "ends in themselves" and participate in a "kingdom of ends." The categorical imperative formulations help us determine our duties.

Duty

We all seem to recognize that we have obligations to others that do not seem to depend on our own desire for happiness. From an early age we are told to respect our elders, not to interrupt, to sit up straight, to behave, and so on. These obligations Kant calls duties, and they form the heart of his moral system.[7] For Kant, the term "duty" has a technical meaning, which can be broken down into two kinds: perfect and imperfect duties.

Perfect Duties

A **perfect duty** for Kant is a duty that is "perfectly determined." It is one that does not admit of any variation or any alternatives in how one goes about fulfilling the duty. Such a duty prescribes or forbids very specific behaviors. If people who were extraordinarily depressed contemplated suicide, then Kant says that the categorical imperative forbids this, since they would be using themselves as a means to their own end. Therefore, there is a perfect duty to avoid suicide.

KINDS OF DUTIES

Perfect Duties *(i.e., those that are perfectly determined)*
  (1) To self: Do not commit suicide.
  (2) To others: Do not lie for personal gain.

Imperfect Duties *(i.e., those that are imperfectly determined)*
  (1) To self: Improve oneself.
  (2) To others: Assist others in need.

---

6. Kant, *Foundations of the Metaphysics of Morals*, 57.
7. Kant, "Grounding for the Metaphysics of Morals," 30–32.

Kant contends that the categorical imperative also prescribes perfect duties to others. Consider whether one should lie in order to get a loan. A person goes into a bank and requests a loan with no intention of ever repaying it. Again, the categorical imperative forbids this action, since the person would be using the bank and the people who work there as means to his or her own selfish end. Thus, there is a perfect duty to others that prevents us from lying in order to obtain a loan.

Imperfect Duties

In addition to those duties that are perfectly determined, there are also those that are "imperfectly determined." An **imperfect duty** is a duty that requires we fulfill the duty but does not specify one particular behavior rather than another. For example, we may have an imperfect duty to help homeless people on the street. We may fulfill the duty by giving them cash, buying them a meal, or giving them a ride to the nearest food bank. We must fulfill the duty, but we may decide how to do it. One way of thinking about the distinction between perfect and imperfect duties is this: when we treat people as means to our own ends, we have violated a perfect duty. When we fail to treat people as ends in themselves, we have violated an imperfect duty. Using explicitly Christian language, we could say that violations of perfect duties are sins of commission, and violations of imperfect duties are sins of omission.[8]

As with perfect duties, imperfect duties also come in two types: to self and to others. For example, we have an imperfect duty to improve oneself. This duty derives from the fact that, if we fail to do this, then we have failed to treat ourselves as an end. We also have an imperfect duty to others. Helping those in need, as we have seen, is an imperfect duty to others, which we can fulfill in a variety of ways. It is left to the individual to determine how best to fulfill that duty, given one's situation and abilities. But in no case can the duty be left unfulfilled.

Heteronomy and Autonomy

Everyone seems to be familiar with the idea of doing the right thing for the wrong reason. Kant uses this intuitive idea to make an important distinction between a will that is good (i.e., one that is autonomous) and one that is less than what it should be (i.e., one that is heteronomous). An **autonomous will** is a will that performs its duty in actions for the sake of duty and for no other

---

8. Kant does not call them "sins." This is merely a helpful way of thinking about the distinction.

reason.[9] The term "autonomous" literally means "self-legislating," and in this case what Kant means is that I should do my duty because my reason "legislates" that I should perform my duty. If it is my duty to assist the homeless person on the street, then I should perform my duty simply because it is my duty and not for any other motive. If I am tempted to do my duty for some other reason, then my will becomes heteronomous.

A **heteronomous will** is a will that does what it does for some motive other than duty.[10] Kant sometimes says that a heteronomous will is one that is determined by "empirical" motives—that is, determined by anything other than duty itself. It may be my duty to help someone who is being robbed and beaten by a gang. However, if I help the person because I recognize the victim as a wealthy philanthropist, and I hope for a reward, then I am performing **actions in accordance with duty** but not **actions for the sake of duty**. Actions in accordance with duty are those that are prescribed by the categorical imperative, but our motive is determined by an idea other than duty for its own sake. The categorical imperative has determined that my duty is to help, but I have failed to act for the right motive.

In addition to acts done for the sake of duty and those done in accordance with duty, there are those that are unrelated to duty. Such activities are merely efficient or aesthetic. Purchasing a painting for my office and going to one restaurant rather than another are examples of amoral activities as prescribed by the hypothetical imperative.

Finally, there are those actions that are prohibited, or immoral, since they violate the categorical imperative. Lying in order to get a loan, murdering a wealthy relative, committing adultery, or failing to help those in need are all examples of **actions contrary to duty**. These actions are all immoral since we can never universalize them, and they always violate the precept to "treat humanity never as means only but always as an end in itself."

We can see in figure 7.1 what these four kinds of actions look like.

Actions done for the sake of duty are the only truly good actions. An example of this would be people who apply the categorical imperative to the question about whether it would be permissible to lie about getting a loan to purchase a new car. They wonder whether it would be morally permissible to misrepresent themselves in order to get the loan. They would determine that they could not request a loan under these circumstances because it would be a violation of their duty. Consequently, they refuse to apply for the loan. Their will is autonomous as they are guided only by the interests of duty.

---

9. Kant, *Grounding for the Metaphysics of Morals*, 42–44.
10. Kant, *Grounding for the Metaphysics of Morals*, 45–48.

Figure 7.1.
Autonomy and Heteronomy in Kantian Ethics

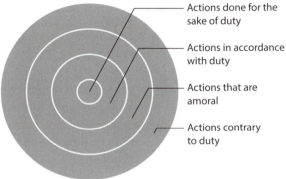

Actions done for the
sake of duty

Actions in accordance
with duty

Actions that are
amoral

Actions contrary
to duty

Now consider people who choose not to get the same kind of loan for a
new car for fear of being discovered. These people do the same action but
have another factor that determines their actions. Their fear, not respect for
duty, is the determining factor, and so their will is heteronomous. This kind
of action is one that is in accordance with duty.

For Kant, the act of securing a loan would be neither moral nor immoral.
Consider other people who want to know the best place to get a loan. The
act of choosing one loan company over another is neither moral nor immoral
but is simply amoral. It is merely a rule of skill. Finally, there are actions that
are contrary to duty. Lying in order to secure a loan violates the categorical
imperative. It not only violates the universalizability criterion, but it is also
using the people at the loan office as means to one's own end.

Kant and Christian Ethics

Although we cannot use happiness as the grounding of ethics, could we not
appeal to God and the commands that God gives us? Kant is reluctant to
introduce God into his arguments for the justification of ethics due to two
considerations. First, if we act for a motive other than duty, then the action is
less than what it should be, and our will becomes heteronomous. If we act for
the purpose of pleasing God, who knows what else we might do if we think
God has commanded an action? We must insist that some actions are always
wrong regardless of God's commands. As we have seen, suicide is wrong
not because it is primarily a sin against God but because it is a violation of
a perfect duty to oneself. It is a case where one fails to treat oneself as an

end. Kant says, "Suicide is not an abomination because God has forbidden it; it is forbidden by God because it is an abomination. If it were the other way about, suicide would not be abominable if it were not forbidden; and I should not know why God had forbidden it, if it were not abominable in itself. The ground, therefore, for regarding suicide and other transgressions as abominable and punishable must not be found in the divine will, but in their inherent heinousness."[11]

Second, we occasionally find things commanded in the Scriptures that seem to violate the requirements of the categorical imperative. For example, God's command to Abraham to sacrifice his son (Gen. 22:2) and God's command to the Israelites to steal whatever they want from the Egyptians (Exod. 12:36) clearly violate perfect duties to others. For Kant, the commands in Scripture must conform to the categorical imperative. If the Scriptures command something other than the categorical imperative, then they must be mistaken.

Regardless of what Kant thinks about the relationship of reason to revelation, there are at least two points of convergence between Kantian and Christian ethics. First, Kant sees the categorical imperative as a formalization of the golden rule. When we do to others as we would have them do to us, we are thinking from the perspective of others. This reflects formulations 1, 3, and 4 of the categorical imperative. The second point of convergence is that Kant sees all people as having intrinsic worth; persons should not be used as means. But we should respect the dignity of all people by treating them in ways that recognize their worth.

Criticisms of Kantian Ethics

Although Kantian ethics seems to correspond in many ways to conventional ethics and Christian morality, it has a number of weaknesses that subject it to important criticisms. First, Kantian ethics fails to respond adequately to conflicts in duty. Let us return to the example we considered at the beginning of the chapter: Do we or do we not lie to the Nazis who are looking for innocent Jews hiding in our house?[12] It would seem, on Kant's view, that there

11. Immanuel Kant, *Lectures on Ethics*, trans. Louis Infield (Indianapolis: Hackett, 1979), 120. He also says, "God is Himself good and Holy because His will conforms to this objective law."

12. The example Kant considers is known as the inquiring murderer. The situation is such that you suppose a friend seeks refuge at your house. You grant it. But then a would-be murderer comes to your door seeking your friend in order to kill the friend. Do you lie to the inquiring murderer? Kant says no. His response to this can be found in Kant, "On a Supposed Right to Lie Because of Philanthropic Concerns," in *The Critique of Practical Reason and Other Writings*, trans. Lewis White Beck (Chicago: University of Chicago Press, 1949), 346–50.

would be two conflicting duties at work here. The first duty would be to tell the truth since this follows from the categorical imperative. But another duty would be to protect innocent life, which also follows directly from the categorical imperative. Kant recognizes no such conflict since moral principles must always be known with certainty. However, our moral lives seem to be complicated by conflicts of duty. In this respect, Kantian ethics fails to make sense out of the real situations in which we find ourselves. Moreover, we occasionally find people in Scripture, such as Rahab, who lie and are praised for their deception. Although Kant would object on the basis of the Scriptures failing to meet his demands for morality, we can see the appeal of prioritizing the good over the right. But even so, the Decalogue does not say, "You shall not lie"; it says, "You shall not bear false witness" (e.g., colluding in deception against another person in a court of law).

A second and related criticism of Kantian ethics concerns the maxim to be universalized. As we have seen, Kant has difficulties adjudicating between competing obligations, but this might be due to the problem of what it is we are trying to universalize. Do I universalize the maxim to always tell the truth or the maxim to always protect innocent life? What this reveals is that there is difficulty ascertaining which maxim one should employ in formulating the categorical imperative.

A third criticism concerns Kant's rejection of happiness as the basis for the moral life. Both secular and Christian sources agree that happiness is indeed the basis for much of our moral lives. Plato, Aristotle, and Mill all agree that happiness is what we desire and that it should play a normative role in our lives. The Psalms and the Beatitudes speak to the importance of happiness, or blessedness, in the life of the person who loves God.

Case Study: Capital Punishment

A famous thought experiment draws into stark relief the various views people have on punishment.[13] A sheriff in a small, racially divided town learns of a murder. Talk around town indicates that the murder was perpetrated by a member of one of the ethnic groups against another. From his experience, the sheriff knows that a riot will ensue, and many people will die. One of his deputies comes to him and offers the following solution: arrest someone with no alibi and try that person for murder. It will prevent the riots, and many

13. Adapted from H. J. McCloskey, "A Non-Utilitarian Approach to Punishment," in *Philosophical Perspectives on Punishment*, ed. Gertrude Ezorsky (Albany: State University of New York Press, 1972), 119–34.

lives will be saved. Should the sheriff do this? In order to answer this question, a person has to have some idea of what punishment is and what it is for.

There are three main theories of punishment: the deterrence theory, the therapeutic theory, and the retributive theory. Although they are not mutually exclusive, they do each have one main idea that is emphasized. The **deterrence theory of punishment** is the theory wherein a punishment is used to deter or prevent future crimes. This theory is usually associated with utilitarian normative theories (see chapter 8) since the basic idea is that overall happiness is to be pursued and unhappiness prevented. The idea is that the punishment is so unpleasant that no one will want to—or be able to—commit the crime in question. For example, if a person is punished in an excruciatingly painful way, then others will not be tempted to commit the crime in question. But it also might be the case that, by killing a perpetrator, he or she will not be able to commit future crimes.

The **therapeutic theory of punishment** is the view that sees punishment as a kind of cure for the perpetrator. The person who commits a crime is an individual who suffers from a kind of disease. Punishment, therefore, is for the purpose of curing the criminal tendencies and behaviors. What this theory shares with the retributivist theory is that the person who commits the crime is the one who needs attention. But this is where the similarities end.

The retributive theory of punishment is based on the idea of just desert. **Retributivism** is the view that we only punish because the perpetrator deserves it. This is Kant's own view.[14] Justice is the only thing that justifies punishment, and justice requires that the criminal pay for the crime committed. Kant argues that anyone involved in the commission of a capital offense deserves the death penalty. So, for example, all the conspirators in the assassination of President Abraham Lincoln were executed by hanging. John Wilkes Booth was the only person who pulled the trigger on the gun that killed Lincoln, and he was later killed by soldiers from a search party. But all those involved in the plot were executed, as they equally shared in the guilt. Kant would have approved. Let us take a look at why.

For Kant, as we have seen, we have a perfect duty not to murder other humans. This is seen by engaging the categorical imperative. According to the first formula, we cannot universalize murder because we could not imagine a world in which *all* people murdered one another. But even if we could universalize it, we cannot will that it become a law of nature in accordance with the second formula because then we would be willing murder as a necessary

---

14. Immanuel Kant, *The Metaphysical Elements of Justice: Part I of the Metaphysics of Morals*, trans. John Ladd (Indianapolis: Bobbs-Merrill, 1965).

law of nature. The third version of the categorical imperative shows that we would be actively treating another person as a means to our own selfish ends, which fails to respect their intrinsic worth. Finally, in accordance with the fourth version, we could not legislate this for a kingdom of ends because as members in the kingdom of ends, we must always think in terms of all people having intrinsic worth and thinking from their perspective as well as our own. So, based on all four versions of the categorical imperative, we see that we have an absolute duty not to murder others. But what do we do about the person who does murder?

We must make certain in the practice of punishment not to violate the categorical imperative, which means that we must take care to universalize our judgments and always to treat others as ends in themselves and never as a means only. It is in appealing to these two ideas that Kant argues in favor of capital punishment. First, Kant claims that we would all universalize our judgments to execute the offender. It would seem that criminals could not will their own execution, and Kant does not argue this point. Instead he argues that even criminals will a system of laws that inflicts punishment on guilty parties. As rational beings (Latin, *homo noumenon*), people can will the universal punishment as a duty. Yet, as criminals who do not desire their own death (Latin, *homo phenomenon*), they wish to avoid it.

Second, Kant argues that we must take care to ensure that we do not treat criminals as a means only and fail to treat them as ends in themselves. We cannot use the criminals and their deaths as means to prevent future crimes. Rather, we must always see punishment as a duty—a duty that respects the dignity and responsibility of the ones who have committed the crimes. Kant asks us to consider the following example: Suppose there are two people found guilty of murder. One of them is a person of noble character, and the other is a person who is a well-known wretch. How should we administer justice to these two? Kant says that they should both be executed because they are both guilty of the same crime. He says, "There is no substitute that will satisfy the requirements of legal justice. There is no sameness of kind between death and remaining alive even under the most miserable conditions, and consequently there is also no equality between the crime and the retribution unless the criminal is judiciously condemned to death."[15]

If one were to let them both live, then Kant argues that the person of noble character would be punished too much as he would have to live with the shame that would attend his every waking hour for the rest of his life. On the contrary, the moral wretch would not be punished enough, according to the magnitude

15. Kant, *Metaphysical Elements of Justice*, 103.

of the crime. This notion of treating criminals as people who are responsible for their actions ties into the means-end formula of the categorical imperative since it means that we must never fail to treat people—even criminals—as persons who are responsible for their actions. To fail to punish them appropriately would be to fail to treat them with dignity, according to Kant.

If we execute all persons guilty of murder, regardless of their moral character, then we are treating them all equally as persons who are worthy of our respect. This last criterion tells us that all people, whether innocent or guilty, should always be treated as ends in themselves and never only as a means. Capital punishment should be employed, not for revenge or for deterrence purposes, but solely because duty requires it.

For Kant, the idea of respect for persons as ends in themselves is an admirable approach to ethics, but we have to wonder whether it fails with regard to the issue of capital punishment. If we truly respect people as beings that have a kind of intrinsic value, can we ever kill them? The problem concerns whether or not it is ever right to take another human's life. Even if a jury could be 100 percent certain that the accused committed the crime—and history shows that well over one hundred people have been convicted and executed for crimes they did not commit in the United States alone—would it still be right to kill another human? In the Gospels, the one time a person guilty of a capital crime (for adultery) is brought to Jesus, he refuses to condemn her to death (John 8:1–11). One reason that many people object to capital punishment is that it is part of the "culture of death" that Pope John Paul II condemned.[16] If every human has incomparable worth, and if every human is made in the *imago Dei*, then to kill another person—even as a punishment—is an attack on God. For many Christians, capital punishment is not merely killing another human but also an act of blasphemy.

Another question concerns the assumptions Kant makes about the judicial system. For Kant, it appears as if systems of justice operate without bias, prejudice, or errors. It is now well established that racial biases profoundly affect the outcome of many trials and the subsequent sentencings. Overwhelming research demonstrates that in the United States young African Americans are twice as likely to be stopped and arrested as their white counterparts.[17] African Americans will serve longer sentences for the same crime committed by a white counterpart, and they are much more likely to be sentenced to death.

16. Pope John Paul II, *The Gospel of Life: Evangelium Vitae* (Mahwah, NJ: Paulist Press, 1995).
17. For more information and other data concerning racial disparities, consult the United States Department of Justice website at https://www.nij.gov/topics/law-enforcement/legitimacy/pages/traffic-stops.aspx.

At every step in the process, African Americans are much more likely to have the system biased against them. Moreover, as we have seen, it is possible to execute innocent people—and this applies to all ethnic groups. Since 1973 at least 144 people who were sentenced to death have subsequently been exonerated by DNA evidence. In light of this, a Kantian theory of retribution—with regard to executing the perpetrator—seems to be theoretically plausible but in practice a clear violation of basic principles of justice since it fails to meet the universality criteria of the categorical imperative.

Discussion Questions

1. Do you think Kant is right when he says that the only unqualified good thing you can imagine is a good will? Why or why not?

2. What is the relationship between happiness and duty?

3. Is it always wrong to lie? If not, then when is it morally permissible to lie, and why? What factors might influence your decision to lie?

4. If you find yourself caught between competing duties, then on what basis do you choose to fulfill the one duty rather than the other?

5. Do you find Kant's argument in favor of capital punishment to be a good one? Why or why not?

6. What theory of punishment do you think is the most just? Why?

EIGHT

Utilitarianism

Actions are right in proportion as they tend to promote happiness;
wrong as they tend to produce the reverse of happiness.

—John Stuart Mill, *Utilitarianism*

Words to Watch

act utilitarianism	*jus in bello*	rule utilitarianism
Christian realism	just war theory	situation ethics
consequentialism	net utility	trolley problem
expected utility	pacifism	utilitarianism
hedonic calculus	principle of utility	
jus ad bellum	proportionalism	

Introduction

In August 1945 the United States military detonated atomic bombs over Hiroshima and Nagasaki in Japan. Tens of thousands of people died in these attacks. The rationale for the use of atomic warfare was that the demonstration of these unbelievably powerful weapons would bring a quick close to World War II. Three days after the second bombing, Emperor Hirohito of Japan chose to surrender. Military scholars and philosophers have debated the morality of this use of atomic weapons. Various questions have arisen in these debates: Would Japan have surrendered anyway? How many lives were saved? How can we know how many lives were saved? Was the cost of innocent life worth the benefit of the bombs' apparent success in ending the war?

Most defenses of the use of the atomic bombs have rested on consequentialist reasoning. **Consequentialism** refers to any ethical theory that views the consequences of an act as its most important moral feature. Consequentialism appeals to the idea of the balance of benefits outweighing the negative costs. In considering the morality of the atomic bomb, then, consequentialist arguments appeal to the idea that many Allied and Japanese lives were saved by the use of these weapons. Their use may have prevented a protracted conventional war that would have cost hundreds of thousands of lives. While the loss of innocent people is regrettable, the value of saving lives seems to be more important.

The most prominent form of consequentialism is known as utilitarianism. **Utilitarianism** is a moral theory in which the greatest happiness of the greatest number is promoted, while unhappiness is avoided. It is important to note here that it may be possible to promote the happiness of the group at the expense of oneself. It is in this way that utilitarianism is distinguished from ethical egoism, which is the view that one can and should promote only one's own happiness. There are two basic forms of utilitarianism: act and rule. They are associated historically with Jeremy Bentham and John Stuart Mill, respectively. In this chapter we consider the main versions of utilitarianism, their development, and to what extent a utilitarian approach to war is morally acceptable among the competing alternatives.

Bentham's Act Utilitarianism

Is it ever morally permissible to break a conventional rule of morality if you know that everyone will benefit from it? Suppose you know that a wealthy family has been robbed. This wealthy family is known for their greed, self-centeredness, and lack of compassion. You also know the thieves, and the thieves have used the money to pay for therapeutic treatment for their child who suffers terribly from a rare medical condition. Should you notify the police? Would not everyone be better off if the thieves were allowed to use their ill-gotten gains to relieve the suffering of their child, especially if the wealthy family's quality of life is not substantially diminished by the robbery? An **act utilitarian** like Jeremy Bentham would answer this question with a definite yes.[1]

1. In contrast to rule utilitarians, who think that we should adopt that set of rules that increase net utility, act utilitarians see the specific action as more important than any rule that generally increases net utility.

Bentham was a social reformer in the eighteenth century who was well known for promoting legislation against child labor. However, today he is best known for developing a normative ethical theory based on what he called the "hedonic calculus."[2] The **hedonic calculus** is a means by which a person could determine the right course of action by figuring out the greatest happiness for the greatest number. For Bentham, one needs to consider each and every act and how it would maximize happiness. The hedonic calculus considers seven different dimensions of pleasure (or happiness): intensity, duration, certainty, nearness, fecundity, purity, and extension. In Bentham's view, it is possible to measure each of these dimensions of pleasure. Intensity and duration are fairly clear elements of pleasure, but fecundity and purity are less so. Fecundity concerned the likelihood that the pleasure would produce more pleasure. Purity considered whether there were associated pains in the pursuit of this particular pleasure.

Bentham held that we should assign a value to each of these elements and then add up the **expected utility** (i.e., the sum total pleasure we expect to achieve) and subtract the pains involved in attaining them. This formula would produce the **net utility** (i.e., the total expected utility minus the associated pains in achieving that particular pleasure) for a given course of action. So, for example, consider a mother who has a Saturday afternoon to do with as she pleases. Which of the following activities should she choose?

1. Go to the office to finish an important project for work.
2. Spend the time at home playing games with her children.
3. Take her children to the local homeless shelter and have them help feed the hungry.
4. Go to the store and buy her children new clothes.

In this decision-making process, the mother needs to calculate the total benefits to everyone affected by the actions and determine which one promotes the greatest overall happiness. Assuming for the moment that we can actually gauge the intensity, duration, certainty, nearness, fecundity, purity, and extent of the actions, what should the mother do? If option 1 results in 14 units of pleasure and 6 units of pain, then we get a net utility of 8 units of happiness. If option 2 results in 20 units of pleasure and 15 units of pain, then we get a net utility of 5 units of happiness. If option 3 results in 9 units of pleasure and 5 units of pain, then we achieve a net utility of 4 units of happiness. If

2. Jeremy Bentham, *The Principles of Morals and Legislation* (Westminster, MD: Prometheus, 1988).

option 4 results in 4 units of pleasure and 2 units of pain, then we get 2 net units of happiness. The decision is clear. She is morally obligated to choose option 1, since it results in the greatest net utility.

Option	Pleasure	Pain	Net Happiness
1	14	6	8
2	20	15	5
3	9	5	4
4	4	2	2

There are numerous problems with Bentham's hedonic calculus, of which we will mention three. First, how are we to determine the intensity of a pleasure? Is there some universal standard to which we might appeal? How do we account for the problem of intersubjectivity (i.e., the idea that any given action might make some people happy, others less happy, and still others unhappy)? Second, do we really have to consider what all of our options are? It would seem that there could be an infinite number of different things we could do on any one Saturday afternoon. Surely a moral theory that cannot be practically applied cannot be obligatory. Third, how are we to define what happiness is? Do all people share the same definition of happiness? If not, then how do we resolve our moral problems? In light of these problems, contemporary act utilitarians have opted for some significant changes to Bentham's approach.

Most contemporary act utilitarians have rejected the hedonic calculus and attempts at defining happiness and instead have opted for a theory that places an emphasis on people's interests. Contemporary act utilitarians also take each act by itself and do not appeal to any rules of behavior, since rules may at times fail to result in the greatest happiness. Sometimes following a rule does not maximize everyone's interests.

On the first point, interests can be understood in a more coherent fashion than the idea of net utility. Units of utility are hopelessly elusive and difficult to define, while interests are not. When making a decision, we can simply ask people to rank their interests. We could ask a group of people, for example, whether they would rather go to a baseball game, work at a homeless shelter, stay home and play games, or listen to jazz. Respondents could then simply rank their interests and act accordingly. Since some possible routes of action hold no interest for people, we need not waste time considering everything we might possibly do.

The second point regards the contrast between **rule utilitarians**, who believe that we should always follow moral rules in order to promote utility, and act utilitarians, who deny the absolute authority of rules. Consider the following scenario, similar to one presented in chapter 7. In a racially divided town, someone has brutally murdered a member of the majority group. The accused are members of a minority group. The judge knows that if the defendants are found not guilty, there will be rioting and looting and a number of innocent people will die. However, if the defendants are found guilty, then peace will prevail. No one will get hurt, and there will be no loss of property. The judge knows the defendants to be innocent and also knows that the rule that people should be treated fairly usually brings about the greatest utility. But in this case the rule does not work. As an act utilitarian, the judge will declare the defendants guilty since this brings about the greatest net utility. In order to see the contrast more clearly, we must first develop an understanding of rule utilitarianism by turning to the work of John Stuart Mill.

Mill's Rule Utilitarianism

John Stuart Mill developed the classical version of utilitarianism, which has become known as rule utilitarianism.[3] Central to Mill's articulation of the theory is the **principle of utility**, which is the idea that actions are right proportionate to the amount of happiness they produce and wrong proportionate to the amount of unhappiness they produce. In his major work on the theory, Mill develops an argument for it as a series of responses to objections and misconceptions about the theory. The first objection Mill considers is what we might call the hedonist objection. In this view, utilitarianism represents an affront to traditional morality when the only basis for moral action is the pursuit of pleasure or happiness. The objector claims that, if pleasure is the only basis for making moral judgments, then the human has been reduced to the level of a mere pleasure-seeking animal. Thus, utilitarianism, the accuser believes, is a theory fit only for swine.

Mill responds to this objection by appealing to an ambiguity in the term "pleasure." There are many different kinds of pleasure, Mill claims. Humans not only have animal pleasures but also rational, or human, pleasures. Viewing art, telling jokes, and reading a good book are all pleasures that only humans can enjoy. As a result, Mill claims, it is the objector, not the utilitarian, who treats the human as nothing more than an animal. Mill writes, "It is better to be a human being dissatisfied than a pig satisfied; better to be Socrates dissatisfied than a fool satisfied. And if the fool, or the pig, is of a different opinion, it is because they know only their side of the question."[4] The reason

3. John Stuart Mill, *Utilitarianism*, ed. Roger Crisp (Oxford: Oxford University Press, 1998).
4. Mill, *Utilitarianism*, 57.

for this, says Mill, is that "human beings have faculties more elevated than the animal appetites, and when once made conscious of them, do not regard anything as happiness which does not include their gratification."[5]

In order to tell the difference between the animal and the human pleasures, Mill introduces the idea of the "moral expert." He claims that, if we are given the choice between two pleasures, then we should consult someone who has had experience of both and has no prior commitment to choosing one over the other. The moral expert, says Mill, will choose the higher pleasure over any amount of the lower pleasure since there is a difference in the quality of the pleasures. The moral expert does not decide on the basis of the mere quantity of pleasure but on the basis of that which ennobles our character. In this respect, Mill differs from Bentham by identifying qualitative differences between various kinds of pleasure that go beyond the mere quantity of pleasure.

The second objection to the theory is the charge that utilitarianism replaces moral duty with happiness. We might call this the Kantian objection since it was Kant who explicitly rejected happiness as a suitable principle on which to base an entire ethical theory. The objector here claims that happiness is unattainable, and even if it were attainable, then we have no right to happiness.

Here we need to have a workable definition of happiness. For Mill, it is not a sustained state of supreme pleasure but a life lived with moments of great pleasure "in an existence made up of few and transitory pains, many and various pleasures, with a decided predominance of the active over the passive, and having as the foundation of the whole, not to expect more from life than it is capable of bestowing."[6] In other words, one can only attain happiness over the course of a well-lived life.

Since we all pursue happiness, we should intend happiness as our motive. Yet the Kantian objector says that this motive vitiates the value of a moral act. From the Kantian perspective, we should always do our moral duty simply because it is our duty and for no other motive. If we permit motives other than duty, for Kant, this opens the door to arguing over competing definitions of happiness and choosing whatever means are most convenient to these ends.

Mill responds to these objections in two ways. First, he argues that ethics, or moral philosophy, tells us what our moral duties are and not the motives we should have when fulfilling them. Mill says that it is unreasonable to expect that the only reason for doing our duty is for its own sake. To ask people to do so is to deny human nature.

5. Mill, *Utilitarianism*, 56.
6. Mill, *Utilitarianism*, 60.

Second, the objector makes a basic mistake in confusing the value of an agent with the value of an act. Suppose a wealthy person makes a large donation to a charitable organization with the intent of getting good publicity and a large tax write-off. This person promotes the greatest happiness for everyone while having selfish motives. The agent's motives have very little value, but the agent's act has tremendous value. Or consider a well-meaning architect who loves children and is the designer of a new orphanage. However, the building is poorly designed and collapses, killing dozens of children. The value of the agent's motive is considerable, but the value of the act increases unhappiness.

A third major objection to utilitarianism is that it is an antireligious moral theory. To this Mill responds by arguing, first, that whether utilitarianism is antireligious depends on what kind of God we have in mind and, second, that we must consider the relationship between divine revelation and utility. Mill says that in Christianity it certainly seems as if God desires our happiness. If this is indeed the case, then utilitarianism is not antireligious but profoundly religious. Thus, one might say that God is a utilitarian. Then Mill claims that "a utilitarian who believes in the perfect goodness and wisdom of God, necessarily believes that whatever God has thought fit to reveal on the subject of morals, must fulfill the requirements of utility in a supreme degree."[7] Since according to the great monotheistic traditions of Christianity, Judaism, and Islam, God desires our happiness, it follows that whatever God commands—whether by means of natural or special revelation—must be for our happiness. According to Mill, a God who does not desire the happiness of creatures is probably not a God worth worshiping.

The primary teaching for Christians is found in the Christian Scriptures where Jesus gives explicit instructions to his disciples. One of the key teachings is the golden rule (Matt. 7:12). Mill says, "In the golden rule of Jesus of Nazareth, we read the complete spirit of the ethics of utility. To do as you would be done by, and to love your neighbour as yourself, constitute the ideal perfection of utilitarian morality."[8] Mill argues that since happiness is the only thing that all people desire, it should be the primary moral principle employed in ethical arguments.

For Mill, all people act on the basis of two kinds of principles: external and internal. The external sanctions for the principle of utility are praise and blame from others. These external principles can make us happy or unhappy, depending on the kinds of choices we make. If we consider God as an Other,

7. Mill, *Utilitarianism*, 68.
8. Mill, *Utilitarianism*, 64.

then we see that God's approval or disapproval can make for powerful motives of action.

Internal sanctions for our behavior go beyond what others think of us. Our conscience can provide an internal sanction of our behavior since it produces psychological pleasure when we act in accordance with it and pain when we act against it. For Mill, a guilty conscience is incredibly painful and provides the necessary proof that we do indeed act on the basis of happiness. To support his argument, Mill offers an analogy. He says that the only way we can tell that something is visible is if people see it. The only way we know that something is audible is if people hear it. Likewise, the only way we know that something is desirable is that people desire it. The one thing that all people desire is happiness. Just as each person desires his or her own happiness, so too all people should desire the happiness of all.

The Trolley Problem

In the 1960s philosopher Philippa Foot developed a thought experiment called the **trolley problem**. This little exercise was meant to draw a sharp contrast between Kantians, who hold to a strict theory of duty, and utilitarians, who hold to the principle that a person should always maximize net utility. The problem takes two different versions. In the first version, you are to imagine a runaway trolley coming down the tracks. From your vantage point you can see that if it continues down the track, it will hit and kill five people. But you are next to the switch that controls the rails. On the other track is one person. If you flip the switch, then the trolley will switch tracks and kill the one person on the other track and thereby save a net total of four lives. Do you flip the switch?

In the second version of the trolley problem, you are standing on an overpass as the trolley comes hurtling down the tracks. Standing next to you is a very large, overweight man who is perched precariously on the edge of the overpass. It is clear to you that (1) he is so large that his body could stop the trolley, and (2) it would be easy for you to push him off the ledge. If you push the man onto the tracks, then you will save the five people down below. If you do not, they will all die. What do you do?

This thought experiment is meant to elicit different feelings about the two scenarios. In the one you are merely flipping a switch, but in the other you actually have to put your hands on the man and push him to his death. However, on further reflection, it is clear that all utilitarians (both act and rule versions) will save four lives at the cost of one since net utility is all that

Figure 8.1.
The Trolley Problem

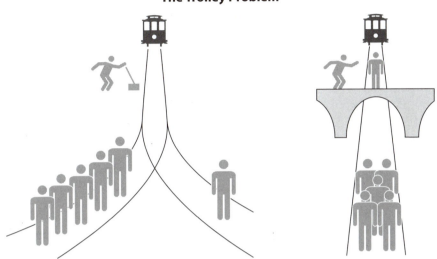

counts. Moreover, no Kantian would flip the switch or push the man since there is a duty not to treat people merely as a means to some other end—no matter how laudable that end is.

There are a number of other factors that people might want to consider. Who are the five people on the tracks? How did they get there? Who is the one person on the other track? Who is the large man on the overpass? What is my relation to all of these people? Answers to these questions might determine how I act. For example, what if the five people on one track are all eighty-year-old convicted felons on a work detail, and the one person on the other track is my five-year old child? What if the five people on the one track are Nobel Prize winners in cancer research, and the person on the other track is a notorious talk-show host known for his ability to incite hatred among listeners? What if the large man on the overpass is my father? Or the beloved pastor or priest at one's local parish? Such questions highlight some of the problems with utilitarianism, to which we now turn.

Criticisms of Utilitarianism

Aside from objections based on the quantification of pleasure we have noted above, there are two major problems with utilitarianism. The first is that utilitarianism has some counterintuitive results regarding our moral relationships.

The second stems from utilitarianism's limited moral epistemology—that is, how we can ever know that our actions will bring about the good consequences we intend.

Bernard Williams has argued that all forms of utilitarianism are problematic because they fail to take account of morally relevant relationships. He offers a thought experiment about an explorer named Jim who has been journeying through the jungle.[9] He stumbles on a clearing where a number of villagers are lined up in front of a firing squad. The sergeant at arms sees Jim and declares that if Jim shoots one of the villagers then the other nineteen can go free. If Jim refuses, then all twenty villagers will be shot. What should Jim do? Williams notes that both rule and act utilitarians will encourage Jim to shoot the one, thereby saving the other nineteen.

Williams claims that the soldiers—whose responsibility it is to obey the sergeant—stand in a different relationship to the villagers than Jim does. Jim has no prior relationship with the sergeant, the soldiers, or the villagers. For Williams, our relationships to a great extent determine our moral responsibilities. For example, I have a greater responsibility to discipline my children—since I am morally and legally responsible for them—than I have to someone with whom I am not related, such as a stranger I see in the grocery store. In Williams's thought experiment, Jim cannot be blamed for the deaths of the nineteen people, even if he refuses to shoot, because there are other agents and relationships in play.

This leads to the second objection to utilitarianism. How does Jim *know* what will happen if he does shoot one villager? Perhaps the sergeant has already determined that all twenty will die regardless of what Jim does, since people are known to lie about what they say they will do. This objection involves what we might call the problem of moral epistemology. For utilitarianism to work, it must be able to anticipate with great regularity the outcomes of various courses of action. However, our actions are only part of a larger constellation of causes that bring about various states of affairs. O. Henry's story *Gift of the Magi* is instructive here. In this short story, a young married couple, deeply in love with each other, think about what they can give to the other. The wife, who has beautiful long hair, knows that her husband desires a chain for his pocket watch. She goes and cuts her hair, sells it, and buys him the chain. Unbeknownst to her, the husband has sold his pocket watch and purchased expensive combs for her hair. The intention to bring about net utility fails since there are other agents at work in the situation.

9. Bernard Williams, *Utilitarianism: For and Against* (Cambridge: Cambridge University Press, 1973), 97–99.

Christian Responses to Utilitarianism

The Hebrew and Christian Scriptures address a number of issues related to utilitarian concerns. Among them are (1) the idea that our actions are goal-directed, (2) the importance of "blessedness," and (3) the well-being of all people. First, throughout the biblical texts, we discover that often there are important consequences for keeping the covenant. Rewards of blessedness, long life, and the benefits of wisdom are all among the motives that are used to persuade people to behave in ways that promote peace, flourishing, and well-being.

Second, in the Sermon on the Mount, Jesus repeatedly states the conditions for blessedness or happiness.[10] He tells his listeners,

> Blessed are the poor in spirit. . . .
> Blessed are those who mourn. . . .
> Blessed are the meek. . . .
> Blessed are those who hunger and thirst for righteousness. . . .
> Blessed are the merciful. . . .
> Blessed are the pure in heart. . . .
> Blessed are the peacemakers. . . .
> Blessed are they who are persecuted for righteousness' sake. . . .
> Blessed are you when people revile you and persecute you and utter all
> kinds of evil against you falsely on my account.
>
> Matt. 5:3–11

The assumption is that those who hear Jesus's words desire to be happy. Yet it may be that contemporary versions of utilitarian happiness (in terms of maximizing interests) are far removed from Christian accounts of blessedness and beatitude.

Third, in the Gospel of John, the high priest makes an interesting statement, full of double entendres, when he says of Jesus that "it is better . . . to have one man die for the people" (John 11:50). On one level, this means that Jesus must die to stop a possible rebellion or to keep the people from turning away from the approved religious practices of the day. On another level, it means that one man's death brings salvation to all humanity. This sounds like an anticipation of utilitarian reasoning.

---

10. Jesus's meaning of "blessedness" is likely not what contemporary utilitarians mean by "happiness," yet there does seem to be a similar teleological orientation and an underlying idea of well-being operating in both uses.

Beyond these three connections found in Scripture, there have been two basic responses to utilitarianism from within the Christian tradition: situation ethics and proportionalism.

Situation Ethics

In the 1960s Joseph Fletcher developed **situation ethics** as a way to combine a Christian ethic of love with utilitarianism.[11] Situation ethics was the idea that the greatest good should be determined not by some universal moral principle but by the amount of goodness produced with reference to the specific circumstances and a motive of love. Fletcher calls his approach the "agapic calculus," which he distinguishes from what he considers the "only two competitors": legalism and antinomianism. Legalism consists in merely following the rules, while antinomianism has no principles whatsoever. For Fletcher, his alternative seems preferable because it takes into consideration what he thinks are the two most important principles: love and the context of the situation.

Situation ethics holds that the motive of love is what ultimately counts. Moral decisions should always aim for the well-being of people rather than the love of principles. In this regard, situation ethics is a kind of act utilitarianism where the net utility of an act is the well-being of persons. From this perspective, there are no absolutes—except for love—that should guide a person's actions. It would thus be permissible to engage in adultery or lying if either of these actions were performed out of a motive of love for the other person and contributed to the other's well-being. Moral rules are merely guidelines and not principles to be worshiped.

The main objection to this view is that there are some activities that can never promote happiness or well-being. Those actions would be the prohibitions found in the Decalogue or violations of the natural law. It is difficult to see how murder or adultery could ever promote well-being, for example. In other words, even if the end is the only thing that can justify the means, the end intended does not justify *any* means whatsoever. Some means are never to be used because of their intrinsically evil nature.

Proportionalism

In the Roman Catholic tradition, when attempts have been made to reconcile natural law ethics with utilitarianism, the results have been mixed. The most notable attempt is known as **proportionalism**, which is the approach that

11. Joseph Fletcher, *Situation Ethics: The New Morality* (Philadelphia: Westminster, 1966).

seeks to weigh the good effects against the evil and find the best proportion between them. This view was rejected by Pope John Paul II in his encyclical *Veritatis Splendor*. He writes, "The teleological ethical theories (proportionalism, consequentialism), while acknowledging that moral values are indicated by reason and by Revelation, maintain that it is never possible to formulate an absolute prohibition of particular kinds of behaviour which would be in conflict."[12] Although the ends we strive for may be good, it does not mean that we can choose any means whatsoever. Not only must the end intended be good (which proportionalism acknowledges), but the circumstances and the act itself must be appropriate (which proportionalism does not acknowledge).

Suppose a suspected terrorist is captured and may have important information about a plot to kill thousands of people in a surprise attack. Would it be morally permissible to torture this person in order to obtain information about the plot? A utilitarian or a proportionalist would answer yes because a greater good would outweigh the relatively insignificant pain the suspect would endure. However, traditional Roman Catholic moral theology indicates that it is always and everywhere wrong to torture human persons since torture itself is an intrinsically evil act. There are no possible ends that can justify means such as torture or other intrinsically evil acts.

Case Study: War

In the early narratives of the Hebrew Bible (e.g., Josh. 6–11), God commands the children of Israel to wage war in order to conquer the land that God had promised them. The context for these commands include the following: (1) the people have been promised this land after departing Egypt and wandering in the wilderness; (2) God wages the war on their behalf; and (3) they see it as their benefit for keeping the covenant with God. In this context, many of the early images of God are those of a warrior. These images are later contrasted with the views that Jesus presents in the Christian Scriptures. In the Gospels Jesus is portrayed as the prince of peace, the good shepherd, and a lamb being led to slaughter. Jesus also tells his followers to be peacemakers (Matt. 5:9) and says that his kingdom is not of this world (John 18:36). He even explicitly warns Peter, who would defend him with violence, that "all who take the sword will perish by the sword" (Matt. 26:52).

There was a tendency in the early church (e.g., Tertullian in the second century) to see war as absolutely incompatible with Christian faith. However,

---

12. Pope John Paul II, *Veritatis Splendor* (Washington, DC: United States Catholic Conference, 1993), 75.

this attitude changed by the time of Augustine in the fourth century, and the idea of just war developed. Just war theory is more clearly articulated in the thirteenth century in the work of Thomas Aquinas, who said that for a war to be just three things must apply: (1) the war has a just cause, (2) it is declared by one who has authority, and (3) its aim is for the purpose of peace. Only when all three conditions are met can one proceed to engage in warfare.[13]

Ethicists usually consider aspects of **just war theory** under two headings: *jus ad bellum* and *jus in bello*. The conditions under which a war may be declared is called ***jus ad bellum***, or the "right to go to war." The right to wage war could only be an act of retributive justice—that is, a kind of morally good punishment when an unjust aggressor has initiated the violence. Preemptive strikes are strictly forbidden under the guidelines of *jus ad bellum* because a just war is an act of retribution, a kind of recompense for a prior act of injustice. The ruler must also think that there is a reasonable chance of winning the war. Politicians in the twenty-first century still appeal to these principles in order to justify wars. A just war is thus one in which a ruler can appeal to the overall justice of the cause against the cause of an aggressor.

A nation's right to go to war is only the first part of just war theory. The means by which a war is waged are also morally relevant, and this is where *jus in bello* considerations come into play. ***Jus in bello*** concerns morally permissible actions once the head of state has declared war, including the right moral actions that serve to constrain, or limit, the evils of war. Traditionally, these principles include a number of rules and regulations. *Jus in bello* forbids targeting noncombatants—for example, civilians, children, people in houses of worship, and the sick. It requires that when combatants offer an unconditional surrender, they cannot be killed (as this would constitute a form of murder). It also provides for proportional responses to aggression—for example, not destroying an entire village or country when disarming the military would be sufficient.

While such moral principles serve as an ideal for which to strive, just war theory faces two critical problems. First, how does one fairly evaluate who started a war? Since many wars and international conflicts have lingered for decades and centuries, how does one determine who committed the first act of unjust aggression? Second, although just war theory may serve as the basis for the subsequent prosecution of war crimes, it has had limited success in curbing wars or the methods used in waging them. The actions in war seem evil in themselves, and it seems likely that there is no way to avoid these intrinsic evils.

13. Thomas Aquinas, *Summa Theologica* 2-2.40, trans. Fathers of the English Dominican Province (New York: Benzinger, 1947).

In contrast to sanctioning wars or providing moral arguments for war, radical reformer Menno Simons argues that a Christian cannot participate in any form of violence, including war. He argues that it is always wrong to kill another person for whom Jesus Christ died. Jesus himself says that "all who take the sword will perish by the sword" (Matt. 26:52), which Simons understands as Jesus's prohibition on political or military violence for Jesus's followers. Simons also appeals to the fact that Jesus did not resist his own death but went willingly to it. Simon's approach is known as **pacifism**, which is the view that it is never appropriate to engage in acts of violence, because Jesus himself did not and taught others not to and because violence begets violence.[14]

The pacifist approach has been criticized for being impractical and for failing to take moral responsibility for letting evil flourish. The pacifist, however, responds that it is not the responsibility of Christian churches to be the state. The function of churches is to show the world that there is another way of being in the world. Nonviolence itself is a witness to the truth Christ embodied.

In the twentieth century, Reinhold Niebuhr offered another alternative. He argued that Christian churches are not, and cannot afford to be, pacifist in the face of the evils that Hitler represented. Yet people can all too easily appeal to just war theory in order to rationalize their own aggression. Niebuhr's approach, which came to be known as **Christian realism**, is a Christian approach to war that acknowledges that war is evil but argues that it is at times a necessary evil—one that requires repentance after the fact.[15]

We see here the three main traditions in Christian ethics: (1) just war theory, (2) pacifism, and (3) Christian realism. The just war theorist sees war as only a defensive act but one that can be justified by another state's aggression. The pacifist sees all acts of war as inconsistent with the teachings of Jesus. The Christian realist sees war as an evil that must be performed to prevent another evil, though still requiring repentance and forgiveness.

In the case of World War II, all three options can be seen. People in the pacifist tradition refused to take up arms. Most people in the Allied countries took the view of a just war, especially after Hitler invaded Poland and France without provocation. Further, Hitler's treatment of Eastern Europeans and Jews added to the rationale. Niebuhr argued that war was a kind of necessary evil since all people sin, and this will inevitably happen when human societies come into conflict. Original sin permeates all human activity. War can never be just, not only because there are no innocent agents but also because innocent

---

14. Menno Simons, "Two Kingdoms," in *War and Christian Ethics*, ed. Arthur Holmes, 2nd ed. (Grand Rapids: Baker Academic, 2005), 185–89.

15. Reinhold Niebuhr, "Why the Christian Church Is Not Pacifist," in *War and Christian Ethics*, 301–13.

people often are killed and because the intentions—even of those waging the war—can often be wrong.

Contemporary developments in war and technology raise further questions. Is the use of remote-controlled drones ever morally permissible? Is the threat of nuclear war a morally good deterrent? Is the use of nuclear weapons ever permissible? In what ways can governments respond to terrorists that do not compromise their own moral principles? What exactly is terrorism, and who decides? Is torture ever a tactic that should be employed as a means to gain a strategic advantage?

Discussion Questions

1. Is it ever possible to do something morally objectionable in order to accomplish a greater good? If so, what are some examples?

2. Is it possible for people to agree on what happiness is? If they cannot agree, then does this reflect the idea that there is no such thing as happiness? Or is it possible that some people are mistaken?

3. How do our relationships with various people determine our obligations to them? Is it ever morally permissible to favor some people over others because of our relationships? Is a utilitarian invariably committed to promoting the welfare of all people and not just those who are near and dear?

4. It is often argued that wars are necessary for the greater good—or at least to prevent significant evil. This is clearly a utilitarian argument. Is it true that wars are morally necessary? Of the three options about war presented in this chapter, which one is the best? How can it be defended on either religious or nonreligious grounds?

5. In war, is it ever morally right or morally permissible to kill some people in order to save the lives of others? Was the use of nuclear weapons by the United States morally justified? If so, then on what basis?

6. Does the use of drone missiles meet the standards of *jus in bello*? Do you think that their use decreases or increases hostilities?

NINE

Continental Ethics

Morality is the herd instinct in the individual.
—Friedrich Nietzsche, *Beyond Good and Evil*

Words to Watch

aesthetic stage	euthanasia	*ressentiment*
bad faith	existentialism	slave morality
double-effect	genealogy	teleological suspension
essentialism	I-Thou relationship	of the ethical
ethical stage	moral stage	*Übermensch*

Introduction

Continental philosophy is an umbrella term that covers a variety of philosophical impulses that grew out of philosophical influences on the European continent in the nineteenth and twentieth centuries. It includes both existentialism and postmodernism as well as other philosophical traditions and greatly influenced much of theology of the twentieth century. In general, it is an approach to important issues that emphasizes meaning, context, authenticity, and personal choice. In this regard, it has a tendency to break free of the confines of interminable analysis and move toward key questions of meaning in an individual's life. This can often be seen in the essays and narratives that these thinkers offer.

The nineteenth-century philosopher Søren Kierkegaard wrote a short story titled "The King and the Maiden" that expresses an important feature in existentialist ethics: authentic action. **Existentialism** is an attempt to defy the preconceived roles that people adopt and achieve a more authentic kind of existence. And so Kierkegaard's story begins with a king who possessed such great power that all his subjects feared him and cowed in his presence. He could not prevent this reaction, since this was how people responded to his title. But one day the king saw a humble maiden with whom he fell in love. He desperately wanted to marry her, but he was afraid that if he came to her as he was in his power and glory, then she might not respond according to her true feelings. The king wanted the maiden to love him for who he was and not because of his power or his fame, so he disguised himself as a peasant and sought her love in that way because it was only in an authentic encounter that genuine love could flourish. Kierkegaard's story shows that, in the genuine encounter with others, we see a kind of unmediated relationship. Yet most of the time we respond to the different masks that we and others wear, and it is in those roles that we think we see the persons themselves.

The existentialist tradition is extraordinarily difficult to define. Many diverse thinkers such as Kierkegaard, Friedrich Nietzsche, Jean-Paul Sartre, Martin Buber, and Dietrich Bonhoeffer belong to this tradition as they highlight the ideas of authenticity, genuine choice, and true encounters with others. In this appeal to authentic existence and encounter, there is not only a rejection of predetermined roles that culture, family, society, and religion often assign to us but also a rejection of **essentialism**—the idea that we all have a basic nature that applies to people universally. The rejection of essences does not necessarily lead directly to moral relativism, but existentialists believe that essences are merely cultural conventions that often restrict us and our freedom to be what we choose to be.

Natural law morality, Kantianism, and utilitarianism each represent a kind of essentialism. In natural law, there are natural essences that predispose us to specific kinds of activities. In Kantianism, we are essentially rational creatures. In utilitarianism people are essentially happiness-maximizing creatures. In the existentialist and postmodern traditions, these essences are rejected in favor of an understanding of persons as choosing their own natures and self-definition. In this chapter, we begin with a consideration of those antireligious figures in the continental tradition. We then move on to Christian and Jewish thinkers. We close with a consideration of euthanasia from both continental and other perspectives.

Nietzsche's Genealogy

Friedrich Nietzsche (1844–1900) represents the beginning of the existentialist approach to ethics in the atheist tradition by a method he calls **genealogy**, which is an unraveling of the moral meaning of a term by giving an account of its origin. For Nietzsche, we must understand that our language does not represent real things or essences in the world; language is fundamentally a way of manipulating people. This is especially true of moral language. According to Nietzsche, the idea that there is truth "out there" is a myth from which we must rid ourselves. Instead of searching for essences of things, we must conduct a genealogy of moral words and trace their origins back to how they were originally employed. Only then can we be free of their tyranny over us. When we do this, we find that moral language has its origins in the *ressentiment*, or moral resentment, of the weak who use moral words to keep the strong subdued. The strong must overcome this moral resentment and become people who move beyond good and evil.

Nietzsche tells us that "truth" has no real meaning. It is simply a leftover from a bygone era, and he sees himself as the one who is bold enough to proclaim, "The emperor has no clothes." He writes, "What then is truth? A mobile army of metaphors, metonyms, and anthropomorphisms—in short a sum of human relations, which have been enhanced, transposed, and embellished poetically and rhetorically, and which after long use seem firm, canonical, and obligatory to a people; truths are illusions of which one has forgotten that this is what they are; metaphors which are worn out and without sensuous power; coins which have lost their pictures and now matter only as metal, no longer as coins."[1] Once we recognize this genealogy of morals, we come to understand that language has lost its power to persuade or control since it no longer has the ability to convince us that there are objective referents that correspond to our names.

Nietzsche contends that every language system (including moral language) is a mistaken reliance on a universal. Kant's appeal to rationality and its fictional idea of universalism is like the attempt of people to pull themselves "up into existence by the hair, out of the swamps of nothingness."[2] The idea of "truth" is merely a construct of our language, and as a result there is no "universal moral system" (as Kant would have us believe) that all people can recognize.

1. Friedrich Nietzsche, *The Portable Nietzsche*, ed. Walter Kaufmann (New York: Viking, 1954), 46–47.
2. Friedrich Nietzsche, *Beyond Good and Evil: Prelude to a Philosophy of the Future*, ed. and trans. Walter Kaufmann (New York: Vintage, 1989), 21.

In the absence of a universal moral law, Nietzsche suggests that we must advocate the morality of the *Übermensch*, the super man whose "will to power" and creative genius forges his own morality or creates his own values. There is no metanarrative other than the one the *Übermensch* creates for him- or herself. Traditional virtues such as faith, charity, justice, and humility are trampled by the will to power.

The history of humanity and its values, according to Nietzsche, consist in the conflict between the **slave morality**, or the herd morality, of the masses and the creative genius of the masters. The herd morality is the result of the masses' appeal to universal moral principles in an attempt to suppress the creative urges of the *Übermensch*. Christianity is a prime example of the slave morality at work by inverting the natural powers of the creative soul. But Christianity grows out of the soil of Judaism, and here Nietzsche gives free reign to his contempt for the slave morality: "It was the Jew who, with frightening consistency, dared to invert the aristocratic value equations good = noble = powerful = beautiful = happy = favored of the gods and maintain, with furious hatred of the underprivileged and impotent, that only the poor, the powerless, are good; only the suffering, sick, and ugly, truly blessed."[3]

The masses have asserted and ultimately established the idea that the weak are somehow the strong. This slave morality is one that says no to the world and to all that is beautiful and creative. But this rejection of the beautiful and the creative is born out of fear of the powerful, who give free reign to their creative urges. This vehement rejection of master morality is based on *ressentiment*, which is the essence of slave morality and is created by those who fear the powerful, creative *Übermensch* and attempt to keep him or her constrained. Nietzsche explains, "The slave revolt in morality begins when *ressentiment* itself becomes creative and gives birth to values."[4] The herd invents moral principles (e.g., honesty and humility) as a reaction to the creative genius of those who are beyond good and evil. According to this interpretation, Christianity, natural law, Kantianism, and utilitarianism all represent *ressentiment* at work. The appeal to a universal morality is a device to keep the powerful in their place. Robert Solomon observes, "Universality, according to Nietzsche, is thus not so much a logical feature of moral judgments, as philosophers from Kant to R. M. Hare have argued, but rather a strategy of the weak to deny the significance of the nonmoral virtues and impose their own morality

3. Friedrich Nietzsche, *"On the Genealogy of Morals" and "Ecce Homo,"* trans. Walter Kaufmann (New York: Vintage, 1989), 7.
4. Nietzsche, *"Genealogy of Morals" and "Ecce Homo,"* 10.

on others."[5] In their appeal to words like "universality" and "necessity," the defenders of the slave morality fail to see that words simply do not have the power that they think they have. Nietzsche's linguistic attack on essentialistic morality was not the only one antireligious continental philosophers would take, as it continues in the work of French existentialist Jean-Paul Sartre.

Sartre's Existentialism

Jean-Paul Sartre (1905–80) was one of the more influential existentialists of the twentieth century. He thought that the Enlightenment did away with God as an explanatory entity and that modern people had no need of God since, as Nietzsche proclaimed, "God is dead! And he remains dead! And we have killed him."[6] However, according to Sartre many people, like Kant, made the mistake of holding on to the idea of a universal morality—as well as the vestigial idea of God that they thought supported morality.

Sartre begins his critique of essentialist theories by noting that the idea of human nature must either be a stand-alone concept or one that preexists in the mind of God. In the former case, we would simply be another kind of animal devoid of choice and self-determination. In the latter case, the idea of human nature would be one constructed according to the prescriptions of a divine legislator who made humans for a specific purpose (e.g., to act in accordance with reason, to maximize net utility, or to worship and glorify God forever). As a result, human nature precedes its existence. God therefore is the cosmic artisan, making humans "according to a procedure and a conception, exactly as the artisan manufactures a paper knife."[7] But the idea of human nature gradually disappeared in the Enlightenment with the result that, by the end of the twentieth century, God was superfluous to ethics.

Instead of buying into an idea of human nature as foisted on humanity by a fictional God, Sartre thinks humans create their own essences. It is here we see the switch. Essence does not precede existence; rather, existence precedes essence. Sartre explains, "Man first of all exists, encounters himself, surges up in the world—and defines himself afterwards. If man as the existentialist sees him is not definable, it is because to begin with he is nothing. He will not be anything until later, and then he will be what he makes of himself. Thus,

5. Robert C. Solomon, *Living with Nietzsche: What the Great "Immoralist" Has to Teach Us* (New York: Oxford University Press, 2006), 206.

6. Friedrich Nietzsche, *The Gay Science*, trans. Josefine Nauckhoff (Cambridge: Cambridge University Press, 2001), 121.

7. Jean-Paul Sartre, *Existentialism and Humanism*, trans. Philip Mairet (London: Eyre Methuen, 1973), 27.

there is no human nature, because there is no God to have a conception of it."[8] Sartre basically thinks that humans create themselves from nothing. It is in their free choice that they make something of themselves.

For Sartre, if humans had a real nature that was somehow given, then we would be bound by some principle external to our freedom. This notion that we would be beholden to a moral principle that was not of our own choosing is the origin of his idea of **bad faith**, which is the attempt of people to appropriate to themselves a false identity. Instead of choosing for themselves, they have simply conformed to some preestablished expectation that has been foisted on them. Authentic existence is self-chosen because the self is condemned to be free. To accept an idea of rational animal, creature, or utility maximizer is to abdicate the responsibility of the self to be free. To permit anyone to take on that responsibility for the self is to act on the basis of bad faith.

For Sartre, all humans have the responsibility to create themselves and to exercise their freedom. Existence must precede essence in order to maintain the freedom that is central to personal identity and meaning. No one else can substitute their authority or theory of human nature and its ethical baggage, since this would undermine human freedom. Sartre writes, "The existentialist finds it extremely embarrassing that God does not exist, for there disappears with Him all possibility of finding values in an intelligible heaven. There can no longer be any good *a priori*, since there is no infinite and perfect consciousness to think it. It is nowhere written that 'the good' exists, that one must be honest or must not lie, since we are now upon the plane where there are only men."[9]

Sartre agrees with a character in one of Dostoevsky's novels who says, "If there is no God, then anything is permissible."[10] Sartre himself says, "Everything is indeed permitted if God does not exist, and man is in consequence forlorn, for he cannot find anything to depend upon either within or outside himself."[11] Because there is no basis for morality in human nature, it must reside in human choice, which is not bound by any principles or authorities external to the self.

Kierkegaard's Stages

Moving from the antireligious approaches to continental ethics to those on the Judeo-Christian tradition, we start with the work of Søren Kierkegaard

8. Sartre, *Existentialism and Humanism*, 27.
9. Sartre, *Existentialism and Humanism*, 33.
10. Sartre, *Existentialism and Humanism*, 33. Sartre here paraphrases a claim made by Dmitri Karamazov, debating with Rakitin, in Dostoevsky's novel *The Brothers Karamazov*.
11. Sartre, *Existentialism and Humanism*, 33–34.

(1813–55), who represents the beginning of the Christian tradition of existentialism and whose work influences many theologians of the twentieth and twenty-first centuries. Kierkegaard was the son of an excessively religious man. His father foisted his own religious neuroses on his children, and so all the children learned to dread God. Kierkegaard at one time was engaged to marry but broke off the engagement and remained a loner for most of his life. His writing reflects his own personal struggles and disgust with the Danish Church and the philosophy of Hegel. Kierkegaard famously made a distinction between Christianity and Christendom and called for a kind of developmental approach to thinking about the moral life.

According to Kierkegaard, there are three basic stages that address the **moral stage** of a human: the aesthetic, the ethical, and the teleological suspension of the ethical. Each of these stages has a representative who serves as a model. Don Juan represents the aesthetic. Socrates represents the ethical. The biblical patriarch Abraham represents the teleological suspension of the ethical.

The **aesthetic stage** is the stage where one is enamored with the pleasures of the senses. Aesthetes live according to their desires. But although desire is often equated with sensual pleasure, it is not merely sensual desire per se but any kind of emotive or sensual experiences. In many respects this represents the attitude of the eighteenth-century philosopher David Hume, whose theory of moral sentiments was based primarily on a kind of restrained hedonism. The fictional example is Don Juan, a sexual seducer who sees the art of seduction and the pursuit of just one more sexual conquest as what gives his life meaning. He lives for this pleasure; however, eventually Don Juan finds that the aesthetic life is ultimately empty. Each new conquest yields diminishing returns on his pleasure, and he lapses into despair. The pursuit of pleasure to the exclusion of all else results in a despair due to boredom. Humans are more than simply pleasure-pursuing animals. In order to overcome this despair, the aesthete must make a choice to be guided by something other than immediate gratification. The only way out of his despondency is to adopt another way of living—to move on to the ethical stage.

The philosopher Socrates represents the **ethical stage**, which is the stage where one lives in accordance with rules and thereby moves beyond the emptiness of the aesthetic life. One could also see Kant's deontological theory of the categorical imperative here—namely, the idea that all people must follow rationally prescribed rules without exception. One must move beyond acting on the basis of mere desire to acting out of the motive of reason and the rules reason itself demands. Ethical individuals have moved beyond acting on their desires. They have bought into universal morality that applies to all people. Ethical people, for example, choose to marry rather than to continue to pursue the merely sensual lifestyle of the Don Juan persona. A life wherein one has stability and follows the rules of society is one that enables people to live peacefully with others and to avoid the despair that the exclusive pursuit of pleasure brings. Yet this stage too cannot satisfy the longing for genuine meaning. Ethical people realize that there is no way to conquer sin merely by an expression of their will. They realize that they know the good but cannot act on it successfully.

The last stage is that of the **teleological suspension of the ethical**, which is the stage in which the moral hero, Abraham, moves beyond the merely conventional life of the ethical. The ethical life is one governed by rules and principles. The one who sees that simply following rules is not enough also sees that it is the existential encounter with God that gives life meaning. Often people have more respect for the rules than they do for persons. When God tells Abraham to offer his only son, Isaac, as a sacrifice, this violates every moral rule we know. It is, in Kierkegaard's words, a teleological suspension of the ethical. It suspends the normal ethical judgments we make in order to have a genuine encounter with God, which can only take place by a leap of faith.

Abraham chose to move beyond the rules and obey God, and so he became an authentic self. Kierkegaard says, "So we stand in the presence of the paradox. Either the Individual as the Individual can stand in an absolute relation to the Absolute, and then ethics is not supreme, or Abraham is lost: he is neither a tragic hero nor an aesthetic hero."[12] The individual who stands in a genuine relationship with God is, in a sense, beyond ethics. The relationship supersedes rule-governed behavior. To refuse to take the leap of faith is to refuse the authentic encounter with God. As a result, faith is more important than rules. Consider the following comparisons:

Stage	Principle	Hero
Aesthetic	Pleasure	Don Juan
Moral	Rules	Socrates
Teleological suspension of the ethical	Radical encounter	Abraham

A hallmark of Christendom is the adherence to rules, which have taken the place of faith. Rules become idols that people worship. They substitute for genuine relationships. Christianity is about an authentic encounter with God without the mediating rules of Christendom.

12. Søren Kierkegaard, *Fear and Trembling*, trans. Walter Lowrie (New York: Anchor, 1954).

Buber's I-Thou Relationship

Martin Buber (1887–1965) was a Jewish philosopher whose most well-known work is *I and Thou*,[13] an extended meditation on what it means to treat others as another self who is worthy of love and respect. Throughout the work, Buber employs a twofold approach to his consideration of persons and their values. By this, he means that our language, the way we situate ourselves in the world, and the way we consider others are always in terms of pairs of ideas: I and Thou, I and It, encounter and experience, mediated and immediate interaction, participation and detachment.

The foundational idea for Buber is that we always find ourselves in relation, and there are two possible ways in which we can relate to the world. He states, "The world is twofold for man in accordance with his twofold attitude."[14] What he means is that there are two basic ways of being in the world: a way that participates, encounters, and acts as a subject and a way that detaches, experiences, and objectifies the world. The first relationship is the I-Thou relationship. The second is the I-It relationship.

An **I-Thou relationship** is a relationship between two persons in which each engages the other person genuinely and freely. It is only in a dialogical relationship with another self that the person becomes what he or she should be. It is only by participating in the lives of one another that people mature morally. The encounter and participation with the other person is one that frees the other of categorization by imposing labels or categories. Buber writes, "When I confront a human being as my You and speak the basic I-You to him, then he is no thing among things nor does he consist of things. He is no longer a He or She, limited by other Hes and Shes . . . nor a condition that can be experienced and described, a loose bundle of named qualities."[15] We stand in relationship to other persons, not to objects. And this is a key difference between the I-Thou relationship and the I-It relationship.

The I-It relationship is one in which the subject is truly alone. He or she sees others as objects to be experienced, analyzed, and manipulated. The self is detached from others and refuses participation in the lives of others. In many respects, the I-It relationship is a kind of moral solipsism—a world that has just one self-contained individual. The other person is reduced simply to an object of one's experience without having one's own individuality as the subject of one's own experiences.

13. Martin Buber, *I and Thou*, trans. Walter Kaufman (New York: Scribner's, 1970).
14. Buber, *I and Thou*, 53.
15. Buber, *I and Thou*, 59.

The two kinds of relationships not only apply to other persons but can also be applied to God. Some people attempt to engage God in an I-It relationship where God is an object to be manipulated. Much of the history of philosophy and theology is the attempt to categorize God using human terms where the experience of God is mediated in ways that are alien to genuine encounter and participation. But Buber says, "By its very nature the eternal You cannot become an It; because by its very nature it cannot be placed within measure and limit, not even within the measure of the immeasurable and the limits of the unlimited; because by its very nature it cannot be grasped as a sum of qualities."[16] God, and the individual's relationship with God, cannot be reduced to mere linguistic categories. In God, a person encounters God without the mediation of language and its labels. Buber's emphasis on the relationship between persons echoes Kierkegaard's emphasis on the encounter with the divine. As a continental thinker, Buber sees the primacy of encounter with persons, treating them with respect, refusing to objectify them, and experiencing them for who they are as central to the task of the moral life.

Bonhoeffer's Christocentric Approach

Dietrich Bonhoeffer (1906–45) was a German theologian who adopted many of Kierkegaard's themes. He was a Lutheran pastor in Germany during World War II and was imprisoned for his part in an attempt to assassinate Hitler. Bonhoeffer sees the idea of Christian ethics as a fundamental mistake. For Bonhoeffer, "Christianity and ethics do indeed have nothing to do with one another; there is no Christian ethic and there can be no transition from the idea of Christianity to that of ethics."[17] In order to understand this claim, one needs to understand that Christianity is fundamentally a knowledge of God and nothing else. Ethics, in contrast, is knowledge of good and evil. In order to understand what Bonhoeffer means, we need to consider his account of original sin, his account of the Pharisee, and his account of what Christianity does to restore the creature's knowledge of God. This knowledge of God invariably resists the temptation to lay down rules and laws.

The Christian narrative begins in the garden of Eden. The man and the woman are told to refrain from one thing: "But of the tree of the knowledge of good and evil you shall not eat, for in the day that you eat of it you shall die" (Gen. 2:17). In this state of innocence, they have knowledge of God and

---

16. Buber, *I and Thou*, 160.
17. Dietrich Bonhoeffer, "What Is a Christian Ethics?," in *Contemporary European Ethics*, ed. Joseph J. Kockelmans (New York: Doubleday, 1972), 451.

may do whatever they will. But they are tempted by the serpent, who tells them that they "will be like God" (Gen. 3:5). They eat of the fruit, "the eyes of both were opened" (Gen. 3:7), and they can now distinguish between good and evil. The result is that they have indeed become "like God" in the sense that they see themselves as the origin of good and evil. They have placed themselves at the center of the cosmos. This is the sin of pride. For Bonhoeffer, "The root of all sin is pride, *superbia*. I want to be my own law, I have a right to myself, my hatred and my desires, my life and my death. The mind and flesh of man are set on fire by pride; for it is precisely in his wickedness that man wants to be God."[18] The knowledge of good and evil makes us proud. To Bonhoeffer, pride is the root of all sin in that it severs us from God and creates disunion.

For Bonhoeffer, the human creature who has knowledge of good and evil is like the Pharisee. Bonhoeffer describes the Pharisee not as a historical figure in the Bible but as an archetype of all people who presume to know good from evil. He writes, "He is the man to whom only the knowledge of good and evil has come to be of an importance in his entire life. . . . The Pharisee is that extremely admirable man who subordinates his entire life to his knowledge of good and evil."[19] Consider the parable of the Pharisee and the tax collector in Luke's Gospel:

> He also told this parable to some who trusted in themselves that they were righteous and regarded others with contempt: "Two men went up to the temple to pray, one a Pharisee and the other a tax collector. The Pharisee, standing by himself, was praying thus, 'God, I thank you that I am not like other people: thieves, rogues, adulterers, or even like this tax collector. I fast twice a week; I give a tenth of all my income.' But the tax collector, standing far off, would not even look up to heaven, but was beating his breast and saying, 'God, be merciful to me, a sinner!' I tell you, this man went down to his home justified rather than the other; for all who exalt themselves will be humbled, but all who humble themselves will be exalted." (Luke 18:9–14)

This parable illustrates a key distinction for Bonhoeffer. The Pharisee justifies himself before God by instructing God on good and evil. He lists his own virtues and shows God that God owes him gratitude. The Pharisee's hubris is based on his knowledge of good and evil. Since he knows what is good and evil, he can demand God's allegiance. In contrast, the tax collector presumes to know nothing but God's mercy offered to a sinful creature.

18. Dietrich Bonhoeffer, *Life Together*, trans. John W. Doberstein (New York: Harper, 1954), 113–14.

19. Dietrich Bonhoeffer, *Ethics*, ed. Eberhard Bethge, trans. Neville Horton Smith (New York: Macmillan, 1963), 26–27.

Sin, as we have seen, is the knowledge of good and evil with pride as that which inevitably separates us from God. Sin severs our relationship not only to God but to all others as well. Separation and disunion is our natural condition. Restoration and union is the only solution, and this can only take place through Christ. This is the only path to authentic encounters with reality since Christ himself is the author of reality. Nothing can be known apart from him, including morality and all its rules.

For Bonhoeffer, any appeal to a law or a rule is one that fails to understand the nature of divine grace. Grace frees us to be the kinds of persons who can respond immediately to God and God's will. This means we release all prior assumptions about what we should and should not do. We are completely free to respond to the will of God. We are in relationship to God and not the law. Grace releases us from the demands of the law. This can be seen in our relationships to other people. Bonhoeffer writes,

> I must release the other person from every attempt of mine to regulate, coerce, and dominate him with my love. The other person needs to retain his independence from me; to be loved for what he is, as one for whom Christ became man, died, and rose again, for whom Christ bought forgiveness of sins and eternal life. Because Christ has long since acted decisively for my brother, before I could begin to act, I must leave him his freedom to be Christ's; I must meet him only as the person that he already is in Christ's eyes. This is the meaning of the proposition that we can meet others only through the mediation of Christ. Human love constructs its image of the other person, of what he is and what he should become. It takes the life of the other person into its own hands.[20]

For Bonhoeffer, it is always wrong to encounter another person based on either our own desires or our sense of what rule must be applied. Rather, we encounter others only through the person and work of Christ because only then can we see ourselves as equally sinful as others and thus as equally in need of forgiveness.

Criticisms of Continental Ethics

Critics have argued that continental approaches to philosophy more generally have substituted an emphasis on the subjective for the objective in ways that undermine itself. This can be seen in two ways: first, with regard to a limited

20. Bonhoeffer, *Life Together*, 35–36.

perspective on moral values and a subsequent subjectivism and, second, with regard to a kind of moral inconsistency.

First, since existentialism places such an emphasis on individual choice validating a person's value, it often regards rules as being an external imposition on a person's individuality and authentic character. One element Kierkegaard, Nietzsche, and Sartre have in common—despite their pronounced disagreements—is their insistence that rules are bad or misguided. Kierkegaard sees following the rules as simply a stage that should be superseded by acting against the rules. Abraham rejected the rules and thus became the father of the faith. For Nietzsche rules are the expression of the slave morality designed to keep truly creative people from becoming what they should become. The *Übermensch* is beyond good and evil—beyond the rules. For Sartre, adopting the rules of religion or of morality is acting in bad faith. It is relinquishing one's moral responsibility to oneself. These thinkers all rightly see that rules can be oppressive and used to manipulate others. However, the alternative is a system of rampant relativism where there are not even some basic principles that all people can affirm. The subjectivism espoused by these thinkers can quickly deteriorate into a kind of rugged self-assertion at the expense of others.

A second problem is that often continental philosophers assume a kind of arrogant resistance to any alternatives to their own views. Alasdair MacIntyre has argued that some continental approaches such as what we find in the work of Nietzsche suffer from an inability to consider critical and sometimes helpful perspectives. At its heart, philosophical reflection is a dialogue among various viewpoints that consider alternatives in a serious manner. Continental approaches often fail in this regard. MacIntyre asks, Does "the genealogist legitimately include the self out of which he speaks in explaining himself within his or her genealogical narrative? Is the genealogist not self-indulgently engaged in exempting his or her utterances from the treatment to which everyone else's is subjected?"[21] The subjective approach offered by many continental philosophers seems to be such that they want to criticize others without letting others criticize them. Thus, they are either omniscient—or at least much wiser than the rest of us—or they are being inconsistent.

Continental Philosophy and Christian Ethics

The neo-orthodox tradition of Christian ethics was deeply indebted to Kierkegaard. Neo-orthodoxy was a Protestant recovery of central themes of the

21. Alasdair MacIntyre, *Three Rival Versions of Moral Enquiry: Encyclopedia, Genealogy, and Tradition* (Notre Dame, IN: University of Notre Dame Press, 1990), 210.

Reformation and a rejection of much of the nineteenth-century theological liberalism. Karl Barth, Emil Brunner, and Bonhoeffer (as we have seen) all looked to Kierkegaard for inspiration for their theologies and consideration of moral issues.[22] For these thinkers, Christianity was not an intellectual assent to a set of propositions about God but an existential commitment of the self to a different way of being. The encounter with God and the individual's response to the divine were central to the faith. As a result, ethics was often seen as problematic since it removed the person from the practice of engaging God and the other, to systematizing principles of right and wrong. If God—in the person of Jesus Christ—was not central to an individual's moral consciousness, then the deliberation could not be understood as Christian. Barth articulates this perspective well: "When we speak of ethics, the term cannot include anything more than this confirmation of the truth of the grace of God as it is addressed to man. If dogmatics, if the doctrine of God, is ethics, this means necessarily and decisively that it is the attestation of that divine ethics, the attestation of the good of the command issued to Jesus Christ and fulfilled by Him. There can be no question of any other good in addition to this."[23]

Echoing this radical connection of ethics to a specifically Christian account of morality, Brunner reiterates this idea when he considers the idea of "the good."[24] Many traditional approaches to moral philosophy, such as those advanced by Plato, Aristotle, Kant, and Mill, contend that the first task of ethics is to define "the good." For Brunner, the good is simply found in the holiness of God. Any attempts to locate the good apart from this is a mistake. He writes, "The Good is based on the Holy. . . . The Holy means God, as the unconditionally sovereign Lord of the world; a thing is holy because, and in so far as, it is His property and is recognized as such. The holiness of man consists in knowing that he belongs to God."[25]

Others have looked not only to Kierkegaard but also to Buber. Jean Vanier, the founder of the L'Arche movement, sees Buber's work as shaping his own deeply held Catholic convictions about social justice and care for those who are marginalized by their disabilities. Vanier writes, "With the death of our false self, we liberate the life of God in us and, in the words of Martin Buber, we allow God to flow through our hearts and our beings and thus to enter our world."[26]

22. See William E. Hordern, *A Layman's Guide to Protestant Theology* (New York: Macmillan, 1968), 113–18.

23. Karl Barth, *Church Dogmatics* II/2, trans. G. W. Bromiley et al. (Edinburgh: T&T Clark, 1957), 518.

24. Emil Brunner, *The Divine Imperative: A Study in Christian Ethics*, trans. Olive Wyon (London: Lutterworth, 1937), 53–58.

25. Brunner, *Divine Imperative*, 53.

26. Jean Vanier, *Becoming Human* (Mahwah, NJ: Paulist Press, 2008), 166.

Case Study: Euthanasia

One of the most famous existentialist philosophers of the twentieth century, Albert Camus, once wrote, "There is only one really serious philosophical problem and that is suicide. Deciding whether or not life is worth living is to answer the fundamental question in philosophy. All other questions follow from that."[27] For Camus, life is absurd, and so one's actions determine the value of the act. This idea of authoring one's own life is critical to his own thinking. He died driving his car into a tree at a high rate of speed, which many think was suicide. But people often consider ending their own lives not as an existential affirmation of their choice but as a means of ending their own suffering caused by some kind of illness.

Consider the tragic case of Brittany Maynard, who in early 2014 was diagnosed with an inoperable malignant brain tumor. Rather than waiting for the brain tumor to destroy her brain and leave her to die a painful death, she chose to end her own life. She was newly married and only twenty years old. She moved from California to Oregon so that she could commit suicide rather than die from the tumor itself. Her action was motivated by a desire to avoid the suffering brought on by the brain tumor as well as a desire to avoid the loss of mental and biological functions that the disease would bring about.

As we have seen, a key idea in continental ethics is the notion of self-determination. The issue of euthanasia thus provides an interesting case study in how continental thinkers practice ethics. The word **euthanasia** comes from the Greek word meaning "good death." There are six types of euthanasia that can be considered according to two dimensions: (1) whether the agent is capable of deciding and (2) whether the death is caused by natural agents or by an external agent.

	Active	Passive
Voluntary	Person desires death and takes a lethal agent that causes death.	Person desires death but lets the disease be the cause of death.
Nonvoluntary	Person is incapable of choosing and is given a lethal agent that causes death.	Person is incapable of choosing and is taken off life support; as a result the disease causes death.
Involuntary	Person desires to live and is given a lethal agent that causes death.	Person desires to live and treatment is withheld causing death.

We can begin with the less controversial kinds of euthanasia. Involuntary euthanasia of both kinds is usually considered a form of murder since it is

27. Albert Camus, *The Myth of Sisyphus* (New York: Knopf, 1955), 3.

a direct violation of the patient's desire to remain alive. A person who kills another innocent person is committing murder since it is always wrong to kill innocent people; to claim that their deaths are for their own good strikes us as absurd. Forms of genocide and murder as a result of medical experimentation during World War II would also count as forms of involuntary euthanasia.[28] There is very little controversy concerning the immorality of both active and passive forms of involuntary euthanasia.

Since voluntary euthanasia fulfills the patient's desires, a number of countries and states have sanctioned its practice. Voluntary active euthanasia is when a patient has an illness and requests to be killed. This may happen by means of a lethal dose of a drug or with a physician's assistance. This latter approach is sometimes known as physician-assisted suicide. Many people believe that this is a form of playing God, and traditional moral theories such as Kantianism and natural law theory oppose this approach. Yet the phrase "playing God" needs to be analyzed. If it means simply making any momentous decision or affecting a person's survival chances, then the phrase is problematic. To place a person on a ventilator, to defend oneself against a rapist, to refuse to give a donation to a charitable organization in the developing world, or to get inoculations may all be instances of playing God on such a broad definition.

There are at least three kinds of approaches that see active euthanasia as a morally viable option: utilitarian approaches, some natural rights approaches, and existentialist approaches. The most notable approach here is the utilitarian perspective as advocated by James Rachels, who has argued that once a person adopts death as the end intended, the means are morally irrelevant.[29] One is morally obligated, on a utilitarian account, to pursue the most painless and efficient means available since the elimination of pain (both for the patients and the patient's loved ones) is the desired end. Yet this approach is not without its own problems. First, it seems that the attitude of intentionally taking an innocent human life could lead to other practices of killing innocents. Second, it seems possible that a patient might decide under duress, have later regrets about the decision, or be misinformed about how long he or she has to live. In such circumstances, ending one's life might not be the act that brings about the most happiness.

---

28. From the perspective of most people, acts of genocide would simply qualify as murder, but from the perspective of the perpetrator, it would be for some notion of "the good of the species." In any case, it is both (1) the intentional killing of another human being, and (2) against the victim's wishes. And for those reasons, it can be seen as fundamentally immoral.

29. James Rachels, *The End of Life: Euthanasia and Morality* (New York: Oxford University Press, 1986).

A second approach is based on one's natural rights. It sees people's lives as their own property—to dispose of as they see fit. The argument is that, if a person has a natural right to life, liberty, and property, then their lives are theirs to do with as they please. To forbid them from taking their own lives is a violation of their liberty. The problem with such an approach is that no one has an absolute right to do as they please in all arenas, and the exercise of this right is final since it cannot be undone.

The third approach is the one sanctioned by existentialists like Camus. A choice about life or death is not the function of utility or of a person's rights but is about a person's self-determination. The political question of a right to end one's life is irrelevant to the existential question of choosing for oneself.

Voluntary passive euthanasia occurs when a patient wants to die but refuses to take steps to end his or her life by something other than natural causes. For example, a patient who suffers from terminal cancer might wish to die and simply refuse treatment. But in this case, the disease itself is the cause of death, not a lethal injection. This becomes complicated, however, from a religious view. In the Catholic tradition people cannot have their own death be the primary intent of their actions. Wanting to die and making death the intent of your action is immoral since it violates a basic precept of the natural law (i.e., that life is to be preserved and any intentional taking of innocent life is always to be avoided). However, a person can appeal to a principle called **double-effect**. Suppose people refuse treatment because they do not want to die in the hospital, incur a terrible financial burden for their family, or face the emotional trauma an extended and painful treatment will cause for both them and their family. In these cases, the intention is not their own death but some other end. However, the action will have a double-effect. It will accomplish the end they intend (e.g., psychological well-being), but it will also bring about their death more quickly. This kind of action is permitted since the intended end is something other than their own death. Any action, whether active or passive euthanasia, that has one's own death as the intended end is not permitted.

The different attitudes toward euthanasia seem to assume that the two greatest evils people face are pain and death. These evils should not be underestimated. It is extraordinarily difficult to understand another person's or one's own pain or to articulate it adequately. Death is also a kind of finality. A person is severed from others, and the grief can be inconsolable. However, it may be that neither pain nor death is the *summum malum* (i.e., the highest evil). William F. May has argued that, at least from a Christian perspective, the *summum malum* is separation from God,[30] whereas the *summum bonum* (i.e., the highest good) is union with God. On this perspective, neither death nor pain—although they are great evils—is the ultimate evil. What this shows is that not only must we give an account of when life ends, what counts as unbearable suffering, and who gets to decide; we must also offer plausible accounts of the significance of human life, what evils must be avoided, and what the ultimate good is in this life.

Discussion Questions

1. Are continental thinkers right to reject essentialism?
2. Does continental philosophy commit itself too much to moral subjectivism and possibly relativism?
3. Does the continental approach to ethics provide a helpful corrective to other approaches that emphasize rules?
4. Is euthanasia ever permissible? If so, under what conditions? If not, why not?
5. If we forbid people from taking their lives, then what other options are available to them?
6. Does the principle of double-effect provide a helpful way of considering euthanasia?

---

30. William F. May, "The Right to Die and the Obligation to Care: Allowing to Die, Killing for Mercy, and Suicide," in *Death and Decision*, ed. Ernan McMullin (Boulder, CO: Westview, 1978).

TEN

Virtue Ethics

Some identify happiness with virtue, some with practical wisdom, others with a kind of philosophical wisdom, others add or exclude pleasure and yet others include prosperity. We agree with those who identify happiness with virtue, for virtue belongs with virtuous behavior and virtue is only known by its acts.

—Aristotle, *Nicomachean Ethics*

Words to Watch

avarice	jocose lie	sloth
cardinal virtues	justice	theological virtues
defect	lust	vices
envy	malicious lie	virtue as a mean
excess	moral virtues	virtues
faith	officious lie	wrath
gluttony	pride	
habit	right reason	

Introduction

Oscar Wilde's book *The Picture of Dorian Gray* narrates the story of an attractive but morally corrupt young man in Victorian England who has his portrait painted one day. He makes the wish that, instead of himself suffering and aging, the portrait would suffer these evils. Remarkably, this is indeed what happens, but not as he expects. Gray displays the portrait prominently in his home for a brief period of time until it starts to transform in unpleasant ways. This transformation coincides with his personal descent into a life of deception and debauchery. He moves the painting to the attic where no one can see it and spends years committed to a life of wickedness. Gray's own countenance never changes—he remains the handsome young man he was at the time the painting was made—but the painting turns into a grotesque caricature of the young man he once was. The reader is left to wonder whether the inconsistency between his outward appearance and his inner corruption eventually became too much to bear.

This story represents the principle that virtue theorists have held since the time of Aristotle: one becomes what one habitually does. In the case of Dorian Gray, we see a kind of direct correlation between moral and ethical evil (as the ugliness of the picture in his attic reflects the moral horror that his life has become), and this gives us a sense of moral vision we never have in real life. Virtue ethics holds that the moral character of a person is built up over time, and we can reasonably expect people to behave in predictable ways. Liars will predictably lie to us. Hospitable people will always take us in. We also take care not to provoke those who have short tempers.

This insight about character and its predictability distinguishes virtue ethics from consequentialism and deontological theories. For a Kantian or a utilitarian, the most important issue is the moral value of the act itself. The Kantian asks, Was this my duty? The utilitarian asks, Did this act produce the greatest happiness for the greatest number? The virtue ethicist maintains that acts are secondary to moral character. The question for the virtue ethicists is not, Is this the right act? It is rather, What kind of person am I to do this sort of thing? And is this the kind of person I want to become?

In this chapter we consider both classical and Christian accounts of the virtues as seen in the work of Aristotle and Thomas Aquinas. After working through the strengths and criticisms of these theories we look at the morality of lying and how virtue ethics—and other views—would approach this topic.

Habit

In the virtue theories of Aristotle and Thomas Aquinas, the human person possesses two natures: a given nature and an acquired nature.[1] We are all born with DNA that, when activated by specific environments, determines how we look, the range of our intellectual capacities, our likes and dislikes, and our natural tendencies. The color of my eyes is determined by my genetics, but

---

1. See Aristotle, *Nicomachean Ethics*, trans. Terence Irwin (Indianapolis: Hackett, 1982); Thomas Aquinas, *Summa Theologica* 1-2.49–54, trans. Fathers of the English Dominican Province (New York: Benzinger, 1947).

my ability to speak Spanish is an acquired ability developed through practice and habituation.

A **habit** is a "second nature" or an acquired disposition that enables us to perform various activities with relative ease. We acquire habits by frequent repetition. As a result, it is only by practicing my Spanish vocabulary, engaging in conversations, being corrected by native speakers, reading books in Spanish, and so on that I develop the capacity to speak with relative ease. Habits require not only repetition but repetition in excellence. Speaking Spanish poorly day after day does not improve proficiency but simply reinforces incompetence. What this requires, therefore, is a community of practitioners who know how to speak and speak well. Not all habits are moral habits. There are aesthetic and intellectual habits as well. I may have the ability to speak Spanish fluently, but it is not what we would call a moral habit, since it is not directed to the good of a well-lived life such as loving relationships and compassion for the hurting.

Virtue

The Moral Virtues

A **virtue** is a good habit of the soul.[2] It is a chosen pattern of behavior that helps us pursue the good in a well-ordered way. There are aesthetic, intellectual, and moral virtues. Painting and sculpting are aesthetic practices that require the practical virtue of art, just as doing logic and analyzing chemical compounds are practices that require the possession of intellectual virtues. Love, patience, and humility are moral virtues. The **moral virtues** are virtues that enable us to act in ways that are truly perfecting of us as persons and not merely as thinkers or artists. They help us pursue the good in ways that are appropriate to us as the kind of beings we are. For Aristotle, humans are "rational animals," and this means that our behavior should conform to what it means to be both rational and animal. In the Christian tradition, humans are understood as creatures made in the "image of God" (Latin, *imago Dei*). From this perspective, since God is love, it follows that to be made in the image of God is to be made in and for love. A virtue, therefore, will reflect the prior understanding of human nature to which a person subscribes. Aristotle claims that there are four moral virtues: prudence, justice, fortitude (or courage), and temperance (or self-control). These are distinguished from intellectual virtues by the idea that the intellectual virtues concern excellences of the intellect

2. See Aristotle, *Nicomachean Ethics*; Thomas Aquinas, *Summa Theologica* 1-2.55–67.

(that is, *thinking*), while the moral virtues concern excellences of character (that is, *doing*). One can be a brilliant thinker and still be a moral wretch. Both kinds of virtues are acquired by training and instruction, but we will focus our attention on the moral virtues that Christians call **cardinal virtues**. They are "cardinal" in the sense that the other virtues hinge on them—as the Latin word for "hinge" is *cardo*. The cardinal virtues, therefore, are the four most important moral virtues. These virtues were handed down and incorporated into the Christian thought of theologians such as Augustine and Thomas Aquinas. However, they were often transformed in ways that Aristotle could not have anticipated.

The first of the cardinal virtues is prudence, or practical wisdom, which evaluates and considers various plans of action in light of what the true goods are. This is the most important of the cardinal virtues because it shapes the other virtues. We cannot be courageous or practice self-control unless we can accurately assess various situations that present themselves to us. Prudence naturally knows the goods we seek and considers them as the starting point for every decision. Prudence requires right reasoning about any and all actions. This **right reason** is the ability to take into account the circumstances of a situation, to perceive the various relationships that apply, and to judge rightly. There can be no moral virtues apart from the right reasoning found in prudence.

If we need to make a decision about some course of action, then we need to be able to deliberate well, to come to a sound judgment, and to act on that judgment. Consider whether I should become a vegetarian. How should I think about this? Our first task is to think about what good we are trying to accomplish. Am I trying to be healthier? Am I concerned about the welfare of the millions of animals that are raised and killed in horrific circumstances? Am I trying to make food more plentiful and accessible for the millions of people starving throughout the world? I can see this action as developing important qualities such as compassion, justice, and practical wisdom. Prudence shows me that we should think about being responsible with our resources, not giving ourselves over to excesses or defects (e.g., gluttony), thinking about issues of sustainability, and considering those who have less than we have. This is a kind of right thinking that gives shape to how we live and act in the world.

The second of the cardinal virtues is justice, which requires that we give to each person what is his or her due. **Justice** is the habit of rendering to others what they deserve. Parents, teachers, siblings, friends, spouses, and business partners all deserve different things, and so we treat them differently. With justice, we see that it may be fair for a parent to treat one child differently from another because the older child has shown greater responsibility and maturity than the younger child. When the younger child complains, the parent can respond, "You have not yet shown that you deserve to be treated in the same manner." Justice takes into account the real relationships that exist among and between persons and acts accordingly. In this way, justice is primarily a virtue about our relationships to others. But there are two other virtues that concern individuals first and foremost.

The third of these cardinal virtues is fortitude, or courage. With this virtue we regulate our fear—or to use Aristotle's term, our "irascible appetites."[3] Our fight or flight instincts can get the best of us, and courage helps us know what to do. We must think clearly about what to do and train our emotions to respond accordingly. We can, for example, be either too cowardly (**defect**) or too rash (**excess**), and we must choose the "mean between the extremes" to guide our actions. Suppose my daughter falls and hits her head, and I need to take her to the doctor for immediate medical care. As I get into my car, I see a large spider on the seat. I have a fear of spiders, and so I pause. What should I do? Aristotle would suggest that the obligation to my daughter, as her parent, should override any fear I have of the spider. There may be other instances, however, where fear tells me I should not act, since to do so would be foolish. Thus, courage represents **virtue as a mean**—that is, finding the balance between too little and too much.

Figure 10.1.

Courage as a Mean between Extremes

Virtuous Mean
courage—concerns fear

cowardice   foolhardiness
Defect   **Excess**

The fourth cardinal virtue is temperance, or self-control, which concerns what Aristotle calls the "concupisible appetite."[4] This appetite is for the things we naturally are attracted to such as food, drink, and sex. Again, there is a mean between extremes, and this mean is relative to the person. Self-control is about consistently finding the virtuous mean between the extremes concerning all of our appetites. If we consider just one of our appetites, for example, our hunger for food, Aristotle says that the appropriate amount one eats is relative

3. Aristotle, *Nicomachean Ethics*, book 2, chapter 5, trans. Terence Irwin (Indianapolis: Hackett, 1982).

4. Aristotle, *Nicomachean Ethics*, book 2, chapter 5.

to the person's size and activities. A person who is large and runs marathons will need a great deal more food than a person who is small and sedentary. Too much food is gluttony, and too little is starvation.

Figure 10.2.

Sufficiency as a Mean between Extremes

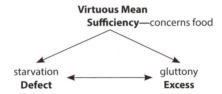

There are other important virtues that Aristotle names, including wit, generosity, patience, and honesty. But the four cardinal virtues are the ones that are central to his theory and that inform the other moral virtues. The importance of prudence cannot be underestimated, since Aristotle says that all the other moral virtues require prudence; without its guidance, a person cannot possess justice, fortitude, or temperance.

Figure 10.3.

The Priority of Prudence among the Cardinal Virtues

The Theological Virtues

The apostle Paul writes, "And now faith, hope, and love abide, these three; and the greatest of these is love" (1 Cor. 13:13). The Christian tradition sees these three virtues as what distinguish Christian views on morality from those of Aristotle and the Stoics, differences that stem from the distinctive Christian views on human nature, sin, and grace. In contrast to the ancient Greek philosophical tradition, Christians saw themselves as alienated from God and from one another. Forgiveness and reconciliation come only through the divine grace offered by Christ. As a result, Augustine says, "No one can have true virtue without true piety, that is without the true worship of God."[5] Pagan virtue, on his account, fails to recognize that God must be the one to whom all human activity is directed. Thomas

5. Augustine, *City of God*, trans. Marcus Dodds (New York: Modern Library, 1950), 173.

Aquinas elaborates: "It is necessary for man to receive from God some additional principles, whereby he may be directed to supernatural happiness, even as he is directed to his connatural end, by means of his natural principles, albeit not without divine assistance. Such like principles are called 'theological virtues': first, because their object is God, inasmuch as they direct us aright to God: secondly, because they are infused in us by God alone: thirdly, because these virtues are not made known to us, save by Divine revelation, contained in Holy, Writ."[6]

Thomas thinks that people need to direct their motivation and intentions to God as the object of these virtues in order to have our lives rightly ordered. **Theological virtues** are thus virtues that are acquired not through our own efforts—as with the moral virtues—but by the infusion of divine grace. They each may grow as a habit—as all virtues can—but they must first be given to us by God. We could not discover these virtues on our own, but we need divine revelation—that is, the life of Christ and the Scriptures reveal to us these supernatural virtues.

The first of the theological virtues is **faith**. The term "faith" can refer to a variety of different but related ideas. Some see faith as simply a private opinion someone has about religion. Others see it as the body of beliefs to which a religious group subscribes. Others see faith as a kind of basic way of looking at the world. The meaning of faith as a theological virtue, however, is the habit of believing God. It is a disposition to believe that what God says is true because it is God who has said it.

From this perspective, faith is not merely wishful thinking but a kind of trust that one has in another person because of that person's character. Faith is not merely an opinion. Opinions are ideas that we have based on either our own experiences or on the reports that others offer us. My friends may tell me that a movie is a good movie, but based on my assessment of the friends and their tastes, I may or may not believe that the movie is good. Opinions can be distinguished from knowledge, which involves a kind of certainty. I do not have the opinion that $2 + 2 = 4$; I know it to be true. There is no uncertainty about this. Faith also has a kind of certainty, not because of the statement itself but because of who tells me what the statement is. In the Gospels Jesus speaks about forgiveness of sins. I may believe that my sins are forgiven, not because just anyone says it but because Christ himself has said it and because Christian churches have affirmed it. This communal assent to the teaching of Christ and his church is not merely a singular act but a habitual believing— and trusting—in God.

6. Thomas Aquinas, *Summa Theologica* 1-2.62.1

The second theological virtue is hope. Thomas Aquinas defines hope as the patient expectation of "a future, difficult, but possible good."[7] There are four generic elements here: (1) Hope is always for a good. We never desire anything unless it is good. We desire water, health, companionship, food, play, and rest because these are all good. Even when we do things that are evil, it is because they appear under some aspect of the good. (2) Hope always concerns the future. We do not hope for what we already possess. We hope for the water we thirst for, the food we smell, and the sleep that beckons to us. But hope is very much an activity we engage in the present, whose object is the future. (3) Hope always concerns a good that is difficult. Under normal circumstances I do not hope to breathe. Unless there is some difficulty one must overcome, hope is not needed. For example, the climb up a mountainside to a waterfall may involve scorpions, overcoming my weariness, and chiding my reluctant children. (4) Hope is always about a good that is possible. I can hope for the water I hear and for losing 10 percent of my body weight because they are within my grasp—or at least within the grasp of my potential reach.

The above examples refer only to the emotion of hope, while the virtue of hope is always *in* God and *for* God. Hope is more than merely the desire for a cold drink, weight loss, or a new promotion at work. It is an expectation that one can achieve and maintain a communion with God, not because of an achievement of one's own but because of God's goodness to humanity.

The third and most important theological virtue is love, or charity. **Charity** is often thought of as unconditional love in the sense that other people are loved regardless of their actions. Augustine, following the apostle Paul, sees love as the most important of all the virtues, the one that gives life to the others. Augustine says, "For beyond any doubt, a man with a right love also has the right faith and hope."[8] For Thomas Aquinas, love is "friendship with God." God is loved for who God is and not for what God "can do for us."[9] God is not loved instrumentally in the way that little children love Santa Claus—for the presents he brings—but is loved for God's own sake.

Charity—another way to talk about love—also enables people to fulfill the greatest commandment, to love God and one's neighbor as oneself. Charity is a participation in the life of God made possible by God's unconditional love for humanity. This love also enables one to love others as we love ourselves. This kind of love even makes possible love for one's enemies. Thomas Aquinas expresses it this way. When we love someone, we love all

7. Thomas Aquinas, *Summa Theologica* 2-2.17.1.
8. Augustine, *Faith, Hope, and Charity*, trans. Louis A. Arand (New York: Newman Press, 1947), 108.
9. Thomas Aquinas, *Summa Theologica* 2-2.23.1.

those people whom that person loves. I have friends whom I love, and so I love their children on account of my love for my friends. If my friends ask me to be their children's guardian in the event of my friends' deaths, then I would gladly do it even if I have never met their children. In a similar way, we love God and all those whom God loves. But God loves all humanity, and so we are called and enabled to love even our enemies because of our love or friendship with God.

Vice

In contrast to the virtues, **vices** are bad habits of the soul. They are dispositions, or patterns, where we fail to be the kinds of persons we should. A vice is a relatively fixed disposition to pursue a good in a fundamentally *disordered* way. A sin therefore is a kind of manifestation of the internal disposition one already possesses. A sin is an act, but a vice is a state of being. Food, sex, justice, self-esteem, and money are all goods proper to humans. However, when we devote our attention exclusively to the pursuit of culinary delights, sexual gratification, revenge, self-aggrandizement, or money, it follows that we neglect other aspects of our lives that make us human. A vice, therefore, is the habitually misdirected pursuit of a truly human good.

The seven deadly sins, or the capital vices, occupy an important role in the history of Christian moral theology. They are called capital vices (from the Latin *caput*) in the sense that from them spring all the other vices. The capital vices are **pride** (or *superbia*), **envy**, **avarice** (or greed), **wrath** (or anger), **sloth** (or *acedia*), **gluttony**, and **lust**.[10] They are the primary vices that seem to afflict humanity to a greater degree or more seriously than other types of vices.

The capital vices arise out of our creaturely condition and our given nature. In the tradition of Augustine and Thomas Aquinas, the vices are a natural result of love gone wrong. Pride is the perverse love of self to the exclusion of all others. Envy is the excessive desire for the goods that others possess. Avarice is the mistaken judgment that money is a good in itself and not merely an instrumental good. Wrath is the perversion of the desire for justice and the failure to control our anger. Sloth is the perverse desire for rest of the soul or a failure to fulfill the demands of love. Gluttony is the excessive desire for the pleasures of eating. Lust is the distortion that sex can substitute for genuine love. These vices are

10. For an excellent discussion of the capital vices, see Rebecca Konyndyk-DeYoung, *Glittering Vices: A New Look at the Seven Deadly Sins and Their Remedies* (Grand Rapids: Brazos, 2009).

not things that people desire in themselves but are the result of our desires for the good gone wrong. Each of these capital vices has a corrective virtue, which is the appropriate way people should regulate their behavior.

All people desire the good for themselves. The desire for the good is not in itself evil but part of our creaturely nature. In order to sustain our existence, we must pursue those things that God has designated for us. However, it is possible that we may desire too much or desire in inappropriate ways. We can desire not only the good but also to be in control of our own good in ways that exceed our capacities. This is the vice of pride.

In Milton's *Paradise Lost*, Satan is a creature who overreaches what is appropriate for him. Satan is not satisfied to be a creature but wants to be God. He desires his own good and his own excellence, but he desires too much for himself. Satan proclaims that it would be "better to rule in hell than to serve in heaven."[11] Pride is directly opposed to the order God has established. The divine order requires love of God and of neighbor. Pride upsets the order, as the proud person wants to be God. When this happens, one has replaced the love of God with an inordinate love of self. Since we were created to love God as our supreme end, we are unable to achieve that end if we live in pride. Further, when we set ourselves over and against our neighbors, we have no choice but to look down on them.

Envy, according to Thomas Aquinas, is "sorrow over another's good."[12] We all believe we deserve to possess specific goods in life, including self-esteem, status, and personal abilities. This desire is not evil in itself. However, when we become obsessed with the good fortune, possessions, talents, abilities, or success of others, it turns to envy. We acquire the vice of envy through the repeated comparison of the self to others in a way that is destructive of the self since the self discovers that it cannot compete successfully with the other person. Envy cuts people off from one another since the comparison of the self to others results in a person wanting evil things to happen to other people. To practice envy means to will another evil so that one can feel better about oneself. A community is thus destroyed by envy since the one who practices envy can only be satisfied when others have been subjugated or destroyed.

Avarice, or greed, is the excessive desire for money or possessions. Possessions enable us to live as embodied creatures since they provide us with the necessities of life. However, the desire for these goods can become an all-consuming desire for more. Avarice is an internal disposition to pursue the

11. John Milton, *Paradise Lost* 1.3, ed. John Leonard (New York: Penguin Classics, 2003).
12. Thomas Aquinas, *Summa Theologica* 2-2.36.2.

instrumental good of wealth to the exclusion of healthy human relationships. An instrumental good, money, or property becomes an intrinsic good, and as a result human relationships are sacrificed for economic success. We become preoccupied with the acquisition of wealth rather than with concern for others. Avarice thus undermines the capacity to love God and one's neighbor. Paul's warning that "the love of money is a root of all kinds of evil" (1 Tim. 6:10) teaches us that we can replace love with acquisition. According to John Wesley, greed is "destructive of that faith which is of the operation of God; of that hope which is full of immortality; of love of God and of our neighbor, and of every good word and work."[13]

The vice of wrath has its roots in our emotions. Emotion is not necessarily a vice, so we must make a distinction among three kinds of anger: emotional anger, virtuous anger, and vicious anger. Emotional anger is a visceral response to a threat to ourselves or to another. I am angered when my neighbor's dog comes charging at my child, and I jump in to protect the child by striking the dog. The anger in this case is one that is prompted by my emotions—by my parental instinct to protect my child from a threat. The second kind of anger is a good kind of anger, as when I am angered by the systematic exploitation of children as cheap labor in many countries. This reflects a reasonable judgment about how children should and should not be treated. The third kind of anger is vicious anger, or wrath. Wrath occurs as a kind of unbridled rage such as when the emotion takes control of me, and I shoot the dog and yell angrily at the dog's owner. Here the desire to protect my child is no longer subject to thoughtful reflection but is more akin to a kind of fearful ferocity. This anger does not appear out of nowhere but is the result of a lifetime of failure to control oneself and think through difficult situations with patience. When this kind of anger becomes a relatively fixed feature of my character, it has become a vice.

Sloth, traditionally known as *acedia*, is numbered among the seven capital vices because it calls us to an excessive rest. As popularly conceived, sloth denotes a kind of laziness or even apathy. If this captured the nature of sloth, then the cure would seem to be a kind of industriousness. Many Christian thinkers have also included a kind of busyness as a form of sloth. But sloth can best be understood as resisting the demands of love. It can do this by busying the self with trivialities and amusements. But it can also become callous to the demands of love since it is a vice consumed with avoiding the difficult work to which love calls us. In both cases the striking feature is one's

---

13. John Wesley, "The Danger of Riches," in *The Works of John Wesley*, ed. Albert C. Outler (Nashville: Abingdon, 1986), 3.234.

resistance to participate in the life of the other. We can refuse to participate in the lives of our family, friends, or God.

Gluttony is the excessive desire for the pleasures that only food can provide. As in the case with lust, the focus here is on the desire itself, which makes it more difficult to participate in relationships that require an other-regarding focus. For Thomas Aquinas, "Gluttony denotes, not any desire of eating and drinking, but an inordinate desire."[14] Food and drink are genuine goods. We require food for our survival. But when our desire for the pleasure of eating exceeds its appropriate order, we become fixated on the desire. Instead of eating to live, we live to eat. We have taken a good intended as a means to good living and made it the end in itself. If our sole purpose is to gratify our own pleasures of the palate, then by necessity other selves must have a secondary status.

Like the desire for food, the desire to protect ourselves, and the desire for rest, lust has its origin in our animal nature. Just like these other desires, sexual desire itself is not evil; it is the desire gone wrong that makes it evil. The lustful person desires the experience of sex and not the other person considered as a person. The lustful person thus objectifies another person and thereby profanes the sacred. Love, as a relationship to the other, is replaced with sex, as an act with an object. Paradoxically, sex without love is an act of intimacy that drives persons further apart than they were before. The more there is sex without love, the more isolated the individual becomes since one achieves only the semblance of intimacy. As Josef Pieper has remarked, for the person consumed with lust, "the aim should be a maximum of pleasure with a minimum of personal involvement."[15] With lust, the other person is used as a means and then promptly discarded when convenient. The problem with lust is that pleasure cannot deliver what it promises. It diminishes with each and every sexual conquest. But while pleasure without love must inevitably diminish, a life of genuine love can be unlimited.[16]

Each of these capital vices has a corrective virtue that enables one to resist the temptations of that particular vice. For pride, the corrective virtue is humility, which is a right estimation and valuing of oneself; for envy, the corrective virtue is kindness; avarice is corrected by charity; anger by forgiveness; gluttony by temperance; sloth by diligence (especially in responding to the demands of love); and, finally, lust by chastity—conceived of in terms of sexual fidelity and not mere abstinence.

14. Thomas Aquinas, *Summa Theologica* 2-2.148.1.
15. Josef Pieper, *Faith, Hope, Love* (San Francisco: Ignatius, 1986), 262.
16. See Stephen Post, *Unlimited Love: Altruism, Compassion, and Service* (Philadelphia: Templeton, 2003).

Vice	Corrective Virtue
Pride	Humility
Envy	Kindness
Avarice	Charity
Anger	Forgiveness
Sloth	Diligence
Gluttony	Temperance
Lust	Chastity

Criticisms of Virtue Ethics

Even though virtue ethics seems to offer a plausible alternative to rule-based theories of ethics, it is not without its critics. Two main criticisms have been leveled against it: First, is there really a unity to the virtues as Aristotle, Aquinas, and others have argued? Second, can it really offer helpful guidance in specific situations?

The first objection here is relevant to both contemporary and classic accounts of the virtues. If a person really possesses one of the virtues, then does that person really possess all of them? It would seem that a person might be courageous but not prudent. A person might practice self-control but not justice. Recently, John Doris has challenged the idea that virtue ethics can lay claim to the idea that they are interconnected in any significant way.[17] His argument is based on social psychology experiments that suggest individuals do not possess the virtues in the way Aristotle described. Rather, behavior is always disproportionately influenced by context or "situations," and as a result people often behave inconsistently. But the virtue ethicist could reply that virtue might be so rare that we cannot expect social scientists to verify it. Another response is one offered by Robert Adams, who claims that people often do exhibit consistent behaviors in various domains of their lives and these domains can—and do—demonstrate consistency even if the person does not possess each and every one of the virtues.[18]

The second objection appeals to the ambiguity inherent in virtue ethics. If virtues are character traits and based on a person's moral character, then how can that possibly guide the rest of us who might not possess that kind

17. John Doris, *Lack of Character: Personality and Moral Behavior* (Cambridge: Cambridge University Press, 2002).
18. Robert Merrihew Adams, *A Theory of Virtue: Excellence in Being for the Good* (Oxford: Oxford University Press, 2006).

of character? Suppose, for example, someone asks you how their clothing looks: Do you tell the truth, or do you lie? Do you apply a principle of honesty, kindness, or some other virtue? The problem here is one of practical reason; that is, it is a problem of how to apply moral principles. In addition, critics say that virtue ethics are culturally relative, dependent on how they have been conceived in different times, places, cultures, and so on. How does one account for the varieties of virtue lists proposed by Christians as well as by non-Christians, and what of different conceptions of virtues around the world? But here the virtue ethicist can simply say, "This is a problem for all moral theories including Kantianism, natural rights, utilitarianism, and divine commands. Which moral principle ought I to apply in any given situation?"

Virtue and Christian Ethics

Although the Christian Scriptures do not use the term "virtue," they do view various character traits as praiseworthy or blameworthy. Jesus's teaching in the Beatitudes praises qualities such as peacemaking and compassion, while elsewhere he encourages love of one's neighbor and even love of one's enemy. Paul makes lists of the "fruit of the spirit," which include love, patience, kindness, and self-control (Gal. 5:22–23). As a result, the Christian tradition—especially the work of Augustine and Thomas Aquinas—easily synthesized the language of Aristotle and the Stoics with the teachings of Jesus and Paul.

The lists of admirable qualities Jesus and Paul gave their listeners need to be contextualized within the cultural settings of the early Christian churches. However, one issue that seems universal—regardless of a particular time and place—is the narrative structure of these values. Jesus's teachings are often in story form. The parables of the good Samaritan and the prodigal son are powerful narratives that give shape and meaning to the ideas of forgiveness, grace, charity, and compassion.

The development of narrative ethics in the twentieth century arose from reflection on the centrality of the narrative in the biblical accounts of the children of Israel and the life and teachings of Jesus. H. Richard Niebuhr's work signaled this development, and he makes an important distinction between history as external events and history as shaping people in a community: "Events may be regarded from the outside by a non-participating observer; then they belong to the history of things. They may be apprehended from within, as items in the destiny of persons and communities; then they belong to a life-time and must be interpreted in a context of persons with their resolutions and devotions."[19] In other words, when biblical narratives speak about events, they act in the story itself. And the language of "our Father" and "our Lord" speaks to how events are internalized and incorporated into the community's identity.

This idea of history as functioning not merely as an accounting of events but as a form of communal remembering and meaning has been picked up by Stanley Hauerwas and Gregory Jones, who identify four ways narrative functions in Christian ethics: (1) our lives take a narrative form, (2) our ideas of rationality are shaped by narrative, (3) personal and communal identities cannot be understood apart from their narrative structure, and (4) virtues are socially located and find meaning only within narratives, and narratives require the virtues for their ongoing vitality.[20] The upshot of this approach is that narrative ethics requires virtues such as memory, honesty, faithfulness, charity, and hope in order to create and sustain a community of believers. Without the cultivation and practice of the virtues, the narrative is just a story.

Case Study: Lying

Most people value honesty in themselves and in other people. It is one particular value that seems to hold universally across cultures. Yet how one employs honesty is open to discussion. For Kant, people have an absolute duty to practice honesty regardless of the circumstances or the consequences. Kant famously argued that even in the case of possibly saving another person's life, one had an obligation to tell the truth regardless of the anticipated consequences. In contrast, for utilitarians, honesty should be practiced only when it increases net utility because in most cases honesty helps facilitate overall happiness. Yet if an individual could save another person's life by lying—and if this promoted net utility—then lying is obligatory. This raises the question: How do I know what will happen if I lie?

Jean-Paul Sartre wrote a famous story about just this issue.[21] Pablo is a prisoner during the Spanish Civil War. His interrogators question him about the location of his collaborator Ramon. If he tells them, then he will go free and Ramon will be executed. After some time, he relents and tries to misdirect his captors, giving them a location where he believes Ramon will not

19. H. Richard Niebuhr, *The Meaning of Revelation* (New York: Macmillan, 1941), 47.

20. Stanley Hauerwas and L. Gregory Jones, eds., *Why Narrative? Readings in Narrative Theology* (Grand Rapids: Eerdmans, 1989).

21. Jean-Paul Sartre, *Nausea: The Wall and Other Stories*, trans. Lloyd Alexander (New York: Fine Communications, 1999).

be. However, it just so happens that Ramon has chosen that location. The authorities find Ramon, arrest him, and execute him. Pablo is subsequently set free for cooperating and must deal with the guilt of betraying his friend. One might read Sartre's story as a vindication of Kantian ethics. Or one could read it as defending the idea that no matter what a person chooses, the result is absurd. Yet a virtue ethicist will reject the Kantian, the utilitarian, and the Sartrean interpretations.

For the virtue ethicist, honesty is the virtue not only of telling the truth but of being morally transparent with others. Honest people develop a reputation for their virtue of trustworthiness. Their character determines their decisions. Honesty is not the only virtue but is shaped by prudence, loyalty, courage, compassion, and an array of other virtues. In this light, honesty is a function of practical reason in the sense that it requires clear thinking about the situation and the ability to act on one's decision. Lying also requires the use of practical reason since it means acting against a basic obligation to tell the truth. People can either avoid telling a lie or simply lie and then attempt to justify the lie.

One way to avoid lying is to employ what Augustine called a "mental reservation."[22] Consider the following case: As you are leaving a store, your child sees a toy and asks if you have any money. Although you do have money, you say no. However, you add silently to yourself, "Not for that." This is the act of making a mental reservation in order to avoid a lie. Many oaths that people take involve the phrase "without any mental reservation" in order to avoid such kinds of attempted falsehoods. Another way of avoiding telling a lie is simply to refuse to answer a difficult question. In some ways, this is like refusing to answer in a court of law in the likelihood that the person's answer might be self-incriminating. Finally, a third option is simply to lie and deal with the consequences.

According to Thomas Aquinas, there are three kinds of lies: (1) jocose, (2) officious, and (3) malicious. All three kinds of lies should be avoided, but there are important differences among the three. The jocose and officious lies are less evil than malicious lies. (Thomas says that the former are merely venial sins while the latter is a mortal sin.)

---

22. The tradition of mental reservation traces to Augustine's *Enchiridion on Faith, Hope, and Charity* (trans. Thomas Hibbs [London: Aeterna Press, 1996], 12), where he does not include the intent to deceive as part of a lie. Sissela Bok comments that this "took its lead from Augustine's definition of lying as having one thing in one's heart and uttering another, but it left out the speaker's intention to deceive as part of the definition. It thereby allowed the following argument: If you say something misleading to another and merely add a qualification to it in your mind so as to make it true, you cannot be responsible for the 'misinterpretation' made by the listener." *Lying: Moral Choice in Public and Private Life* (Vintage, 1989), 35.

A **jocose lie** is a lie told as a joke. For example, I tell my friend that we are going out for a nice quiet dinner, but many of his friends and I have planned a surprise party for him at his favorite restaurant. I tell him the lie to get him to come with me, and when he arrives at the restaurant, we all laugh as he realizes I have lied to him. Here, I have told a lie in good fun. No one is harmed by this lie, and we enjoy the look of surprise on his face when he sees so many of his friends gathered around to celebrate with him. The lie is both to please him and amuse his friends. Aquinas says that this kind of lie is minor and weighs very lightly on the moral scales.

An **officious lie** is a lie told for the purpose of achieving some important good result and not for the sake of amusement. Here, the lie is told for a much more serious reason than a surprise party. Another person's life or well-being may be at stake. If we consider the case of lying to the Nazis who are looking for Jews during World War II, then we can see this as an instance of an officious lie since the protectors are lying in order to save the lives of innocent people. Once again, this kind of lie may be seen as bad, but the end intended is so much more important than the sin committed.

The last kind of lie is the malicious lie. A **malicious lie** is a lie told for some evil purpose, and it is a seriously evil kind of lie. Shakespeare's play *Othello* provides a clear example of a malicious lie. The narrative tells of Othello, who is married to Desdemona. Othello's supposed friend Iago decides to inflict pain on Othello because Iago feels slighted. He decides to lie to Othello about Desdemona's faithfulness in order to cause mayhem.

Whereas Thomas distinguishes various kinds of lies, Dietrich Bonhoeffer argues that the context—and a person's unique relationships—is more relevant than the kind of lie told.[23] Bonhoeffer offers an example: Suppose a very young child is at school and the teacher, who knows the family, asks, "Isn't it true that your father comes home drunk every night?" If the child lies, then the responsibility of the lie rests on the teacher for asking such an embarrassing question of a child who rightly feels an immediate sense of loyalty to his or her family. The teacher has overstepped the moral boundaries and has violated the child's relationship to his or her family. It may be appropriate for teachers to intervene in some cases, but Bonhoeffer's point is that there are often unequal power relationships that affect a person's practical reasoning.

Another factor involves the consequences of lying. These can be considered either collectively or individually. Utilitarians and others point out that if people lie habitually, it can erode the trust that ties a society or a community

---

23. Dietrich Bonhoeffer, *Ethics*, ed. Eberhard Bethge, trans. Neville Horton Smith (New York: Macmillan, 1955), 354–72.

together. G. J. Warnock has observed that the lie is not merely about false information but about issues wider in scope. He says, "It is . . . not the implanting of false beliefs that is damaging, but rather the generation of the suspicion that they may be being implanted. For this undermines trust; and, to the extent that trust is undermined, all co-operative undertakings are also undermined."[24]

Finally, on a virtue ethics approach, the more a person lies, the easier lying comes for the individual. Lying becomes habitual; it becomes a vice. As a vice, it undermines not only the trust society needs to operate successfully but also a person's ability to tell the truth. A person might need to be able to tell the truth as an act of courage or justice; and so, if the virtue of honesty is lacking, it can undermine these other virtues as well. The virtuous person thus asks, Is this the person I want to become?

Discussion Questions

1. Does a virtue ethics approach offer a better way to think about normative ethics than the rule-based theories such as Kantianism or utilitarianism? Why or why not?

2. How culturally relativistic are virtue ethics? To what degree does the conception of virtuous living differ from person to person, and culture to culture?

3. Is love the most important of the virtues? Why or why not?

4. Of all the vices, which one seems to be most popular in the twenty-first century?

5. How important is honesty as a virtue? Is it the most important virtue?

6. Is lying ever permissible? If so, under what conditions? Does a virtue approach to honesty and lying offer a better alternative than a Kantian or utilitarian approach?

24. G. J. Warnock, *The Object of Morality* (London: Methuen, 1971), 61.

Epilogue

Love and Christian Ethics

Love, and do what you will.

—Augustine, *Sermon
on the First Epistle of John*

Dante's *Divine Comedy* stands out as one of the truly great works in litera-ture.[1] While on one level it is a fictional tour of hell, purgatory, and heaven, it also encompasses history, politics, mythology, art, and philosophy in addition to offering theological insights on moral issues. It provides a kind of moral encyclopedia for those studying ethical issues from both philosophical and theological perspectives. The work is composed of three books corresponding to the three locales—the *Inferno* (hell), the *Purgatorio* (purgatory), and the *Paradiso* (paradise or heaven).

The *Inferno* has nine levels or circles that descend with respect to the vi-ciousness of the sin committed. The further Dante descends, the greater the sins and the greater the punishments. He starts in Limbo where he encounters people such as Aristotle, who were bereft of the benefits of Christianity. Dante then proceeds through the other levels of hell, encountering the lustful, the gluttons, those consumed with avarice, the wrathful, those guilty of heresy, the violent, the fraudulent, and finally—the worst of them all—the traitors. The last level of hell is particularly interesting in that it includes those who

1. Dante Alighieri, *The Divine Comedy*, trans. Robin Kirkpatrick (New York: Penguin, 2007).

betray their "lords." Here we find Satan, Judas, and Brutus. They are all individuals who once loved their lords but betrayed that love. From Dante's perspective, a betrayal of love is the worst sin a person can commit.

As Dante exits hell and moves through purgatory—where the souls of those destined for paradise must be cleansed—he sees that it is a mountain that must be climbed. At the lowest level of the mountain he first encounters the proud since pride is the first obstacle that prevents us from seeing God. From there, Dante moves up the mountain and sees the envious, the greedy, the wrathful, the slothful, the gluttons, and the lustful. The higher he goes, the less damaging the sins.

Finally, Dante arrives in paradise. Here he sees various saints rewarded according to their virtue. He ascends up the levels of heaven according to the various virtues with the highest sphere associated with charity. For Dante, love is the greatest of the virtues, and the betrayal of love is the worst of the vices. In a famous passage, he proclaims that God is "the love that moves the sun and the other stars."[2] In other words, the love of God is the reason for all that exists; it animates all creation. Dante's poetic narrative has its roots in the Gospels and their emphasis on love. In this epilogue, we suggest that love is the virtue that ties together Christian ethics and moral philosophy. In contrast to some of the more philosophical approaches, for a number of the more particularly theological approaches we have studied in this book, the aim of ethics can be seen as a call to love others since God is love and calls all people to loving relationships with one another. Here we briefly review the more significant theories and how each one engages this most central aspect of Christian ethics.

Love and Philosophical Ethics

Philosophical approaches to love and ethics, with rare exceptions, have not offered nearly as much as their theological alternatives. In the *Symposium*, Plato presented an account of *eros* that focused on the beauty of its object where the lover longs to possess the beloved. Although Aristotle does not develop a theory of love, he offers a helpful account of friendship that Thomas Aquinas will later use and transform for his own purposes.[3]

The modern philosophers also seem to show relatively little interest in love. Love plays no role in Locke's account of natural rights. It may be a

2. Dante, *Divine Comedy*, canto 33.
3. See Aristotle, *Nicomachean Ethics*, book 8; Thomas Aquinas, *Summa Theologica* 2-2.23–27, trans. Fathers of the English Dominican Providence (New York: Benzinger, 1947).

motivating factor in his account of tolerance, but for him love is relegated to the private domain of religion. For Kant, love would need to be a duty as prescribed by the categorical imperative and would thus have little to do with a person's affection. For utilitarians, love could be a motivation to increase net utility, but people's intentions have little to do with the moral worth of their actions.

The upshot of this analysis is that the theological tradition offers much more in terms of the centrality of love, and there are at least four of these approaches that consider love and its place in a person's moral life. These four are divine command, continental approaches, natural law, and virtue ethics. And each one draws on the teachings of Jesus in the Christian Scriptures.

Love and the Christian Scriptures

The Synoptic Gospels (Matthew, Mark, and Luke) all indicate that, when asked what the greatest commandment is, Jesus answers that it is love of God and of one's neighbor.[4] The centrality of love is also found in John's Gospel where Jesus says that "no one has greater love than this, to lay down one's life for one's friends" (John 15:13).

The other writings in the Christian Scriptures reflect this centrality as well. Paul proclaims that love is the greatest of all qualities a person can possess (1 Cor. 13). The author of the Letters of John proclaims that love is the only true test of whether a person is a disciple of Jesus or not. He exhorts his readers, "Beloved, let us love one another, because love is from God; everyone who loves is born of God and knows God. Whoever does not love does not know God, for God is love" (1 John 4:7–8). These writers did not have a philosophy or theology of love. Rather, they encouraged specific behaviors, the following of various rules, the cultivation of positive attitudes toward others, and the imitation of Jesus. The task of developing these ideas and applying them in the midst of new social, cultural, and intellectual contexts was therefore left to the moral theologians who followed.

Love and Divine Commands

Although divine command theorists see obedience as their starting point, love is the aim of obedience. They argue that we need the command because our

---

4. The wording is slightly different in each: Matt. 22:34–40; Mark 12:28–34; Luke 10:25–28.

natural inclinations are insufficient to recognize and fulfill the requirements of love. This is true for at least two reasons. First, although we love ourselves naturally, we fail to love others as we should. Second, even if we do manage to love some others, Jesus's command to love our enemies is impossible to recognize and fulfill without the explicit command and the work of divine grace.

Augustine sees the command to love as central. But we are to love God and others for their own sakes and not merely instrumentally. His distinction between "use" and "enjoyment" points to an important element in his account of love.[5] Enjoyment is to have a kind of satisfaction in something for its own sake, while use is merely to employ something for a further end. Augustine says, "The things which are to be enjoyed, then, are the Father and the Son and the Holy Spirit, and the Trinity that consists of them, which is a kind of single, supreme thing, shared by all who enjoy it."[6] This love of God—and subsequently of one's neighbor—gives the appropriate shape to the Christian life.

Because Augustine saw enjoyment of God in teleological terms—and as a compromise with pagan approaches to Christian morality—Anders Nygren drew a sharp distinction between Greek understandings of love, *eros*, and specifically Christian understandings of love, *agapē*.[7] For Nygren, much of Christianity—at least since the time of Augustine—had capitulated to Greek philosophical ideas in ways that were harmful to Christian moral life. Instead of acquisitive desire, *agapē* focuses on sacrificial giving; instead of grasping for things above itself, *agapē* lowers itself; instead of a human attempt to ascend to God, *agapē* is God's descent to humanity; instead of being based on human effort, *agapē* originates in God's grace; instead of operating from an egocentric perspective, *agapē* practices unselfish love; and instead of recognizing the value already present in its object, *agapē* creates value in its object. From Nygren's perspective, no human effort at determining what is good and achieving it will ever be sufficient. A command to love—a divine command to "love one another" (1 John 4:7)—must be issued from the divine lawgiver, and only this can enable us to love as we ought.

Love and Natural Law

Some Protestant and Catholic thinkers have seen the command to love not as a divine command needed because of human sinfulness but as a completion

5. Augustine, *On Christian Teaching*, trans. R. P. H. Green (New York: Oxford University Press, 1997).

6. Augustine, *Christian Teaching*, 10.

7. Anders Nygren, *Agape and Eros* (New York: Harper and Row, 1969).

and perfection of the natural order. They take seriously the Thomistic idea that "grace does not destroy nature but perfects it."[8] They appeal to natural law ethics, which points to some basic moral principles that all people can see as operating in their various cultures. This theory appeals to some basic truths about humans that apply universally.

All people have basic physiological drives for such goods as food, drink, shelter, and procreation. But they also have drives that are natural to them as humans, which extend beyond the merely biological. Humans also desire companionship, virtue, and truth. Insofar as people are rational beings, there are goods that correspond to that nature. Thomas Aquinas writes that the natural law points us to these various goods but only generally. Implicit in this pursuit of virtue and the truth about God lies the truth—undisclosed until the agent attains understanding of God and the acquisition of virtue— that all people are called to a life of love. The natural law informs us that we should pursue virtue, but it does not tell us explicitly that we should love one another. It is only when we come to see what virtue truly is that we see that the pinnacle of the moral life is love.

Seeing this idea of the natural law pointing to a law of love, C. S. Lewis develops an argument in three different stages within his work.[9] The first stage is to show that we all have a basic idea of justice about right and wrong in a fairly universal respect. All people recognize that there are some basic demands of and rules for morality. The second stage is to show that morality applies across cultures and that these universal demands require the love of others. Almost all cultures have a law of general beneficence that requires love of parents, children, and neighbors. In the third stage, Lewis moves from a general rule of love to a specification of the various kinds of love humans have for one another, including affection, erotic love, and friendship. He argues that charity is the highest form of love, which is the ultimate way of pursuing the good.

Love and Christian Existentialism

Closely allied to the divine command tradition is the approach that many Christian existentialists take to Christian ethics and love. Where the divine command theorist sees the source of obligation in the command of God, the

8. Thomas Aquinas, *Summa Theologica* 1.8.2.
9. The idea of "developing stages" is not C. S. Lewis's own description but our characterization of his work. The first stage is in *Mere Christianity* (New York: Macmillan, 1952), where he discusses the "law of human nature," 17–39. The second stage can be found in his *Abolition of Man* (New York: Macmillan, 1947) and his discussion of "The Way." The third stage is found in *The Four Loves* (New York: Harcourt-Brace-Jovanovich, 1960), 163–92, in the chapter on charity.

Christian existentialist sees the source of obligation in the genuine encounter with God. The encounter with God is prior to the command of God in the sense that we have been confronted by the divine person who makes claims on us.

For Kierkegaard, love was a command that was determined by love itself. He writes, "Erotic love is determined by the object; friendship is determined by the object; only love to one's neighbor is determined. By love since one's neighbor is everyman and, unconditionally every man, all distinctions are indeed removed from the object."[10] In other words, we are required to love all humans without making any kind of excuses or distinctions among them that would lessen the force of the command. Moreover, for Kierkegaard, genuine love—an authentic love—can only be mediated through the love of and encounter with God. There can be no direct love of another human since that kind of love will attempt to manipulate or coerce the beloved.

Picking up on this theme of unconditional love, Bonhoeffer claims, "When we judge other people we confront them in a spirit of detachment, observing and reflecting as it were from the outside. But love has neither time nor opportunity for this. If we love we can never observe the other person with detachment, for he is always and at every moment a living claim to our love and service."[11] Detachment and judgment distance us from the other because they turn the other into an object. Love, on the contrary, illuminates the other person as another self—a person for whom Christ died. And Christ, as in the case of Kierkegaard, is always the mediator between persons.

Bonhoeffer draws a distinction between human love and spiritual love in that the former is based on its own human desire and immediacy. Because of this, human love is incapable of loving the enemy. In contrast, spiritual love enables the lover to serve and love the other as a brother or sister only through Christ. He says, "I do not know in advance what Love of others means on the basis of the general idea of love that grows out of my human desires—all this may rather be hatred in an insidious kind of selfishness in the eyes of Christ. Spiritual life is bound solely to the Word of Jesus Christ."[12] The existential encounter with Christ and the believer's response of love for God and for one's neighbor open us up to the love that loves without presuppositions or demands on the other.

10. Søren Kierkegaard, *Works of Love*, trans. Howard Hong and Edna Hong (New York: Harper Torchbooks, 1962), 77.

11. Dietrich Bonhoeffer, *The Cost of Discipleship*, trans. Christian Kaiser (New York: Macmillan, 1963), 204.

12. Dietrich Bonhoeffer, *Life Together*, trans. John W. Doberstein (New York: Harper, 1954), 35.

Love and Virtue Ethics

Since the virtues are good qualities of the soul that we can cultivate, love—as the chief virtue—is the most important quality that we can develop. Although the Christian Scriptures rarely use the Greek term for virtue, *aretē* (2 Pet. 1:5), this should not be problematic. Most early Christian writers were working with descriptions of people and their desirable character traits rather than developing theories based on moral psychology and a theory of virtue.

Those thinkers emphasizing love as a virtue—especially Augustine and Thomas Aquinas—saw themselves as inhabiting the Christian world of values while employing Greek and Roman language to express those values. Thomas thus employs Aristotle, saying that charity is a "friendship with God" and that love more generically is the "affirmation of being."[13] This definition encompasses God, the self, others, and even one's enemies.

God's steadfast love for the world and all humanity is the starting point. "For God so loved the world" is not merely a phrase in John 3:16 but a theological orientation for the Christian Scriptures. When we say, "God loves," what we mean is that "God affirms the value of all creation." God's love means that all creation is affirmed and has value without exception. Humans are called, therefore, to love what God loves.

As a theological virtue, charity (1) is located in the will and not the emotions, (2) is a stable disposition, and (3) is a participation in the life of God. The human loves and desires that all people have are often inconsistent and erratic. They are based on familiarity, beauty, or convenience and not on the intrinsic value of the other person. But the theological virtue of charity is not like this. Human loves are often prompted by emotions or desires that can change significantly, but the will is oriented not merely to a specific person or object but to Goodness itself—to God. This is not merely one choice a person makes; it is a tendency to act in a particular manner.

Virtues are stable dispositions, good habits. As habits, they become part of the person as a second nature. We can expect charitable people to behave in a fairly predictable way. The virtue of charity, unlike the Aristotelian moral virtues, is a participation in God. And since God is love, the virtue of charity is our continued participation in divine love. It is only by our participation in God that we are able to love the stranger and the enemy; any attempts to do so by a sheer effort of the will, unaided by divine grace, cannot succeed. God is the source of charity, the necessary facilitator of charity, the end intended by all charitable action, and the one in whom all loving people participate.

13. Josef Pieper, *Faith, Hope, Love*, trans. Richard and Clara Winston (San Francisco: Ignatius, 1986), 207.

Concluding Reflections

In emphasizing the centrality of love, the Christian moral tradition offers something philosophical theories cannot offer: the grace of Jesus Christ, which provides a new way of being and acting in the world. The idea of self-giving love that is made possible only through faithful discipleship presents an alternative to love as duty, net utility, or free choice. Rather, humanity's union with God in love is understood as the ultimate good. As in Dante's vision of heaven, the human creature comes to see and participate in God, who is Goodness itself. Although the divine command theory, natural law ethics, Christian existentialism, and virtue ethics may differ in how love is to be understood, defined, and practiced, they agree on its centrality. Indeed, in the last *cantos* of Dante's *Paradiso*, we find diverse Christians and saints, who in their terrestrial lives differed significantly, all united in the love and worship of God.

Glossary

actions contrary to duty In Kantian ethics, those actions that directly violate the categorical imperative.

actions for the sake of duty In Kantian ethics, those actions that are required by the categorical imperative and performed simply because it is a duty. *See also* autonomous will.

actions in accordance with duty In Kantian ethics, those actions that are required by the categorical imperative but are performed by a motive other than duty.

act utilitarianism The view that for any given action, the net utility must be pursued for that specific action.

aesthetic stage In Kierkegaard's ethics, the moral stage represented by Don Juan that sees the goal of life as sensual pleasure.

agapistic ethics A theological approach to normative ethics that places primacy on the biblical idea of *agapē* (or love).

analytic ethics A philosophical approach to ethics in the past one hundred years that focuses on the meaning of moral language and the validity of the logic employed in ethical argumentation.

anthropocentrism The idea that humans are somehow at the center of the universe both metaphysically and morally.

antireligious objection to utilitarianism The accusation that utilitarianism is a moral theory that directly denigrates religion by being solely concerned with pleasure.

apodictic law Those commands in the Bible that do not permit any exceptions, such as the Decalogue.

applied ethics That discipline that engages specific moral issues from a particular moral perspective, especially issues like capital punishment, environmental ethics, fair trade, and bioethics.

autonomous will In Kantian ethics, it is a will that performs its duty for the sake of duty alone and for no other reason or motive.

avarice Also known as "greed," one of the seven capital vices and an excessive desire for money or possessions.

bad faith In Sartre's ethical theory, the idea that we are somehow responsible to some moral principle that was not of our own choosing.

biblical ethics The approach that emphasizes the authority of the Bible above all other authorities and applies the texts to contemporary situations.

cardinal virtues Also known as the "moral virtues," these are the virtues Aristotle believed that enable us to act in ways that help us to be good human beings; they include prudence, justice, courage, and self-control.

casuistic law In the Hebrew Scriptures, the kind of law that addresses specific cases usually in the form of "If . . . then . . ."; it is often contrasted with the absolute binding force of apodictic laws.

categorical imperative Kant's rational method for determining a person's duty.

ceremonial precepts Those precepts of the Hebrew covenant that were understood by Christians as applying only in the times of the law and the prophets.

charity In Christian virtue ethics, the third and most important of the theological virtues; it is a participation in the life of God and enables us to love God and our neighbors in an unconditional way.

Christian realism The idea associated with Reinhold Niebuhr that in some cases people have two choices that are both evil and must admit that the choice they make is evil and then ask forgiveness for it.

connection of the virtues The theory that in order to possess a particular virtue that a person has to possess all the virtues, to some degree.

conscience The subjective judgment an individual makes about a particular moral issue; in the Roman Catholic tradition, one's conscience is always morally binding whether or not it is objectively true.

consent *See* explicit consent; tacit consent.

consequentialism Any moral theory that emphasizes the good over the right, a theory that sees the results of an action (or system) as having the most moral value.

consistent ethic of life Cardinal Bernardin's idea that a person cannot selectively pick and choose which pro-life positions to support but must embrace them one and all.

counsel of prudence Kant's idea that we can attain happiness in terms of an "If . . . then . . ." formula.

covenant A relationship between two parties based on love wherein the individuals bind themselves to one another.

cultural relativism The idea that people in one culture cannot judge the actions of people living in another culture.

Decalogue (also known as "The Ten Commandments") Those apodictic commands that were central to the Mosaic covenant.

deontological ethics Those normative ethical theories that emphasize right or duty (e.g., Kantianism, natural rights theory, and divine command morality), especially the nature of moral obligation.

depravity The theological idea that all humans are utterly sinful and incapable of knowing truth apart from divine grace.

deterrence theory of punishment The idea that a punishment should primarily deter other crimes.

divine command morality The normative ethical theory that the basis for moral obligation is found in obedience to God's commands.

divine law In Thomistic ethics, those divine precepts that a person could not know from the natural law;

those commands that had to be the product of special revelation.

divine sovereignty In ethical theory, the idea that there can be nothing, no moral rule or principle, that stands over and above God.

double-effect The idea in Catholic moral theology that when an action has two consequences, one good and one evil, the agent is only permitted to will the good result.

duty In Kant's theory, a morally binding obligation as determined by the categorical imperative. Perfect duties are those that are "perfectly determined" and prescribe specific behaviors. Imperfect duties are "imperfectly" determined and can be fulfilled in a variety of ways.

ecojustice The practice of making certain that poor and marginalized groups do not unfairly bear the burden of ecological harm.

egoism An individualistic moral theory professing that people pursue their own self-interest and that they are morally justified in doing so.

envy One of the seven capital vices understood as sorrow over another person's good fortune.

essentialism The idea that all humans have the same basic nature.

eternal law In Christian ethics, the second person of the Trinity, Christ.

ethical stage Kierkegaard's second moral stage that is typified by following moral rules.

ethics The thoughtful reflection and evaluation of various systems of morality around which people organize their lives.

euthanasia *See* involuntary euthanasia; nonvoluntary euthanasia; voluntary euthanasia.

Euthyphro Dilemma Plato's dilemma that attempts to show that either God's commands are arbitrary or that God is irrelevant to the precepts of morality.

excess In Aristotle's account of the virtues the extreme that does too much.

existentialism A philosophical attempt to defy preconceived roles by trying to achieve a more authentic kind of existence.

explicit consent The verbal or written agreement a person makes to the social contract or constitution.

faith In Christian virtue ethics, the first of the theological virtues and the habit of believing God.

First Table The first four commandments in the Decalogue delineating our obligations to God.

fortitude The cardinal virtue that enables us to regulate and moderate our fear.

genealogy In Nietzsche's moral theory, an unraveling of the moral meaning of a term to its psychological and biological sources; an attempt to trace and discredit a term by giving an account of its origin.

general revelation Those truths people can know through their own abilities and by observation of the world without the aid of special revelation.

gluttony One of the capital vices, concerned with an excessive desire for the pleasures that only food can provide.

habit An acquired disposition that enables a person to perform some activity with relative ease.

hedonic calculus Bentham's device for calculating the greatest pleasure that a particular act could provide.

heteronomous will For Kant, any will that was determined (or motivated) by an intention other than one's duty.

holiness code The commandments in the Hebrew Bible that derive from the Decalogue.

hope In Christian virtue ethics, the second of the theological virtues and the patient expectation of a difficult but possible future good.

hubris A kind of moral arrogance, usually in reference to a person's relationship to God.

human law In Thomistic ethics, those laws designed to govern specific societies and political organizations and should not violate the natural laws.

humility In virtue ethics, the virtue that serves as the corrective to pride, a kind of right valuing of the self.

hypothetical imperative In Kantian ethics, those imperatives that take the form of an "if . . . then. . . ." construction. These are nonmoral imperatives for Kant since they are based upon a person's desires.

imago Dei Latin term for "the image of God."

imperative A prescribed rule or duty.

imperfect duties In Kantian ethics, these are duties that are "imperfectly determined" in that they allow freedom in how a person fulfills them; they do not prescribe or forbid specific behaviors.

imperfect happiness In the Christian tradition of Aquinas this refers to the kind of happiness we can achieve in this life on earth, as contrasted with the perfect happiness of the beatific vision in heaven.

individualism Any normative moral theory that prioritizes the individual's good over that of the community's good.

involuntary euthanasia The termination of a person's life against their wishes.

I-Thou relationship In Buber's thought, the idea of a genuine and respectful relationship between two persons.

jocose lie a lie told for an amusing purpose without harm being done to another person.

jus ad bellum The conditions under which a war may be declared just, arguing for "the right to go to war."

jus in bello The "morally permissible actions of war" that serve to constrain, or limit, the evils of war.

justice Rendering to others what they deserve, which deals with right and wrong in a fairly universal respect.

just war theory The moral justification for going to war and for fighting in wars.

Ketuvim "The writings" which represent the third section of the *Tanakh*—the Hebrew Scriptures. The *Ketuvim* consists of a variety of writings, both historical and poetic, including the books of Job, Psalms, and Proverbs.

law of nature The basic moral principle that governs all human interaction, regardless of religious commitments or cultural contexts.

love The guiding principle behind our proper relationship with God, others, and ourselves, characterized by holiness, righteousness, and justice. *See also* charity.

lust The desire for the experience of sex without considering the other person as a person or any habitually uncontrolled sexual desire; one of the capital vices.

malicious lie A lie told for some evil purpose.

means-end formulation of the categorical Kant's rational principle that all people should be treated equally under the moral law.

metaethics The study of moral language and the nature of moral properties.

methodological atheism The idea that our moral deliberations have no need of God.

moral philosophy The philosophical study of ethics.

moral precepts The most basic principles of morality.

moral relativism The idea that there are no universal moral principles that all people, regardless of their culture, recognize as obligatory.

morals The collective values we live by—the values we ascribe to certain activities and goods.

moral stage A distinguishable level of moral development (for example, Kierkegaard talks about aesthetic and ethical stages).

moral theology Theological reflection on ethical issues. There are various types of moral theology: biblical, divine command, agapistic, narrative, and natural law ethics.

moral virtue A good habit of the soul that enables its possessor to live and act well.

narrative ethics Ethics in which narrative is primary; rules and principles are secondary in the sense that discipleship is more about being a certain kind of person than it is about discovering the right rule that we should apply in any given context.

natural law ethics The idea that there are abiding moral principles in human nature that all people can and do understand.

natural laws Those basic moral principles that all people—regardless of culture or custom—can see as operating in their own and other cultures.

natural right to life, liberty, and property The argument that people have a natural right to life, liberty, and property, and that their lives are theirs to do with as they please.

net utility Ethical thinking in terms of "the greatest good" (or "net utility," maximizing interests) that can be accomplished.

Nevi'im "The prophets," which represents the second section of the *Tanakh*—the Hebrew Scriptures. The *Nevi'im* consists of a variety of major and minor prophetical books.

nonvoluntary euthanasia The termination of a person's life when that person is incapable of expressing his or her personal choice

normative ethics The theory about central moral principles that should guide everyone's lives.

objectivist ethics The theory associated with Ayn Rand that holds people's lives as the standard of value—and their own lives as the ethical purpose of every individual person.

officious lie An untruth told for the purpose of achieving some important good result and not for the sake of amusement or malice.

ownership The possession of an object wherein the only interests belong to the owner.

pacifism The theory that it is never appropriate to engage in acts of violence because violence begets violence.

perfect duties A "perfect duty" for Kant is one that is "perfectly determined." That is, it is one that does not admit of any variation or any alternatives in how one goes about fulfilling the duty.

perfect happiness The beatific vision of God, according to Christianity, in contrast to imperfect happiness that anyone may experience in this life.

pride The chief of the capital vices that inevitably separates us from God, sometimes considered the root of all sin.

primary precepts Precepts of natural law that do not change and are binding on all people regardless of culture.

proof of the principle of utility Mill's argument that just as each person desires his or her own happiness, so too all people desire the happiness of all.

proportionalism The ethical theory that seeks to weigh the good effects against the evil and find the best proportion between them.

quadrilateral A paradigm for understanding issues of religious authority for Christian theology and ethics, which includes the authorities of Scripture, tradition, reason, and experience.

relativism The idea that morals have no objective basis.

ressentiment The "moral resentment" of the weak, according to Nietzsche, who use moral words to keep the strong subdued. But it is the strong who must overcome this and become people who are "beyond good and evil."

retributivism The theory of punishment based upon the idea of just deserts.

right reason Reason's ability to see important relationships to guide our actions, according to Aristotle.

rules of skill Activities where our "end" (i.e., our reason for action) is variable and therefore our "means" to that end will also be variable.

rule utilitarianism The belief that we should always adopt those moral rules that promote net utility.

Second Table The latter half of the Ten Commandments, which include all the obligations toward one's neighbor, including the exhortation to honor one's parents and the prohibitions on murder, theft, adultery, and false witness.

secondary precepts In natural law ethics, those human laws that generally benefit society.

selfishness The central virtue in the moral life, according to the objectivist ethics of Ayn Rand.

situation ethics A kind of theistic act utilitarianism associated with Fletcher where the "net utility" of an act is the well-being of persons. From this perspective, there are no absolutes—except for love—that should guide a person's actions.

slave morality A herd morality of the masses, according to Nietzsche, which appeals to "universal" moral principles in order to keep the powerful from exercising their genius.

sloth One of the capital vices; resistance to the demands of love.

special revelation God's disclosure of particular knowledge, not naturally known, for example, as found in Scripture regarding salvation.

state of nature The original condition of people, according to Locke, consisting of a precontractual (and presocietal) state, wherein all people are free and equal.

stewardship The habitual care of a gift entrusted to a person or persons.

strong divine command morality The contention that God can command anything whatsoever, since God's power, or strength, is not inhibited by any constraints.

tacit consent An agreement that is understood to apply to persons born into a society where, by continuing to live there, they agree to abide by the principles of that society as articulated in the social contract.

Tanakh The Hebrew Scriptures; an acronym of the Hebrew letters of the three major sections: *Torah* ("instruction" or "teaching"), *Nevi'im* ("prophets"), *and Ketuvim* ("writings").

teleological suspension of the ethical The suspension of normal ethical judgments we make in order to have a genuine encounter with God, according to Kierkegaard, which can only take place by a "leap of faith."

telos The way in which our activities presuppose some particular end, or goal.

theological virtues The Christian tradition considers faith, hope, and love to be the virtues constituent for morality.

therapeutic theory of punishment The view that sees punishment as a kind of cure for the perpetrator.

Torah The "instruction" or "teaching," which represents the first section of the *Tanakh*—the Hebrew Scriptures. The Torah consists of five books: Genesis, Exodus, Leviticus, Numbers, and Deuteronomy.

trolley problem A thought experiment devised in order to determine how to decide who to save, and consequently who not to save, from an impending trolley accident.

Übermensch The morality of a "Super Man," according to Nietzsche, whose "will to power" and creative genius forges his or her own morality, thereby creating values.

universalizability formulation of the categorical imperative The idea that any maxim, that is, a subjective principle of action, according to Kant, must in principle be universalized.

vice A bad habit of the soul. Vices are dispositions, or patterns, where we fail to be the kinds of persons we should.

virtue A good habit of the soul. Virtues are a chosen pattern of behavior that helps us pursue the good in a well-ordered way.

virtue as a mean Virtue is "a mean between two extremes," according to Aristotle. For example, the virtue of courage is the mean between cowardice and foolhardiness.

voluntarism The will is considered the central element of moral decision-making, including obedience to God's commands.

voluntary euthanasia The willing termination of a person's life.

weak divine command morality A version of divine command theory that asserts that God's commands are constrained by God's character.

wrath One of the capital vices; when the emotion of anger becomes habitually vicious.

Further Reading

General Ethical Resources

Christian Ethics and Moral Philosophy

Augustine, *On Christian Teaching*. Translated by R. P. H. Green. New York: Oxford University Press, 1997.

Gill, Robin, ed. *The Cambridge Companion to Christian Ethics*. New York: Cambridge University Press, 2001.

Gushee, David P., and Glen H. Stassen. *Kingdom Ethics: Following Jesus in Contemporary Context*. 2nd ed. Grand Rapids: Eerdmans, 2017.

Hauerwas, Stanley. *The Peaceable Kingdom*. Notre Dame, IN: University of Notre Dame Press, 1981.

John Paul II, Pope. *The Splendor of Truth*. New York: United States Conference of Catholic Bishops, 1993.

MacIntyre, Alisdair. *Three Rival Versions of Moral Enquiry*. Notre Dame, IN: University of Notre Dame Press, 1990.

Mattison, William C., III. *Introducing Moral Theology: True Happiness and the Virtues*. Grand Rapids: Brazos, 2008.

Moore, G. E. *Principia Ethica*. Cambridge: Cambridge University Press, 1903.

Murdoch, Iris. *The Sovereignty of Good*. New York: Routledge, 2001.

Niebuhr, Reinhold. *The Nature and Destiny of Man: A Christian Interpretation*. 2 vols. Louisville: Westminster John Knox, 1996.

Nygren, Anders. *Agape and Eros*. Translated by Philip S. Watson. New York: Harper and Row, 1969.

Rawls, John. *A Theory of Justice*. Cambridge, MA: Harvard University Press, 1971.

Sartre, Jean-Paul. *Existentialism and Humanism*. Translated by Philip Mairet. London: Eyre Metheun, 1973.

Thomas Aquinas. *Summa Theologica*. Trans. Fathers of the English Dominican Province. New York: Benziger, 1947.

Troeltsch, Ernst. *The Social Teaching of the Christian Churches*. 2 vols. Louisville: Westminster John Knox, 1992.

Williams, Bernard. *Ethics and the Limits of Philosophy*. Cambridge, MA: Harvard University Press, 1986.

Ethics in the Hebrew Scriptures

Amdt, Emily. *Demanding Our Attention: The Hebrew Bible as a Source for Christian Ethics*. Grand Rapids: Eerdmans, 2011.

Barton, John. *Understanding Old Testament Ethics: Approaches and Explanations*. Louisville: Westminster John Knox, 2003.

Birch, Bruce C. *Let Justice Roll Down: The Old Testament, Ethics, and Christian Life*. Louisville: Westminster John Knox, 1991.

Brueggemann, Walter. *Theology of the Old Testament*. Minneapolis: Fortress, 1997.

Copan, Paul. *Is God a Moral Monster? Making Sense of the Old Testament God*. Grand Rapids: Baker Books, 2011.

Green, Joel B., and Jacqueline Lapsley, eds. *The Old Testament and Ethics: A Book-by-Book Survey*. Grand Rapids: Baker Academic, 2013.

Gutiérrez, Gustavo. *On Job: God-Talk and the Suffering of the Innocent*. Maryknoll, NY: Orbis, 2005.

Trible, Phyllis. *Texts of Terror: Literary-Feminist Readings of Biblical Narratives*. Philadelphia: Fortress, 1984.

Ethics in the Christian Scriptures

Harrington, Daniel, SJ, and James Keenan, SJ. *Jesus and Virtue Ethics: Building Bridges between New Testament Studies and Moral Theology*. New York: Sheed and Ward, 2005.

———. *Paul and Virtue Ethics: Building Bridges between New Testament Studies and Moral Theology*. New York: Sheed and Ward, 2010.

Hays, Richard P. *The Moral Vision of the New Testament: A Contemporary Introduction to Christian Ethics*. San Francisco: HarperCollins, 1996.

Meeks, Wayne. *Origins of Christian Morality: The First Two Centuries*. New Haven: Yale University Press, 1995.

Ogletree, Thomas W. *The Use of the Bible in Christian Ethics*. Philadelphia: Fortress, 1983.

Witherington, Ben, III. *New Testament Theology and Ethics*. Downers Grove, IL: InterVarsity Press, 2016.

Divine Command Ethics

Brunner, Emil. *The Divine Imperative: A Study in Christian Ethics*. Translated by Olive Wyon. London: Lutterworth, 1937.

Davitt, Thomas E. *The Nature of Law*. St. Louis: Herder, 1951.

Evans, C. Stephen. *God and Moral Obligation*. New York: Oxford University Press, 2014.

Hare, John. *God's Call: Moral Realism, God's Commands, and Human Autonomy*. Grand Rapids: Eerdmans, 2000.

Helm, Paul. *Divine Commands and Morality*. New York: Oxford University Press, 1981.

Idziak, Janine Marie, ed. *Divine Command Morality: Historical and Contemporary Readings*. Lewiston, NY: Mellen, 1978.

McInerny, Ralph. *Ethica Thomistica: The Moral Philosophy of Thomas Aquinas*. Washington, DC: Catholic University of America Press, 1989.

Mouw, Richard J. *The God Who Commands*. Notre Dame, IN: University of Notre Dame Press, 1991.

Plato. *Plato: The Collected Dialogues*. Translated by Lance Cooper. Edited by Edith Hamilton and Huntington Cairns. Princeton: Princeton University Press, 1961.

Quinn, Philip. *Divine Commands and Moral Requirements*. Oxford: Oxford University Press, 1978.

Natural Law Ethics

Boyd, Craig A. *A Shared Morality: A Narrative Defense of Natural Law Ethics*. Grand Rapids: Brazos, 2007.

Donagan, Alan. *The Theory of Morality*. Chicago: University of Chicago Press, 1978.

Fuchs, Joseph. *Natural Law: A Theological Investigation*. New York: Sheed and Ward, 1965.

George, Robert. *In Defense of Natural Law*. Oxford: Oxford University Press, 2001.

Laing, Jaqueline A., and Russell Wilcox, eds. *The Natural Law Reader*. Oxford: Wiley-Blackwell, 2013.

Lewis, C. S. *The Abolition of Man*. New York: Macmillan, 1954.

———. *Mere Christianity*. New York: Macmillan, 1949.

Maritain, Jacques. *Natural Law: Reflections on Theory and Practice*. South Bend, IN: St. Augustine Press, 2001.

Porter, Jean. *Nature as Reason: A Thomistic Theory of Natural Law*. Grand Rapids: Eerdmans, 2005.

Simon, Yves. *The Tradition of Natural Law: A Philosopher's Reflections*. New York: Fordham University Press, 1992.

Natural Rights Ethics

Finnis, John. *Natural Law and Natural Rights*. Oxford: Oxford University Press, 2011.

Laing, Jacqueline A., and Russell Wilcox, eds. *The Natural Law Reader*. Oxford: Wiley-Blackwell, 2013.

Maritain, Jacques. *Natural Law: Reflections on Theory and Practice*. South Bend, IN: St. Augustine Press, 2001.

Strauss, Leo. *Natural Right and History*. Chicago: University of Chicago Press, 1999.

Tuck, Richard. *Natural Rights Theories: Their Origin and Development*. Cambridge: Cambridge University Press, 1982.

Individualistic Ethics

Hobbes, Thomas. *Leviathan*. Edited by C. B. MacPherson. New York: Penguin, 1982.

Locke, John. *A Letter concerning Toleration*. Buffalo, NY: Prometheus, 1990.

———. *Two Treatises of Government*. Edited by Peter Laslett. New York: New American Library, 1963.

Nozick, Robert. *Anarchy, State, and Utopia*. New York: Basic, 1977.

Rand, Ayn. *The Virtue of Selfishness*. New York: Signet, 1964.

Kantian Ethics

Acton, H. B. *Kant's Moral Philosophy*. New York: St. Martin's, 1970.

Grenberg, Jeanine. *Kant and the Ethics of Humility: A Story of Dependence, Corruption, and Virtue*. New York: Cambridge University Press, 2010.

Kant, Immanuel. *Critique of Practical Reason*. Translated by Lewis White Beck. New York: Macmillan, 1985.

———. *Ethical Philosophy*. 2nd ed. Translated by James W. Ellington. Indianapolis: Hackett, 1995.

———. *Lectures on Ethics*. Translated by Louis Infield. Indianapolis: Hackett, 1980.

Kosgaard, Christine M. *Creating the Kingdom of Ends*. New York: Cambridge University Press, 1996.

Nell, Onora. *Acting on Principle: An Essay on Kantian Ethics*. New York: Columbia University Press, 1975.

Sullivan, Roger J. *An Introduction to Kant's Ethics*. New York: Cambridge University Press, 1994.

Wood, Allen W. *Kant's Ethical Thought*. Ithaca, NY: Cornell University Press, 1970.

Utilitarian Ethics

Bentham, Jeremy. *The Principles of Morals and Legislation*. New York: Prometheus, 1988.

Eggleston, Ben, and Dale E. Miller, eds. *The Cambridge Companion to Utilitarianism*. Cambridge: Cambridge University Press, 2014.

Fletcher, Joseph. *Situation Ethics: The New Morality*. Philadelphia: Westminster, 1966.

Kazcor, Christopher, ed. *Proportionalism: For and Against*. Milwaukee: Marquette University Press, 1999.

Mill, John Stuart. *On Liberty and Utilitarianism*. New York: Knopf, 1906.

Sen, Amartya, and Bernard Williams, eds. *Utilitarianism and Beyond*. Cambridge: Cambridge University Press, 1982.

Smart, J. J. C., and Bernard Williams. *Utilitarianism: For and Against*. Cambridge: Cambridge University Press, 1973.

Continental Ethics

Bonhoeffer, Dietrich. *Ethics*. Edited by Eberhard Bethge. Translated by Neville Horton Smith. New York: Macmillan, 1963.

———. *Life Together*. Translated by John W. Doberstein. New York: Harper, 1954.

Buber, Martin. *I and Thou*. Translated by Walter Kaufman. New York: Scribner's, 1970.

Calarco, Matthew and Peter Atterton, eds. *The Continental Ethics Reader*. London: Routledge, 2003.

Kierkegaard, Søren. *Fear and Trembling*. Translated by Walter Lowrie. New York: Anchor, 1954.

Nietzsche, Friedrich. *Beyond Good and Evil: Prelude to a Philosophy of the Future*. Edited and translated by Walter Kaufmann. New York: Vintage, 1989.

———. *The Gay Science*. translated by Josefine Nauckhoff. Cambridge: Cambridge University Press, 2001.

———. *"On the Genealogy of Morals" and "Ecce Homo."* Translated by Walter Kaufmann. New York: Vintage, 1989.

Sartre, Jean-Paul. *Existentialism and Humanism*. Translated by Philip Mairet. London: Eyre Methuen, 1973.

Virtue Ethics

Adams, Robert Merrihew. *A Theory of Virtue: Excellence in Being for the Good*. Oxford: Oxford University Press, 2006.

Aristotle. *Nicomachean Ethics*. Translated by Terence Irwin. Indianapolis: Hackett, 1985.

Foot, Philippa. *Virtues and Vices and Other Essays in Moral Philosophy*. Oxford: Clarendon Press, 2003.

Hauerwas, Stanley. *The Peaceable Kingdom*. Notre Dame, IN: University of Notre Dame Press, 1982.

Hauerwas, Stanley, and Charles Pinches, eds. *Christians among the Virtues: Theological Conversations with Ancient and Modern Ethics*. Notre Dame, IN: University of Notre Dame Press, 1997.

Konyndyk-DeYoung, Rebecca. *Glittering Vices: A New Look at the Seven Deadly Sins and Their Remedies*. Grand Rapids: Brazos, 2009.

MacIntyre, Alasdair. *After Virtue: A Study in Moral Theory*. 3rd ed. Notre Dame, IN: University of Notre Dame Press, 2007.

———. *Dependent Rational Animals: Why Humans Need the Virtues*. LaSalle, IL: Open Court, 1999.

Pieper, Josef. *Faith, Hope, Love*. San Francisco: Ignatius, 1986.

Porter, Jean. *The Four Cardinal Virtues*. Notre Dame, IN: University of Notre Dame Press, 1966.

Thomas Aquinas. *Disputed Questions on the Virtues*. Translated by E. M. Atkins. New York: Cambridge University Press, 2009.

Timpe, Kevin, and Craig A. Boyd, eds. *Virtues and Their Vices*. New York: Oxford University Press, 2014.

Relativism

Beckwith, Francis, and Gregory Koukl. *Relativism: Feet Planted Firmly in Mid-air*. Grand Rapids: Baker, 1998.

Fletcher, Joseph. *Situation Ethics: The New Morality*. Philadelphia: Westminster, 1966.

Harman, Gilbert, and Judith Jarvis Thompson. *Moral Relativism and Moral Objectivity*. New York: Wiley-Blackwell, 1996.

Mackie, J. L. *Ethics: Inventing Right and Wrong*. New York: Penguin, 1977.

Ratzinger, Joseph, and Marcello Pera. *Without Roots: The West, Relativism, Christianity, Islam*. Translated by Michael F. Moore. New York: Basic, 2006.

Specific Ethical Resources

Obligations to One's Neighbor

Aiken, William, and Hugh Lafollette, eds. *World Hunger and Morality*. New York: Prentice-Hall, 1995.

Hallett, Garth. *Priorities and Christian Ethics*. New York: Cambridge University Press, 1997.

Held, Virginia. *The Ethics of Care: Personal, Political, and Global*. Oxford: Oxford University Press, 2007.

Sowle-Cahill, Lisa. *Global Justice, Christology, and Christian Ethics*. New York: Cambridge University Press, 2015.

Unger, Peter. *Living High and Letting Die*. New York: Oxford University Press, 1997.

Wisor, Scott. *The Ethics of Global Poverty: An Introduction*. New York: Routledge, 2016.

Environmental Ethics

Blanchard, Kathryn, and Kevin O'Brien. *An Introduction to Christian Environmentalism: Ecology, Virtue, and Ethics*. Waco: Baylor University Press, 2014.

Carson, Rachel. *Silent Spring*. New York: Houghton-Mifflin, 1962.

Francis, Pope. *Laudato Si—On Care for Our Common Home*. New York: Our Sunday Visitor, 2015.

Marlow, Hilary, and John Barton. *Biblical Prophets and Contemporary Environmental Ethics*. New York: Oxford University Press, 2009.

Northcott, Michael S. *The Environment and Christian Ethics*. New York: Cambridge University Press, 1996.

Pojman, Paul, and Louis P. Pojman, eds. *Environmental Ethics*. New York: Oxford University Press, 2011.

Rolston, Holmes, III. *A New Environmental Ethics: The Next Millennium for Life on Earth*. New York: Routledge, 2011.

Singer, Peter. *Animal Liberation*. London: Cape, 1990.

White, Lynn. "The Historical Roots of Our Ecological Crisis." *Science* 155 (1967): 1203–7.

Human Sexuality

Grabowski, John S. *Sex and Virtue: An Introduction to Sexual Ethics*. Washington, DC: Catholic University of America Press, 2003.

Grenz, Stanley. *Sexual Ethics: An Evangelical Perspective*. Louisville: Westminster John Knox, 1997.

Pinckaers, Servais. *The Sources of Christian Ethics*. Washington, DC: Catholic University of America Press, 1995.

Salzman, Todd A., and Michael G. Lawler. *Sexual Ethics: A Theological Introduction*. Washington, DC: Georgetown University Press, 2012.

Thatcher, Adrian, ed. *The Oxford Handbook of Theology, Sexuality, and Gender*. New York: Oxford University Press, 2015.

Via, Dan O., and Robert Gagnon. *Homosexuality and the Bible: Two Views*. Minneapolis: Fortress, 2003.

Abortion

Bernardin, Joseph L. *The Seamless Garment: Writings on the Consistent Ethic of Life*. Edited by Thomas A. Nairn. New York: Orbis, 2008.

Grisez, Germain. *Abortion: The Myths, the Realities, and the Arguments*. New York: Corpus, 1970.

Noonan, John T., ed. *The Morality of Abortion*. Cambridge, MA: Harvard University Press, 1970.

Paul VI, Pope. *Humanae Vitae*. New York: Pauline Books, 1968.

Thompson, Judith Jarvis. "A Defense of Abortion." *Philosophy and Public Affairs* 1.1 (1971): 54–66.

Tooley, Michael. *Abortion and Infanticide*. Oxford: Oxford University Press, 1983.

Warren, Mary Anne. "On the Moral and Legal Status of Abortion." *The Monist* 57.4 (1973): 1–9.

Wennberg, Robert M. *Life in the Balance: Exploring the Abortion Controversy*. Grand Rapids: Eerdmans, 1985.

Punishment

Alexander, Michelle. *The New Jim Crow: Mass Incarceration in the Age of Colorblindness*. New York: New Press, 2012.

Brugger, E. Christian. *Capital Punishment and Roman Catholic Tradition*. Notre Dame, IN: University of Notre Dame Press, 2014.

Cone, James. *The Cross and the Lynching Tree*. New York: Orbis, 2012.

Glover, Jonathan. *Causing Death and Saving Lives*. Harmondsworth, UK: Penguin, 1977.

Kramer, Matthew. *The Ethics of Capital Punishment: A Philosophical Investigation of Evil and Its Consequences*. Oxford: Oxford University Press, 2014.

Lewis, C. S. "The Humanitarian Theory of Punishment." In *God in the Dock: Essays in Theology and Ethics*, edited by Walter Hooper, 224–30. Grand Rapids: Eerdmans, 1970.

War

Allhoff, Fritz, Nicholas G. Evans, and Adam Henschke, eds. *Routledge Handbook of Ethics and War: Just War Theory in the Twenty-First Century*. New York: Routledge, 2015.

Bell, Daniel M., Jr. *Just War as Christian Discipleship: Recentering the Tradition in the Church Rather than the State*. Grand Rapids: Brazos, 2009.

Coates, A. J. *The Ethics of War*. Manchester, UK: Manchester University Press, 2006.

Holmes, Arthur, ed. *War and Christian Ethics*, 2nd ed. Grand Rapids: Baker Academic, 2005.

O'Donovan, Oliver. *Just War Revisited*. Cambridge: Cambridge University Press, 2003.

Reichberg, Gregory, Henrik Syse, and Nicole M. Hartwell, eds. *Religion, War, and Ethics: A Sourcebook of Textual Traditions*. Cambridge: Cambridge University Press, 2014.

Shaw, William H. *Utilitarianism and the Ethics of War*. New York: Routledge, 2016.

York, Tripp, and Justin Bronson Barringer, eds. *A Faith Not Worth Fighting For: Addressing Commonly Asked Questions about Christian Nonviolence*. Eugene, OR: Cascade, 2012.

Euthanasia

Badham, Paul. *Is There a Christian Case for Assisted Dying? Voluntary Euthanasia Reassessed*. London: SPCK, 2007.

Beville, Kieran. *Dying to Kill: A Christian Perspective on Euthanasia and Assisted Suicide*. Cambridge, OH: Christian Publishing House, 2014.

Cholbi, Michael J., ed. *Euthanasia and Assisted Suicide: Global Views on Choosing to End Life*. Santa Barbara, CA: Praeger, 2017.

Hyde, Michael. *The Call of Conscience: Heidegger and Levinas, Rhetoric and the Euthanasia Debate*. Columbia: University of South Carolina Press, 2001.

May, William F. *Testing the Medical Covenant: Active Euthanasia and Health Care Reform*. Eugene, OR: Wipf & Stock, 2004.

McMahan, Jeff. *The Ethics of Killing: Problems at the Margins of Life*. Oxford: Oxford University Press, 2003.

McMullin, Ernan, ed. *Death and Decision*. Boulder, CO: Westview, 1978.

Lying

Augustine, Mary Sarah Muldowney, and Mary Francis McDonald. *The Fathers of the Church: Treatises on Various Subjects—Lying, Continence, Patience*. Washington, DC: Catholic University of America Press, 1952.

Bok, Sissela. *Lying: Moral Choice in Public and Private Life*. New York: Vintage, 1999.

Carson, Thomas. *Lying and Deception: Theory and Practice*. Oxford: Oxford University Press, 2012.

DeLapp, Kevin, and Jeremy Henkel, eds. *Lying and Truthfulness*. Indianapolis: Hackett, 2016.

Griffiths, Paul. *Lying: An Augustinian Theology of Duplicity*. Grand Rapids: Brazos, 2004.

Tollefsen, C. F. *Lying and Christian Ethics*. Cambridge: Cambridge University Press, 2014.

Scripture Index

Old Testament

Genesis

1:24 77, 81
1:25 81
1:26 38
1:26–27 14
1:28 38, 51
2:17 56, 146
3:5 147
3:7 147
17:12 56
22:1 56
22:2 114
22:7 55
22:8 55

Exodus

3:22 57
12 57
12:36 114
15:13 48
20:1–17 10, 24, 56, 77
20:2 12
20:4–5 34
20:10–11 31
20:13 6
23:19 56
34:6 48

Leviticus

11:9–12 56
18:22 32

19:18 41
20:13 32

Numbers

14:18 48

Deuteronomy

5:1–22 24
5:6–21 10
5:10 48
5:16 6
7 57
7:1–2 31
14:8 56

Joshua

6–11 133

Ruth

4:1–22 34

Psalms

19:1 13

Proverbs

8:15–21 29
9:10–11 29

Isaiah

1:23 27

Ezekiel

16:49 35

Hosea

1 57

Amos

5:21–24 28

Micah

6:8 6, 21, 28

New Testament

Matthew

5–7 10
5:1–12 14
5:3–11 131
5:9 133
5:13–14 43
5:17 32
5:20 40
5:21–22 42, 59
5:27–28 59
5:27–30 43
5:31–32 59
5:33–34 59
5:38–39 42
5:42 42
5:44 42, 59
5:48 42, 44
6:1–4 43

7:12 41, 104, 127
8:5–13 34
16:14 59
19:17 44
19:20 44
19:21 44
22:34–40 175n4
22:37–40 12
25:34–40 48
26:52 6, 133, 135

Mark

12:28–31 6, 49
12:28–34 175n4

Luke

6:27–28 12
6:31 17
10:25–28 175n4
18:9–14 147

John

1:3 61, 78
3:16 48, 179
3:19 49
3:35 49
5:20 49
8:1–11 118
8:11 81

11:50 131
12:43 49
15:13 175
18:36 133

Romans

1:18–19 13
1:19–21 78
1:20–21 14
3:23 60
12:10 49

1 Corinthians

12:31 49
13:13 39, 49, 160

Galatians

3:28 11, 31
5:6 47
5:8 48
5:13 47
5:14 47
5:19–21 47
5:22–23 168
5:22–26 47

Ephesians

2:8–9 43, 44
2:10 46

1 Timothy

6:10 165

James

1:22 48

1 Peter

3:9 59

2 Peter

1:5 179

1 John

4:7 176
4:7–8 175

Revelation

20:1–6 44

Subject Index

abortion, 87, 96, 97, 98–100
Abraham, 24, 55–58, 66, 94, 114, 143–44, 149
actions contrary to duty, 112–13
actions for the sake of duty, 111–12
actions in accordance with duty, 112–13
aesthetic stage, 143
agapē, 49, 176
agapistic ethics, 11–12
analogy of Scripture, 42
analytic ethics, 9
anthropocentrism, 36
apodictic law, 25
applied ethics, 8–9, 15–16
Aquinas. *See* Thomas Aquinas
Aristotle, 3–4, 9, 36, 60, 74–76, 106, 115, 150, 155–60, 167–68, 173–74, 179
atonement, 43, 46
Augustine, 2–4, 9–11, 12, 72, 75, 78, 134, 158, 160, 162–63, 168, 170, 176, 179
autonomous will, 111
autonomy, 111–13
Ayer, A. J., 9

bad faith, 142, 149
beatitude(s), 14, 40, 115, 131, 168
Bentham, Jeremy, 122–24, 126
Bible, 5, 10, 12–13, 15–18, 22–23, 27, 30–35, 37, 42–43, 45, 48, 50–51, 55–58, 66, 77, 81, 83, 133, 147. *See also* Christian Scripture(s); Hebrew Scripture(s)
biblical ethics, 10–11, 24, 34, 35, 37, 51
bigotry, 51
Bonhoeffer, Dietrich, 92, 95, 104, 138, 146–48, 150, 171, 178
Brunner, Emil, 150
Buber, Martin, 9, 138, 145–46, 150
business ethics, 8

Calvin, John, 4, 10, 45–46, 55, 59, 63
capital punishment, 8, 32, 100, 104, 115–19
cardinal virtue(s), 158–60
Catechism of the Catholic Church, 11
categorical imperative, 104–5, 108–19
chesed, 48
Christian ethics. *See* ethics: Christian
Christian realism, 135
Christian Scripture(s), 48–51, 59, 67, 77, 127, 131, 133, 168, 175, 179. *See also* Bible; Hebrew Scripture(s)
church(es), 10–12, 14–15, 43–45, 49–50, 77, 81, 91, 133, 135, 161, 168
confession, 1–2, 26, 77
conscience, 3, 66–68, 91, 128
consequentialism, 5, 122, 133, 156
consistent ethic of life, 100
context, 11–15, 17–18, 25, 27–28, 33, 40–41, 50, 56–57, 66, 77, 88, 132–33, 137, 167–68, 171, 175
counsel of prudence, 106–7
counsels of perfection, 44
courage, 4, 157, 159–60, 167, 170, 172
covenant(s), 22–27, 29, 31, 43–44, 46, 77, 83, 131, 133
creation, 10, 13–14, 36–37, 51, 58, 61–62, 77–79, 87, 174, 179
cultural relativism, 16–17

Decalogue, 10–11, 24–26, 56–58, 66, 77, 81, 115, 132
Declaration of Independence, 85–86, 97
defect, 158–60
deontological ethics, 5
Derrida, Jacques, 9
descriptivism, 8
deterrence theory of punishment, 116

disciple(s), 10, 12, 47–48, 60, 127, 175
discipleship, 12, 180
divine command, 11–12, 57, 59–65, 67, 94, 168,
    175–76
divine command dilemma, 61–63
divine command ethics, 11–12, 63
divine law, 79–80, 86
divine sovereignty, 61
double-effect, 153
duty, 5–6, 60, 67, 98, 104, 107–8, 110–18, 126,
    128–29, 156, 169, 175, 180

ecojustice, 36
education, 76, 96, 100
egoism, 87, 91–95, 122
emotivism, 8
Enlightenment, 86, 104, 141. *See also*
    modernism
environment, 7–8, 22, 35–38, 50–51, 53, 156
environmental ethics, 8
essentialism, 138
eternal law, 45, 72, 78–79
eternal life, 46, 48, 148
ethical egoism, 92, 122
ethical stage, 143
ethics, 1–5
    Christian, 2, 6–7, 9, 11–12, 14, 18, 41, 45,
        50–51, 76, 97, 113–14, 132, 135, 146, 149,
        168–69, 173–74, 177
    of love, 48–49
euthanasia, 100, 151–54
Euthyphro Dilemma, 62–63, 65
evil, 12, 27–28, 56, 59, 64, 66, 75–76, 78, 80,
    82, 105–6, 131–35, 139–40, 146–49, 153–56,
    162, 164–66, 170–71
evolution, 81
excess, 49, 82, 159–60, 163–66
existentialism, 5, 137–38, 141, 143, 149,
    177–78, 180
    Christian, 177–78, 180
    ethics, 8, 138
expected utility, 123
explicit consent, 89–90
exploitation, 25, 30, 50, 104, 165

faith, 4, 10, 18, 43, 45–47, 49, 59–60, 62, 77, 79,
    87, 94, 133, 140, 144, 149–50, 160–62, 165
family, 35, 48–50, 59, 77, 103, 122, 138, 153,
    166, 171
First Table, 25
Fletcher, Joseph, 132
forgiveness, 43, 135, 148, 160–61, 166–68
Foucault, Michel, 7, 9
Franklin, Benjamin, 86
freedom, human, 37, 47, 82, 88–91, 93, 96, 138,
    142, 148

genealogy, 139
general revelation, 13, 15
God, 3–4, 6–7, 9–10, 12–15, 21–36, 38, 43–50,
    52, 55–68, 72, 74, 77–80, 83, 86–89, 91,
    94, 97, 106–7, 113–15, 118, 127–28, 133,
    140–44, 146–48, 150, 152, 154, 157, 160–66,
    174–80
golden rule, 41, 104, 114, 127
good, the, 5, 8, 30, 53, 60, 90, 94–95, 97, 105,
    115, 142, 144, 150, 157, 162, 164, 177
grace, 14, 26, 43, 45–47, 49, 60, 77, 148, 150,
    160–61, 168, 176–77, 179–80
greatest commandment, 6, 41, 162, 175
Grotius, Hugo, 86
guidance, 3, 6, 10–11, 17, 44, 47, 76, 160, 167
guilt, 58, 116–18, 125, 128, 170, 173

habit(s), 14, 156–58, 161, 163, 179
happiness, 74, 85–86, 93, 97, 99, 106–8, 110,
    113, 115–16, 121–28, 131–32, 138, 152,
    155–56, 161, 169
Hare, R. M., 9, 140
heaven, 13, 40, 44, 61, 103, 142, 147, 164,
    173–74, 180
Hebrew Scripture(s), 14–15, 21–24, 25,
    29–35, 41, 46, 48, 50. *See also* Christian
    Scripture(s)
hedonic calculus, 123–24
hell, 42–43, 164, 173–74
heteronomous will, 112
heteronomy, 111, 113
Hobbes, Thomas, 92–93
holiness, 23, 26–28, 31, 41, 49–50, 150
Holiness Code, 26, 32
Holy Spirit. *See* Spirit, Holy
homosexuality, 32–33, 81–83
hope, 48–49, 64, 81, 106, 112, 160, 162, 165,
    169
hubris, 60, 147. *See also* pride
human law, 71, 79–80
human nature, 13, 71–76, 80–81, 93, 95, 126,
    141–42, 157, 160
Hume, David, 4, 143
hypothetical imperative, 105–7, 112

image of God, 14, 157
imperfect duty, 110–11
imperfect happiness, 74
individualism, 87, 97
integrity, 3, 37, 95
intellectualism, 58
intuition, 6, 65, 93, 95, 109
intuitionism, 8
I-Thou relationship, 145

Jefferson, Thomas, 86
Jesus Christ, 6–7, 10–12, 14, 17, 25, 31–33,
     40–51, 59–60, 77–78, 81, 92, 97, 104, 118,
     127, 131, 133, 135, 150, 161, 168, 175–76,
     178, 180
jocose lie, 171
John (apostle), 75, 78, 175
judgment, 13, 30, 42, 47, 64, 66–67
jus ad bellum, 134
jus in bello, 134
just war theory, 134–35
justice, 4, 6, 10, 13, 23, 26–30, 32, 34–37, 43,
     48–50, 56, 58, 68, 74–76, 78–81, 95–97,
     116–19, 134, 140, 150, 157–60, 163, 167,
     172, 177
justification, 8, 113

Kant, Immanuel, 4, 7, 9, 103–19, 126, 139–41,
     143, 150, 169, 175
Kantianism, 2, 8, 138, 140, 152, 168
Ketuvim, 23, 29
Kierkegaard, Søren, 4, 9, 12, 138, 142–44, 146,
     149–50, 178
King, Martin Luther, Jr., 72

Lacks, Henrietta, 85–86
law of nature, 77, 87–89, 91, 108–9, 116–17
Levinas, Emmanuel, 9
Lewis, C. S., 13, 58, 64–65, 71–72, 75, 77, 177
liberation, 24, 31, 33, 50
Locke, John, 86–91, 93, 96, 174
love, 3, 6–7, 12, 21, 23, 26–29, 32, 39–44, 47–51,
     58–60, 63–65, 80, 97, 127, 130, 132, 138,
     145, 148, 152, 157, 160, 162–66, 168, 173–80
love chapter, 49
Luther, Martin, 10, 45–46, 59, 63
lying, 5, 13, 111–13, 156, 169–72

malicious lie, 170–71
marginalization, 50
means-end formulation, 109, 118
medical ethics, 8
mercy, 31, 105, 147
metaethics, 8–9
methodological atheism, 80–81
Mill, John Stuart, 7, 115, 121–22, 125–28, 150
modernism, 36, 50, 86–87, 141, 174. *See also*
     Enlightenment
Moore, G. E., 9
moral philosophy, 3–4, 8, 13–14, 17–18, 25,
     109, 126, 150, 174
moral precepts, 74
moral relativism, 16–17, 75, 81, 138
moral responsibility, 47–48, 135, 149
morals, 3–4, 6, 75, 127, 139

moral stage, 143
moral theology, 4, 7, 10–11, 13, 16–17, 67, 133,
     163
moral virtue, 157–58, 160–61, 179
Moses, 24, 31

narrative ethics, 10–12, 168–69
nation(s), 31, 39, 47, 50, 82, 89, 134
natural law, 2, 11, 13, 65, 71–81, 83, 94, 132,
     138, 140, 152–53, 175–77
     ethics, 2, 11, 13, 71–77, 80–81, 132, 177, 180
     Christian, 76–80
     theory, 65, 72–75, 80, 152
natural rights, 2, 8, 17, 86–88, 90–91, 96–98,
     152–53, 168, 174
     theory, 87–89, 187
nature, 13, 36–37, 43, 59, 65, 71, 77, 81, 83,
     87–92, 108–9, 116–17, 177
net utility, 94, 123–25, 128, 130, 132, 141, 169,
     175, 180
Nevi'im, 23, 27
Nietzsche, Friedrich, 4, 7, 9, 137–41, 149
normative ethics, 8–9, 91

obedience, 12, 24, 26, 45–47, 56, 60, 63, 65
obey, 12, 44, 46–47, 53, 55, 62, 64–67, 76, 109,
     130, 144
objectivism, 93–96
objectivist ethics, 93–94
officious lie, 171
oppression, 50, 68
original sin, 135, 146
ownership, 31, 37, 87

pacifism, 42, 135
Paul (apostle), 11, 13, 23, 41, 45–49, 75, 77–78,
     160, 162, 165, 168, 175
peace, 6, 73, 125, 131, 133–34
perfect duty, 110–11, 113, 116
perfect happiness, 74
Peter (apostle), 6, 133
philia, 49
philosophical ethics, 2, 4, 9, 174–75
philosophy, moral. *See* moral philosophy
Plato, 3–4, 9, 60–61, 75–76, 115, 150, 174
poor, the, 27–28, 30, 34–36, 40, 44, 51–53, 86,
     131, 140
postcolonial interpretation, 33
postmodern tradition, 137–38
poverty, 34–35, 40–41, 51
power, 7, 9, 13, 36, 46, 58–59, 63–64, 66, 72, 77,
     89, 91, 106, 138–41, 171
prayer, 40, 42, 59, 147
prejudice, 18, 118
prescriptivism, 8

pride, 95, 147–48, 163–64, 166–67, 174. *See also* hubris
primary precepts, 79
principle of proportionality, 34
principle of utility, 125, 127
property, 3, 26, 56, 88–91, 93, 96, 125, 150, 153, 165
proportionalism, 132–33
prudence, 106–8, 157–58, 160, 170. *See also* wisdom
psychological egoism, 92, 95

quadrilateral (Wesleyan), 14–18

racism, 68, 72
Ramsey, Paul, 23, 26
Rand, Ayn, 93–97
Rawls, John, 9
reconciliation, 4, 160
redemption, 23
relativism, 2, 8, 16–18, 75, 81, 138, 149
ressentiment, 139–40
retributivism, 116
right, the, 5–6
right reason, 76, 158
rights, 2, 8, 17, 31, 68, 82, 85–91, 96–100, 152–53, 168, 174
rule utilitarianism, 124–28

saint(s), 95, 174, 180
salvation, 4, 14, 31, 40, 43–46, 131
sanctification, 4, 23
Sartre, Jean-Paul, 4, 9, 138, 141–42, 149, 169–70
Satan, 164, 174
Scripture. *See also* Christian Scripture(s); Hebrew Scripture(s)
secondary precepts, 79–80
Second Table, 25
selfishness, 49, 93, 178
Sermon on the Mount, 10, 25, 40–44, 131
sexism, 68
sexuality, human, 7, 13, 72, 81–83
sin, 14, 32, 35, 42–43, 46, 58, 60, 81, 111, 113, 135, 144, 146–48, 160–61, 163, 170–71, 173–74
sinfulness, 3, 13–14, 23, 33, 60, 147–48, 176
situation ethics, 132
slave morality, 140–41, 149
social contract, 89–91, 93–94
Socrates, 3, 61–62, 75–76, 125, 143–44

soul(s), 3, 6, 12, 37, 40, 49, 76, 78, 140, 157, 163, 174, 179
special revelation, 13–15, 32, 57, 79, 127
Spirit, Holy, 46–47, 49, 168, 176
state of nature, 87–92
stewardship, 22, 36–38
strong divine command morality, 63

tacit consent, 89–90
Tanakh, 23, 29
teleological suspension of the ethical, 143–44
telos, 36, 74, 82
temperance, 157, 159–60, 166–67
Ten Commandments, 10, 12, 24–26, 34, 56, 58. *See also* Decalogue
theological virtue(s), 49, 160–62, 179
therapeutic theory of punishment, 116
Thomas Aquinas, 4, 13, 58, 72, 74–75, 78–79, 134, 156–58, 160–64, 166, 168, 170–71, 174, 177, 179
Torah, 23
trolley problem, 128–29
trust, 109, 147, 161, 171–72

Übermensch, 140, 149
universalizability, 109, 113
unqualified good, 104–5
utilitarianism, 2, 8, 36, 94, 121–22, 125–27, 129–32, 138, 140, 168

vice(s), 47, 95, 163–67, 172, 174
violence, 16–18, 30–31, 133–35
virtue(s), 2, 5, 8–10, 12, 47, 49, 59–60, 63, 65, 74–76, 79, 93–95, 104, 106, 140, 147, 155–72, 174–75, 177, 179–80
  as a mean, 159
voluntarism, 58

war, 6, 97, 121–22, 133–36
weak divine command morality, 63
Wesley, John, 4, 10, 58, 165
Wesleyan quadrilateral, 14–18
William of Ockham, 58, 63
Williams, Bernard, 130
wisdom, 3, 23, 29–30, 32–33, 58–59, 74, 127, 131, 158. *See also* prudence
works, 43, 45–47
worship, 34, 36, 58, 65, 77, 80, 91, 127, 132, 134, 141, 144, 160, 180
wrong, the, 5–6